You Can Adopt

above: Will, United States

top: Garrett, Russia
bottom: Hadarya, United States

facing page: Zachary, United States

You Can Adopt

An *Adoptive Families* Guide

Susan Caughman and Isolde Motley

with the editors and readers of *Adoptive Families* magazine

BALLANTINE BOOKS | NEW YORK

To our children,
Hope, Charlotte, Senai, Ian, and Hannah.
Without them, this book would have
been finished much sooner.

A Ballantine Books Trade Paperback Original

Copyright © 2009 by New Hope Media, LLC

All rights reserved.

Published in the United States by Ballantine Books,
an imprint of The Random House Publishing Group,
a division of Random House, Inc., New York.

BALLANTINE and colophon are registered
trademarks of Random House, Inc.

Acknowledgments for contributed
material may be found starting on page 277.

LIBRARY OF CONGRESS CATALOGING-IN-PUBLICATION DATA

Caughman, Susan.
You can adopt : an adoptive families guide /
Susan Caughman and Isolde Motley with the editors
and readers of Adoptive Families magazine.
p.   cm.
ISBN 978-0-345-50401-2
1. Adoption—Handbooks, manuals, etc.   2. Adoptive
parents—Handbooks, manuals, etc.   I. Motley, Isolde.
II. Adoptive families.   III. Title.
HV875.C369 2009
362.734—dc22   2009020252

Printed in the United States of America

www.ballantinebooks.com

9 8 7 6 5 4 3 2 1

Book design by Jo Anne Metsch

What a difference it makes to come home to a child.

—Margaret Fuller

Foreword

For more than thirty years, *Adoptive Families* magazine has served as the leading source of authoritative, trusted parenting information for families before, during, and after adoption. The magazine's editorial advisory board includes America's leading adoption attorneys, pediatricians, psychologists, and social workers, all experts who can share the latest research, legislation, and policy. But the real experts are the hundreds of thousands of *Adoptive Families* readers, the women and men who have walked every possible path to parenthood, who have adopted children from every imaginable situation, and who tell their stories in our pages.

You Can Adopt walks you through the practical steps of adoption: Where do I start? Do I need an attorney? How do I make sure the child is healthy? Where do I find a social worker? Which are the best adoption agencies? For each stage, it gives clear options and honest, unvarnished advice. More crucially, it walks with you as you make the decisions only you can make: When do I stop treatment for infertility? How do I persuade my spouse? How important is it to me to parent a newborn baby? How do I tell my parents? Do I want a child who looks just like me? In this book, our readers write about the choices

above: Matthew, United States

they made before you; they share their reasoning and the results. Sometimes they made mistakes; by reading about them, you can avoid their errors. Some had a smooth, easy path; others changed direction and found themselves in a place they never expected to be. But all of them ended up saying, "This is my child." And they sent us these photographs—every one an adopted child brought home by one of our families—to prove it.

THE EDITORS
Adoptive Families

Contents

above: Carolyn, United States

Brian, United States

A Note from the Editors

While it is our intention that the content of *You Can Adopt* be timeless, there will always be new circumstances to consider. Adoption laws and practices change constantly, at the international, national, and state level; it is important that you keep abreast of developments that will affect your particular situation. This book should be used for informational purposes only, and is not meant to take the place of advice from attorneys, medical doctors, social workers, or other professionals with whom you consult as you go through the adoption process.

Introduction

Once upon a time, we were in your shoes—beginning to think about adoption, not sure what to do next, not even sure we wanted to adopt. Now, so many years later, we are helping our children fill out college applications, teaching them to drive, learning to like their boyfriends and girlfriends, and beginning, ever so subtly, to hint about grandchildren. Our children are not adopted; they *were* adopted, and now they're just our children. Happy, smart, loving, successful, gorgeous children.

People say that you forget about the pain of childbirth. Once the baby arrives, nothing else matters. Adoption is, remarkably, the same. The agonizing decisions, the piles of paperwork, the absurd, time-wasting bureaucracies—they all fade away. Here is your child, and you are a family. How you came to be a family doesn't matter at all.

We are not here to talk you into adopting a child. But we can make you a promise, from our own personal experiences and from our time at *Adoptive Families* magazine: You can create a family. You can fall in love with a child and be loved in return. You *can* adopt.

SUSAN CAUGHMAN
ISOLDE MOTLEY

above: Gabriel, United States

The Top Ten Myths About Adoption

1 There are no babies, especially American babies.
Of the 100,000 or so adoptions that take place in the United States every year, about 25,000 are of American newborns.

2 Children adopted from abroad are all disabled or disturbed.
The vast majority of international adoptees are healthy, happy children.

3 Adoption takes years (unless you're a celebrity).
Most of our families brought their children home within two years of submitting their paperwork—for many, the process takes less than one year.

4 Adoption costs hundreds of thousands of dollars.
The average cost of an adoption, before grants and reimbursements, is about the same as the price of a midsized car. It is possible to complete an adoption for a few hundred dollars.

5 Only perfect couples can adopt.
Whether you are gay, straight, single, married, divorced, disabled, rich, poor, professional, unemployed, retired, aged twenty-one or sixty, a pillar of the community or a person with a slightly spotty past, you can adopt a child.

6 Adopted children are "stolen" from their birth families.
Laws in America have multiple safeguards to ensure that a birth mother cannot be coerced or bribed into placing her child for adoption. Some international adoptions have involved bribes, deceit, or downright theft, but there are plenty of adoption agencies that can guide families to absolutely ethical international adoptions.

7 All birth mothers are unstable teenagers.
Most birth mothers are women in their twenties making a well-thought-out choice to give their child a better life than they themselves can provide.

8 **Birth parents can come back and take your child.**
Once an adoption has been finalized in court, the child is as much yours as if you had given birth.

9 **All adoptees are troubled.**
Recent long-term studies of adoptees in America show that they are no different in self-esteem and attachment to family from children raised by their biological parents.

10 **Adoption always ends in tears.**
After thirty years of working with adoptive families, we can promise you that most adoptions end in joy, triumph, and love.

Aleksandra, Russia

Adoption at a Glance: *The Decision Tree*

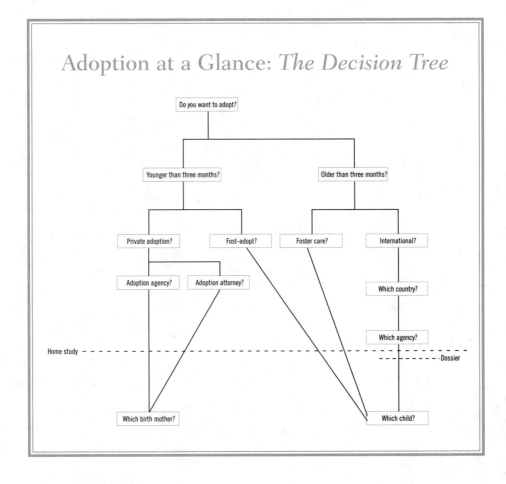

PART I

Thinking About Adopting?

above: McIntyre, United States

Can I Do This?

Making the Decision to Adopt

Do I really want to adopt?

When you bear or raise children, you step into the un-known. If you adopt, you take a step further. You can't predict what baby would come from your own genetic mix, but you might recognize traits as the child grows up: "He's got Grandpa's ears." With an adopted child, there's an element of mystery: "Where did that nose come from?"

The parents who read *Adoptive Families* magazine say that they love watching their children's traits and talents unfold: A family of clumsies embraces an award-winning gymnast; bookworms welcome the math genius. Before you adopt, understand that it means loving your child for who he or she really is, not as your own small replica.

Can I adopt?

The practical answer is: Yes, almost any American adult can adopt a child. The real question is: When

> *The love I feel for my son is real. Who cares if I didn't give birth? When he looks at me with those beautiful brown eyes and says, "Mommy," that's all I need. Like the saying goes, you didn't grow under my heart but in it.*
> —NANCY

above: Aidan, Russia

Although I knew I would love our new baby deeply, I was secretly worried that I would love my biological son more. Now that our daughter is home, it's hard to believe I ever felt that way! I am so attached to her and love her so deeply that I don't know how I would cope if something ever happened to her.

—KIARA

From the minute we received our daughter, we had comments that she was meant to be with our family. Her personality, likes, and interests are, amazingly, the same as ours. I often say that she just naturally fit into our family. She was destined to be ours.

—KAREN

you think about adopting, what kind of child do you imagine? A baby? A toddler? A teenager? A child who looks just like you, or a child of another background?

The decisions may seem overwhelming at first, but we will guide you through them one by one. We've taken this journey ourselves—and so have the hundreds of other adoptive families who tell their stories in this book. We will also help you answer what may be the most important question of all: Are you *ready* to adopt?

Will I love a child who "isn't mine"?

Most adoptive parents secretly worry that they won't be able to bond with a child who's not related by blood. In our thirty years of experience at *Adoptive Families*, we have found that this worry disappears once the child is home. In fact, we have heard from hundreds of parents with both biological and adopted children who say they often forget which they adopted and which they birthed.

Are adopted children more likely to be "problem" kids?

While the "troubled adoptee" is a soap-opera staple, academic study offers a different picture. The Sibling Interaction and Behavior Study, launched in 1999 by the University of Minnesota's Center for Twin and Family Research, is the most comprehensive, authoritative study ever conducted that includes adoptees. Each round of data has shown that the vast majority of adopted children do just as well psychologically and socially as children raised in their biological families.

TECH SUPPORT: To read more about the long-term study of adoptees (Sibling Interaction and Behavior Study—SIBS—at the University of Minnesota's Center for Twin and Family Research), go to adoptivefamilies.com/sibs.

How long will it take?

Believe it or not, most adoptive parents bring their children home within two years of submitting their paperwork. However, this doesn't mean your adoption will take two years; time lines vary. (One editor of this book, through a combination of special circumstances and sheer luck, completed an adoption in three months, from the first, tentative phone call to an agency to actually bringing the baby home.)

As a general rule, adopting from foster care is the fastest process; international adoption varies greatly by country; private, infant adoption in the United States is the most unpredictable.

> To see time lines for the ten most popular countries for international adoption, go to adoptivefamilies.com/internationaladoption.

How much will it cost?

You can spend tens of thousands of dollars on your adoption, or you can spend next to nothing. An annual survey of fifteen hundred *Adoptive Families* readers shows that the average cost of an adoption is about the same as that of a midsized car ($23,000 in 2008). For many, reimbursements from employers and the federal government brought the net outlay down to a few thousand dollars. Lack of money won't stop you from adopting, though it will affect the kind of adoption, and possibly the kind of child. (Yes, we agree, that's not fair, but it is reality.)

> To see actual budgets from families who have completed their adoptions, go to adoptivefamilies.com/cost.

How do I get a healthy child?

Whether they are born to you or adopted, children do not come with guarantees. However, as with preg-

It feels like we four are peas in a pod, and I can't imagine our little family garden blooming any other way.
—DAWN

There are so many "ifs" I cannot possibly list them all. But there is one fact with no if, no uncertainty, attached: My daughter is simply, positively, my daughter. As she snuggles by my side, she feels like a pure miracle—whether placed there by mere chance or by divine intervention.
—BONNIE

nancy, there are steps you can take to improve the odds that your child will be healthy. If you adopt in the United States, you can identify a mother before birth and help ensure that she receives good prenatal care; if the child has already been born, you can review medical records before proceeding with the adoption. In international adoption, you can choose a country known for a high standard of infant care and work with an adoption pediatrician to decode the medical report before agreeing to accept the child. Chapter 6, "Can I Adopt a Healthy Child?," gives more detail.

Can I adopt a newborn?

Whatever kind of adoption you do, at some stage you will be "chosen" by either a social worker or a birth mother. Social workers and birth mothers generally want to place newborn babies with middle-class couples (gay or straight) in their late twenties to late thirties. If you don't fit this profile, you may find it harder to adopt an infant. But it's still possible; see chapter 3, "Can I Choose a Child?"

Marisa, United States

STRAIGHT TALK: If you have been thinking of adoption as something you'll do if you grow too old to have a biological child, think again. The odds of adopting an *infant* drop dramatically with each year you are over thirty-five. If you are between thirty-five and fifty, and still trying for a biological child, you should simultaneously research adoption, so you don't lose any additional time. If you are over fifty, your best chance of adopting an infant may be through a fost-adopt program.

Can I adopt a child who looks like me?

No matter what your ethnicity, you can find a "matching" child. If you are a really exotic mix, it may take longer, and some groups (Native Americans, for example) have specific processes. But there are adoptable children of every background.

Adoption 101

The best way to understand the adoption process is to focus first on the children available:

- American newborns: **Babies born in the United States to mothers who have arranged to place them directly for adoption. Most can go home with their new parents within days of their birth.**
- Foster children: **Children who are in the care of a state agency because their birth parents cannot care for them. More than half of U.S. adoptions in any given year come from this group, and this is generally the most affordable route to adoption.**
- International orphans: **Children who are eligible for "orphan visas" through adoption by U.S. parents because their parents have died or cannot provide care.**

After you think about the child who's right for your family, you can choose the right partner:

- Private attorney
- Adoption agency

Different agencies and attorneys specialize in different kinds of adoption, so you need to think about what kind of child—what age, what race—is right for you before you make any commitment to an agency or attorney. You may also end up using a combination of partners, or you may choose to work independently.

We chose to adopt our first child from Russia, because there were many children in need of homes and we felt we'd actually be doing some good in the world to adopt one of those children. Plus, we didn't have to market ourselves to birth mothers, as is often the case in domestic adoptions. That would have been too much for me, already humiliated by my infertility.
—COLLEEN

Meeting my birth mother and the family of my birth father, who had passed away, made me realize that if life had been different, I would not be who I am, and I would not be connected to the people, including my parents, whom I love so much. I felt grateful for all of my history.

—BRENDA

TRIED AND TRUE: While you think about the family you want to create, keep notes of your thoughts. If an attorney or agency suggests going in a different direction, our adoptive families say you should look back at your notes and remind yourself why you made the original decision.

Will they want to find their birth parents?

These days, more and more adoptive families meet and communicate with their child's birth family (this is called "open" adoption), so the search question doesn't arise. Our experience is that about half the children from old-fashioned "closed" adoptions eventually choose to search, often when they are old enough to begin thinking about having children of their own. The vast majority of those who succeed in finding their birth parents report that it made no difference to their relationship with their adoptive parents.

> Laws on confidentiality in adoption are in constant flux. To learn about the situation in each of the fifty states, go to: adoptivefamilies.com/statelaws.

Can I love a child of another race?

Would-be parents are sometimes embarrassed to ask this question. Don't be. Society assumes that parents and children will look alike. If you are going to build a family that's different from the norm, you will draw extra attention, and you will need extra support, so you need to think about how it will affect your life.

REALITY CHECKLIST
Are You Ready to Adopt a Child of Another Race?

❑ Do you live in an integrated neighborhood, so that your child will be able to attend an integrated school? If not, are you willing to move?

❑ Do you have friends of different races and ethnic groups? Do you visit one another's homes regularly?

❑ How will you react to people who make negative comments or stare? Can you respond in a way that will help your child feel good about himself?

❑ Are you ready to help your family deal with the racial bias you might face together?

When our boys were little, it was very tempting to pretend that raising an African American child is the same as raising a Caucasian child, but it is not. The better answer is that skin color should not matter, and we, as a family, are working toward helping the world to learn this basic truth.

—JESSICA

Can the birth parents take the child away?

All states give birth mothers time (days to months) to reconsider their plans before adoptions are finalized, and a significant number of birth parents do end up choosing to keep their babies. Adoption attorneys tell parents pursuing the private adoption of an infant to expect one "miss" before a successful adoption. Our families say you can reduce the chances of a missed adoption by making sure that all members of the birth family support the adoption and that the birth mother has had professional counseling.

Finalized adoptions are very rarely contested. Fewer than 0.1 percent end up in court.

We chose to go the route of fully open domestic adoption through an agency. We wanted to have as complete a medical history of our children as possible, as well as a relationship with our children's birth parents. We are now the proud parents of two beautiful children. We have had our daughter since birth, and our son since he was about thirteen days old. We have open relationships with our children's birth mothers, as well as their birth fathers, and we feel very fortunate.

—BONNI

❑ Did the birth mother receive counseling?

❑ Did the birth father consent?

❑ Do the birth grandparents (on both sides) support the adoption?

If you can't bear to think about any uncertainties with birth parents, you should consider either adopting from foster care or international adoption.

How do I avoid scams?

True adoption frauds are rare. Adoption incompetence is the real problem; there are well-meaning adoption facilitators, consultants, attorneys, and agencies who want only to help but who simply aren't equipped to do the work. Chapter 4, "Where Do I Start?," will help you pick reliable partners.

TRIED AND TRUE: The best way to make sure your adoption succeeds is to work with a nonprofit adoption agency or an adoption attorney who has completed lots of adoptions just like yours—same kind of parents, same kind of child, same state, same circumstances.

How can I persuade my spouse to adopt?

Many, many couples are deeply divided about adoption. Marriage counselors and social workers say the reluctant partner is usually the male, whose concerns may range from simple ambivalence about parenthood in general to specific concerns about loving a child who's not related by blood. Most of the couples who were initially divided say that spending time with adoptive families—especially watching adoptive dads with their children—eased the reluctance, but you must also work through the issues within the framework of your own marriage.

We've Been There: The Reluctant Spouse

1. Acknowledge your spouse's concerns and fears.

2. Air and discuss the differences between you, rather than trying to cover them up or smooth them over.

3. In your discussions, maintain balance between the reasons for your spouse's resistance to adoption and your reasons for wanting to adopt.

4. Don't take a spouse's initial reaction as the final word. When a subject is emotionally charged, people often say things they don't really mean.

5. Give your spouse time and space to consider issues as they arise; recognize that people approach change at different speeds.

6. Don't expect your spouse to react to developments in the adoption process the same way you do.

7. Find a support group of other couples considering adoption. Hearing that they, too, have reservations may help both of you.

8. If your spouse isn't providing the support and encouragement you need to cope with the adoption process, seek support from a sympathetic friend or relative.

9. See a marriage counselor if you have trouble navigating any of these issues. A reluctant spouse may hear questions and advice better from a neutral observer.

Looking back on our journey to parenthood, I see that this is how it was meant to happen for us. All the twists and turns along the way were life-learning experiences, preparing us for the wonderful relationship we have and for the daughter who is ours.
—LISA AND TIM

I Needed This All Along

Dennis Kneale

KATHY AND I MET WHEN WE WERE NEWSPAPER REPORTERS, SIT-
ting four desks apart and feigning disinterest in each other. We had our
first date over Memorial Day weekend. Sixteen months later we married;
she was thirty-two, I was thirty-five. She warned that if we wanted to have
children, we had better start "trying" soon. We waited two or three years.
That brilliant idea was mine—I wanted some time for the two of us.

Five years on: We have been "trying" for three years and now are deep
into the medical crapshoot of infertility treatment. Kathy is one of four
hundred women undergoing an in vitro cycle this month at New York–
Cornell Hospital. But the process fails. Soon it becomes clear that we will
never have our own children.

Kathy awakes one morning looking hollow and haunted. "If we can't
have children, why be married at all?" she says. To Kathy, it is as simple as
plan B: If we can't have a baby, of course we should adopt. To me, it is as
simple as "Never mind": If we can't have our own, why bother? Let's just
have an epic romance instead.

We go into marriage counseling, but soon it becomes an inquisition
into why I am afraid to adopt, so I quit. I dwell on darkness. What if the
baby has medical problems? What if she has attachment disorder? My
deepest fear: What if she just doesn't love me?

The fertility struggle left me drained and in retreat. Kathy reacts to our
tragedy with resolve instead of resignation: Let's make this right. One
morning I tell her maybe we should give up—let's just enjoy each other
and dote on our nieces and nephews. Kathy, in tears, says, "But I want a
family with you." In the ensuing weeks, Kathy comes to fear that the real
reason for my reluctance is a lack of love for her. I begin to suspect that
Kathy's quest isn't driven by love for me at all—she wants a baby, with or
without me.

Late that same year, Kathy gets a new ally in this fight: my mother.
Mom sends me a letter adorned with a photo of me at age six. "If you
choose never to be a father out of fear," she writes, "you'll be missing an
experience that will add great joy and excitement to your life." Enclosed is

a Father's Day card I made at about the same age, addressed "to the best father of all." Even this doesn't work.

Weeks later, the kid chasm explodes into a fight so furious, it frightens me. We are on a drive; she's at the wheel and I'm talking, again, in vaguely negative tones about adoption. She screeches to the side of the road and goes nuclear. "GET OUT! I NEVER WANT TO SEE YOU AGAIN!" She screams so loudly that a blood vessel bursts in her right eye.

And in that moment, it finally becomes clear that there is no way out of this. My mind runs the cold calculus. Refuse to adopt and break up now. Refuse and stay with her for thirty years—and in our seventies, explain why I deprived the love of my life of the one thing she needed most. Adopt and end up getting divorced anyway. (But at least we'd have done something good that links us forever. Score.) Adopt and live happily ever after. (I like that one best.) For all my foreboding, I feel afraid not to adopt, fearful of missing out on something wonderful. "Dennis, just open your heart," a friend tells me one night. This tears me up. Maybe I need this more than I know.

Still uncertain, we enter the labyrinth of adoption paperwork, and by year's end our documents are stacked a foot high and growing. The Chinese government clocks in our application on May 12. Seventeen days later, unbeknownst to us, our daughter is born.

During the wait, I plunge into my work and stay out late, drinking too much. I waver between worrying about the enormous responsibility if the adoption goes through—and dreading the devastation to Kathy if it doesn't.

One year later, my phone rings at work. Kathy excitedly announces: "Her name is Jing Jing. She's twelve months old, and we just got her picture. She's beautiful!" We both choke up, sharing happiness for the first time in months. Weeks later, we fly to China to bring Jing Jing home. Knock, knock! We open the door to see a Chinese woman holding a staring, tiny tyke. It jolts me: Wow, she's so cute, and she's ours. Jing Jing has arrived cranky, dirty, and disoriented after the bus ride with the stranger who is now handing her into Kathy's arms. The escort leaves all too quickly, and Jing Jing erupts into heartbreaking cries of abandonment. We tackle the first goal of parenting: Get the kid to stop crying.

Kathy tries to distract her with a parade of plush toys. Jing Jing only cries harder. Panicking, we turn to a gift from a friend: a wee backpack filled with knickknacks. Inside, we discover a box of Cheerios. Kathy feeds one to Jing Jing, then another, and suddenly our new daughter is smiling sweetly.

Then Jing Jing steals my heart. Tired and hungry and a stranger only half an hour before, this delightful little girl—this culmination of years of struggle and hope and heartache—looks me in the eye and smiles shyly. She picks out a Cheerio, holds it up to my lips, and feeds it to me. My heart swells with tenderness, and I tell her, "Oh, my Jing Jing. I will love you for the rest of my life."

Kaelynn, South Korea

My parents and in-laws hate the idea of adoption. Should we go ahead?

Lots of *Adoptive Families* readers report that at least one grandparent was opposed to their adoption. Some can't give up the idea of biological grandchildren; others even insist that any child placed for adoption must be a "bad seed." Most parents report that the concerns disappear as soon as the child is home, but a few grandparents (and other family members) simply never come around. Only you can decide if building your own family is worth the possibility of rupture with other family members.

The Grandparents-to-Be
Lois Gilman

TO ANYONE ELSE, IT'S A FAMILY SNAPSHOT: MY CHILDREN stand on the front porch of their paternal grandparents' home, arms entwined. But this photo, like so many others, records a cherished scene that I once thought would never be mine to treasure. I had no children to include in family pictures after a decade of marriage and an intense desire for a baby. Despite numerous tests, tubal surgery, and drug therapy, I had never become pregnant. My mother, who lived nearby, was aware of my efforts and had even gone with me to doctors' offices. But my in-laws had been spared my husband's and my struggle with infertility, since they lived far away. I dreamed about the day when I could disclose to them the happy news about the expected arrival of a grandchild.

When that day finally dawned, I worried about how they would react to the fact that their first grandchild would be adopted. For Jack and Dorothy Gilman were first-generation Americans, and their only child, Ernie, was born when they were both in their forties, after a stillbirth and several miscarriages. How would they come to accept and love a grandchild not of their own blood and also from Chile, a country and culture so unlike their own?

My anxieties were not entirely misplaced. After we told my in-laws about our plans, they wrote us a letter begging us to reconsider. They didn't oppose adoption per se, but they were wary of intercountry adoptions and especially of health problems a child from abroad might have. We wrote long letters and enclosed newspaper clippings about adoption. For every question they raised, we came up with an answer. But it was their rabbi's assurances that helped my in-laws finally change their minds. "Our grandchild, Seth, will be a joy to his parents and to his grandparents," wrote Jack, "and will keep the name of Gilman alive for generations to come."

I've learned that my in-laws' reaction to adoption was quite typical. When I wrote *The Adoption Resource Book*, a guide to adoption, prospective adoptive parents confided to me the difficulties they had when discussing adoption with their parents. On reflection, much of the unease makes sense. Prospective adopters have often lived with the possibility of adoption for years, and mulled over their final decision for months. Yet we ask our parents to endorse our plans from the moment we break the news, and to love as their own a grandchild whose origins they know little about. Even the most eager grandparents-to-be might be expected to harbor a few doubts under the circumstances. Adoptive grandparents need preparation and a chance to vent their feelings.

If you're thinking about adoption, try to talk with your parents in advance about your plans. You might ask them to join you at a meeting of an adoptive-parents group, subscribe to a newsletter, or talk with experienced grandparents by telephone. A local parent group might offer a special workshop or panel discussion for adoptive grandparents. (For several years, I offered a grandparent workshop at conferences, bringing in several grandparents through adoption to be the panelists, and asking the local group to invite members to bring their parents.) A comment from one prospective grandparent who attended a workshop I ran underscored just how important that can be: "I've been so in the dark. This is the first time my daughter has shared her adoption plans with me."

Now you know the special resonance our family photographs have for me. In May 1979, three generations gathered, and we took the first of many portraits for the Gilman family archive. Two years later, Jack and Dorothy welcomed a second grandchild, Eve Claire Rose, from South Korea. Sadly, they did not live to see both their grandchildren graduate from high school and go on to college, but my children have many memories of their loving grandparents, who came to love them as their own. These memories are the true legacy.

I'm single. How will this affect my adoption?
All U.S. states permit adoption by single parents, and about 20 percent of adoptive parents are unmarried. However, some U.S. agencies and foreign countries don't accept applications from singles; when you choose an agency or attorney, pick one that explicitly encourages adoption by singles and talk to other singles who have already adopted.

Adoption 101: Your Identity and Your Adoption

Your marital status

- Some countries don't permit singles to adopt.
- Some U.S. agencies don't accept applications from singles; others steer single parents toward specific kinds of children (special needs, older).
- Few foreign countries and U.S. states permit unmarried couples to adopt together. If you and a partner (gay or straight) both want to adopt a child, one of you must adopt first, then the other completes a "second-parent" adoption, similar to adoption by a stepparent.

Aleksandr, Russia

Your sexual orientation

- Many sending countries forbid adoption by gays and lesbians. Some follow a "don't ask, don't tell" policy. Others actually require would-be parents to swear they're not gay.
- Whether you can complete an adoption as an openly gay parent will depend on the laws in your state, which change depending on political pressure. To check

if your state permits gays to adopt, go to adoptivefamilies.com/statelaws.

- Some U.S. agencies will not accept applications from gays and lesbians.
- Some birth mothers will not choose gay parents for their children; others (disenchanted with their own heterosexual relationship) distinctly prefer to place a child with a gay family.

The gay adoptive families among our readers recommend that you find an agency or attorney with whom you can be completely honest, and let them decide how much information to pass along to the sending country or birth family.

Sonora, United States

How do I know when to stop trying for a biological child?

Social workers recommend that parents attend counseling as they make the decision to end infertility treatment; the rationale is that they do not want parents to see adoption as a second-best way to have a child. Many agencies require that clients stop all attempts to have biological children before they start the adoption process. If you want to continue trying for a biological child while pursuing adoption, choose an agency, attorney, or social worker who will support you. They do exist—it may just take some hunting. If you are adopting internationally, some countries do not permit pregnant women to adopt; if you are working on a private infant adoption, pregnancy reduces the chance that a birth mother will choose you.

We were both reluctant, and endured twelve years of infertility treatments. Finally, I realized I did not want to live the rest of my life without being a parent. It took another year to convince my husband, and then only after a psychologist asked him if he was afraid that he couldn't love a child not biologically related. He said yes. She asked him if he loved his wife. He looked at me and said that he loved me with all his heart. Then the psychologist asked if he was biologically related to his wife. Naturally, he responded "No." We signed up to adopt the following week, and our son was born the next year. We love him more than we could ever imagine was possible.

—LIZA

Josephine, United States

Through the Glass
Leah Van Divner

"ARE YOU STILL GETTING THE GIRL?" PEOPLE WOULD ASK, within minutes of learning that I was pregnant. Getting the girl? Did they think it was like ordering furniture? Did they think that, after flying halfway around the world to meet our daughter, a tiny, little . . . humongous thing like pregnancy would change our desire to adopt? When I informed the airport security officer that I was there to greet my newly adopted daughter, her gaze landed on my obviously pregnant belly, and I saw confusion and surprise wash across her face.

I hadn't seen my daughter for nine months, since visiting her orphanage. A few months after that, another family from our agency had traveled to the same orphanage and agreed to take some photos for us. Propped up side by side on our table sat ultrasound shots of my soon-to-be-born son curled up inside me and photos of my soon-to-be-home daughter, in oversized, mismatched clothes, Bozo the Clown shoes, and a wild haircut, sitting alone on a worn couch.

I watched passengers stream from the plane, then, finally, I saw their outline in the doorway. My husband was laden with shoulder bags and a five-year-old girl the size of a skinny toddler half her age. Her skin was pale, her expression blank. She clung to his neck as he struggled to walk. One look at his face was all I needed to feel his utter exhaustion.

I moved closer to the wall of glass that separated the waiting area from the arrival hallway and smiled at my husband. Only half of his mouth managed to smile back, but his gratitude at being home shone in his eyes. Through the glass, I could hear his muffled voice: "There's Mommy," he said, pointing at me. "There's Mommy," he said again, and she looked in my direction. I reached out and pressed my hand against the cool glass. Nothing in her eyes changed, but she reached out and placed her palm against mine on the other side. All I could think, with our hands pressed together through a thick pane of cold glass, was that at that moment, she and I were nothing more than two strangers about to embark on a long, uncharted journey.

Just the other day, I watched my eleven-year-old daughter play in the backyard, her shiny, dark hair tumbling from her ponytail, her long legs dangling from the crossbar of a play set. When she saw me through the window, she ran toward the house, yelling, "Mom, wanna come out and play horseshoes?" Her six-year-old brother was not far behind. I placed my hand on the thin screen between us. She reached up and pushed her palm against mine. I could feel the warmth of her skin, see her eyes bright with anticipation. She smiled and wiggled her brows, enticing me to play. "There's Mommy" echoed softly in the back of my mind. There was nothing between us now but the love of a mother and child.

Will I always mourn the biological child I didn't have?

Even parents who have adopted by choice tell us that they sometimes grieve for unborn biological children. However, *all* adoptive parents we know, including those who adopted after infertility, say, "But this is the child I was meant to have."

What happens if I get pregnant?

Most of our adoptive mothers say that when they announced their adoption, at least one friend or relative said, "Of course, now you'll get pregnant." In reality, adoption doesn't increase your chance of conceiving—but adoptive mothers do get pregnant. If you are working with an agency that discourages parents from having biological children while adopting, you will be asked to leave the adoption program. If you are working independently, or your agency has a different policy, it is up to you. At *Adoptive Families*, we know a startling number of women who adopted in the last months of pregnancy.

Do I have to tell the child he was adopted?

Fifty years ago, adoptive parents often pretended that their children had been born to them. (Some adoptive mothers even wore padded maternity clothes for

With adoption, there is a child at the end. With infertility treatments, there may not be.
—JANIECE

While I still feel a pang when I hear a woman tell her labor-and-delivery story, I jump right in when the talk turns to the intensity of the mother-child bond. My attachment is so fierce, it takes my breath away.
—JUDY

To my amazement, anniversary dates of heartbreaking miscarriages are no longer in my memory bank, and I actually find myself glad that my fertility efforts failed. While the struggle and long waits were, at times, debilitating, I now realize that it was all necessary to bring the right children into my life. It is truly miraculous.
—MARYANN

months before the baby came.) Adult adoptees who grew up with secrecy talk about feeling that something wasn't "right" about them, about feeling both betrayed and relieved when they learned the truth.

Nowadays, the growth in open adoption (in which the birth parents keep in touch with the adoptive family) and transracial adoption (let's face it, it's hard to pretend that two Caucasian parents gave birth to a Chinese baby) means that it's almost impossible to keep an adoption secret. Our adoptive families rarely report having to tell a child about their adoption—because their children have always known, and their personal adoption story has always been an integrated part of their identity.

WISE WORDS: *Lois Melina, an adoptive parent who has been writing and lecturing about adoption for thirty years and has seen it go from a taboo topic to a source of pride, says: "We cannot build healthy relationships with our children on secrecy and lies—and this includes lies of omission. Rather, we must help them discover who they are in an atmosphere of unconditional love."*

How will I know I'm ready to adopt?
There is only one good reason to adopt, just as there is only one good reason to bear a child: Your desire to be a parent is greater than your fear. Having a child means giving up control of your life, your emotions, your future. When you're ready to let your heart walk around outside your body, you're ready for adoption.

Will my child love me as much as if I had given birth?
Yes. It's that simple.

WHAT DO I DO NEXT?

Read. Especially memoirs by adoptive parents; for our favorites, go to adoptivefamilies.com/adoptionmemoirs.

Watch. Spend time with adoptive families. Many adoption agencies and support groups host gatherings for parents and children; to find a local agency or group, go to adoptivefamilies.com/support_group.

Share. Talk to your partner, if you have one, about your feelings on adoption. If you are dealing with infertility, contact Resolve, the National Infertility Association, about attending one of its "exploring adoption" sessions.

Our bond is real, extending beyond a biological relationship between mother and child. I love her because I am her life, and she is mine.

—ALLISON

Nicolas, United States

Where Is
My Child?

Choices in Adoption: Domestic
and International

Where do adoptive parents find their children?

In any given year, there are about 100,000 adoptions in the United States (not counting adoption by step-parents). About half the children are adopted from U.S. foster care, often by their foster parents. About one quarter are "domestic newborns," placed at birth by their mothers. About one quarter are adopted from other countries. More media attention is paid to international adoptions, but the statistics have been remarkably consistent for the past twenty years: More than three quarters of adoptees are United States–born.

STRAIGHT TALK: While just about anyone can adopt, your choices—Which country? What age?—will be shaped by your own identity. Many foreign countries have age limits for would-be parents and will not accept applications from those younger

above: Hannah, United States

than twenty-five or older than forty-five. Some American adoption agencies also have specific limits. Older parents will have better luck with private adoption through an attorney (no age limits at all), adopting from foster care, or adopting an older child—either domestic or international.

ADOPTING FROM THE UNITED STATES

How do children get placed for adoption in the United States?

While children adopted from other countries are called "orphans" (more on this later), virtually all U.S.–born adoptees have living parents.

In some cases, birth parents choose to place children for adoption at birth; their parental rights can be transferred directly to the adoptive parents with the approval of the state. Other U.S. adoptees have been relinquished to the state by birth parents who are ill or incarcerated, or have been removed from their birth parents because of abuse or neglect; in these cases, parental rights are transferred first to the state, then from the state to the adoptive parents.

Adoption 101: "Private" Adoption

We use the term "private adoption" to mean that parental rights are transferred directly from the birth family to the adoptive family. It's often called "domestic infant adoption" because almost all children adopted this way are American newborns. Some people also use the term "private adoption" to mean an adoption facilitated by an attorney rather than an agency, but in fact many adoption agencies do private adoptions.

My wife and I had a good idea of what we were looking for in a child. We wanted someone who would demonstrate a love of life, an unquenchable thirst for knowledge, and a sweet yet powerful disposition. That is exactly who our daughter is. I feel that it would be naïve and ungrateful of me to ask the universe for a child with such wonderful traits, for that child to come with these traits and more, and for me to call it dumb luck or a destiny that was determined before I was able to ask for the gift. I am learning that the universe is a very strong force.

—WILLIAM

We chose domestic adoption because we really wanted a newborn. We wanted to experience parenthood from as near the start of life as possible. From there, it was a matter of picking the right agency. Domestic newborn adoption comes with an emotional as well as a financial cost. You need to prepare for the possibility that, after you pay the birth mother's expenses, she might change her mind. That's the reality of adoption.

—NANCY

Are there really American babies to adopt?

Of the 25,000 or so private adoptions that take place every year, most are of babies placed at birth or soon after. In fact, the number of domestic newborns available for adoption has risen slightly in the past few years. The idea that there are no babies comes from a quirk of history: Just after World War II, adoption of American infants reached a high point (returning GIs + lack of contraception = lots of unplanned babies) and then declined steeply, leading to long waits and the still-current myth that healthy American infants are scarce.

Who are the birth parents?

The majority of birth mothers relinquishing children are over eighteen (one study puts the average age at twenty-four). Most are single (though about 5 percent of babies are relinquished by married couples). About a quarter have children already. Interestingly, the women who place their children for adoption are more likely to have intact families, higher incomes, and higher educational levels than mothers who choose to keep their babies. The average age of relinquishing birth fathers is twenty-seven; about one quarter of them take an active role in placing their children.

Why do they choose to place a child for adoption?

About three quarters of placing birth mothers say they cannot give the child the life it deserves; the rest say they want to continue their own education.

The Day I Gave My Heart Away
Jill

WHEN I FIRST FOUND OUT THAT I WAS PREGNANT, I WAS TER-
rified. I told my mom in the only way I could—I wrote her a letter. She responded better than I had hoped. I was sure that my father would kick me
out of the house when he found out. Instead, he sat still for a while, then
he got up and hugged me, assuring me that he would be there for me. The
way Steve, the baby's father, reacted to the news totally blew my mind.
His first question was "Who's the father?"

Steve was my supervisor at a new job that I had just started. I was immediately attracted to him—I felt like a schoolgirl with a crush. We
started dating a few weeks later and were together just about every day
after that. When he first told me that he loved me, I was ecstatic. But
when he found out about the baby, it was as if a war had erupted between
us. At first Steve wanted me to have an abortion, but I insisted that I was
going to keep my baby. Then he started pushing for adoption, which to me
seemed coldhearted. I couldn't understand how someone could just hand
over his or her child for someone else to raise.

One night I woke up suddenly. I felt as if I had somehow been told that
adoption was the best choice for everyone involved—especially the baby.
I went back to sleep, finally feeling some peace within myself. Other than
my family, few people agreed with my decision. People asked me why and
how I could do such a thing, but, deep down, I knew that adoption was
the best option for me, for Steve, and, most important, for the baby.

My family and I heard about an adoption agency from friends who'd
adopted a baby boy. The agency staff treated me kindly and with respect.
They gave me complete control over how things were done. I was able to
choose the adoptive parents, which helped me feel more comfortable
about my decision. The staff asked me for a list of qualities that I wanted
the prospective parents to have. From that list, and from Steve's and my
physical descriptions, the agency chose three couples in their files that
"matched" and gave me their profiles to read. The letters provided information about what each person did for a living, what their interests were,
and what their extended families were like. These letters gave me some

insight into each couple, and somehow, the process of picking out the adoptive parents helped me cope with my emotions.

Although I read each letter at least twenty times, one of them caught my eye from the very beginning. The couple seemed sincere, and they clearly expressed how much love they had to share with a baby. I was touched by what they had gone through to become parents and how long they had been waiting. Then I had to decide whether or not I wanted to meet this couple. I was glad the decision was mine to make.

I asked my mother to go with me. The beginning of the meeting was a bit rocky. We exchanged gifts, little things that helped relieve some of the tension. As the meeting went on, we all began to relax. We talked about our families and my pregnancy. This meeting put my mind at ease about what kind of home and family my child would be growing up in. I knew I had made the right choice for my child.

Throughout the rest of my pregnancy, John and Caren checked to see how I was doing, through the agency. They also sent me cards and letters of encouragement. At first I thought that the letters would do more harm than good, because they would show me exactly how much this couple wanted my baby. But in reality they helped me more than I could have imagined, showing me not only how much they wanted my baby but how much they would love him or her.

Although my pregnancy seemed to go by quickly, the bond between my baby and me grew steadily stronger. I began to realize how hard it was going to be to give him or her to the adoptive parents. As the due date got closer, I tried to block out the fact that this child would not leave the hospital with me.

At 2:45 A.M. on October 17, my labor began. My father drove me to the hospital—about thirty miles away—while my mother held my hand. I kept telling them that the baby was coming, but they didn't believe me. By the time we pulled up outside the hospital emergency room, the baby's head was crowning. A nurse jumped into the backseat and helped me deliver my beautiful, healthy baby girl. The labor and delivery, which my parents thought would take hours, took only one hour and fifty-five minutes, start to finish.

I was given the choice of whether I wanted to be the one to hand the new parents their precious baby. At first I wasn't sure if I could do so without wanting to run, taking the baby with me. But as I looked down at her beautiful face, I knew I had to be the one to give her to John and Caren. I couldn't have gotten through that day—or any other for that matter—without the help and support from my parents and sister.

Although I still think about Samantha every day, I am thankful that she has parents who are keeping her safe and happy when I couldn't. As a birth mother, I know that placing a child for adoption—a child that you cannot take care of properly—is the most unselfish thing that any woman can do for her child.

Elizabeth, United States

I went into a place deep inside of me, my "heart of hearts," that tells me who I am and what I need to do in my life. My heart of hearts told me, even though I knew it was going to hurt, that I needed to place my babies for adoption. And I am happy to know that both of my children are happy, they are loved, and they are in wonderful, wonderful families.

—VICTORIA

How do I find a birth mother?

How you go about searching for a birth mother will depend on the laws in your state. You'll have to decide whether you feel comfortable talking to and screening women who are still in the process of making a decision about their pregnancy. If you'd rather work through an intermediary, an agency or attorney can do the screening for you. Some of our families have enjoyed the direct contact with expectant mothers; others find the process too emotional and draining.

We started attend-ing foster-care classes because we were certain we couldn't afford to adopt a newborn. The day of our first class, we received a call from an old ac-quaintance telling us that she had heard we were hop-ing to adopt, and that she had a good friend who was pregnant and want-ing to plan an adop-tion for her baby. I am an extremely private person and really hated the idea of broadcasting to friends and family about our desire to adopt, but I guess it does pay to network. Make sure everyone knows what you are planning. Someone always knows some-one else.

—AF READER

Adoption 101: How to Find a Birth Mother

- Apply to an adoption agency that will send your biography (along with those of others) to a birth mother; she makes the choice.
- Apply to an adoption agency that prescreens birth mothers and makes the choice for you. (This is increasingly rare; more and more birth mothers want to make the choice themselves, and agencies want to facilitate them.)
- Retain an adoption attorney who will search for a birth mother for you.
- Search independently for a birth mother by posting your profile on an adoption website, advertising in the newspaper, posting flyers, and mailing letters to people who may have contact with birth families.

Many parents end up taking a combination of routes. If legally permitted, they may advertise inde-pendently, then use an attorney to screen the birth mothers. They use an attorney to find the birth mother, then complete the adoption through an agency, and so on. Chapter 4, "Where Do I Start?," will help you pick your method.

STRAIGHT TALK: Some states do not permit attor-neys to match birth parents to adoptive parents; in other states, would-be adoptive parents can't advertise to birth mothers directly. To check the laws in your state, go to adoptivefamilies.com/statelaws.

What should I say to a potential birth mother?

If you are adopting privately, you will end up writing a "Dear Birth Mother" letter or making a Web profile that describes you and the life you can offer a child. You will want to offer details on your home, career, finances, circle of friends, faith, extended family—and, most of all, your plans for her child.

We've Been There: Birth Mothers' Tips for Family Profiles

1. Inject humor. Include an amusing anecdote or funny photo that shows that humor is one way you deal with life. "They had a picture of the whole family wearing 3-D glasses and watching fireworks," said Kelly of the family she chose to parent her baby. "This family had a good time just being around one another."

2. Show something special about yourself. Have a horse? Share a picture of it. Bilingual? Write a few words in your second language. You want to differentiate yourselves from the others in the stack. "The mother I chose proposed to her husband at an NFL football game on the big scoreboard," says Jessica. "I liked her chutzpah."

3. Find balance. Let potential birth parents know that your life is full enough, that you aren't depending on a baby to make it "complete." "I didn't want my baby to be the one thing that saved these people from a life of misery," explains Sara, "so I passed on them." Yet don't make it seem so full that you would have no room for a child. Shelly recalls one couple she didn't choose: "Both people had high-powered jobs and were involved in so

I remember how nervous we all were! I think that it helps to know that the birth mother wants you to like her as much as you want her to like you. Try to think of her as an old friend, and be sincere. You will have a forever bond with this amazing woman.
—ALLISON

Lily, United States

many things that I just couldn't see how they'd fit in another responsibility."

4. Accurately represent yourselves and avoid playing to your audience. One birth mother might love dogs, while another might be allergic. One might want her baby to be the couple's first, while another might want the baby to have older siblings. To bring about the best match, simply be truthful about who you are and what your lives are about.

5. Ask a trusted friend to look over your masterpiece before turning it in to your agency. Ask this person to be candid about the photos, letters, and tone. "In one picture, taken at a family picnic, they all had red eyes," explains Gwen. "I know it was just the photo, but my impression was 'How demonic!' "

6. Tinker. Advertisers know that tweaking just a word or an image can dramatically change results. If you've been waiting a while, make a minor change, such as the stationery or the lead photo.

WISE WORDS: *Susan Watson, director of the domestic adoption and birth-parent services programs at Spence-Chapin, which has been placing children since 1908, says: "Adoptive parents should meet expectant mothers with honesty and integrity. In our experience, birth mothers exercise incredible wisdom when they choose adoptive parents."*

Christopher, United States

Dear Birth Mother . . .
Nelson Handel

MY WIFE AND I WANTED TO HAVE A CHILD. BUT AFTER FOUR
fruitless years in the gristmill of infertility treatments (drugs, insemina-
tions, in vitros, donor eggs), after exhausting our resources (physical, emotional, financial), after burying the monthly hope that our bodies would
bring forth children, we accepted the fact that we are infertile. Biology
has been quietly put to rest, a haunting memory.

After examining our options, we decided to pursue an open adoption.
We liked the idea of connecting with our birth mother, of having her
choose us to parent her child, and of choosing her in return. To find
prospective parents, we learned, birth mothers contact agencies or adoption attorneys, answer classified ads in Sunday newspapers, and, sometimes, surf the Web. Soon they find themselves reviewing what are known
as "Dear Birth Mother" (DBM) letters, documents that introduce adopting couples and explain why they want to adopt. From these, birth mothers narrow their choices.

So we needed to write one, a DBM letter. Quite suddenly, we found
ourselves trying to sell ourselves as parents and, just as quickly, realizing
the impossibility of the task. If I asked you to tell me, with some measure
of certainty, what your life will look like in five years, could you do it? Ten
years? Eighteen? Will you still be married? Employed in the same profes-
sion? Living under similar circumstances? And how will you raise your
child? Can you articulate a cogent philosophy governing the stages of your
life to come? Nanny, day care, or stay-at-home parent? Private school or
public? When asked, who can truly predict more than his intention to
live, love, thrive, and grow old in the most positive circumstances he can
muster? This letter should be simple, right? "We're nice people and we'll
do our best. What more can you ask?" Lots, it turns out.

We studied letters written by other couples and analyzed their approaches. How were they targeting the market? We coldly analyzed the
"competition" and attempted to position ourselves in the field, capitalizing
on our strengths (education, humor, compassion) and smoothing over our
weaknesses (Los Angeles, working mom, forty years old). We honed our

pitch to the perceived interests of the consumer pool and tried to be all things to all people. Could we be fun yet firm, stable yet fluid, Caucasian yet multicultural, urban yet safe, Jewish yet Christian? How could we translate the left-coastal lifestyle of a couple of former artists into that of an archetypal American home? We're urban cynics, but the sample letters we saw were lush with what we termed goo-goo. Fill your letter with teddy bears, snuggles, and references to "tummy mommies," the goo-goo school suggested. Be as cute and cuddly as you can; birth mothers are suckers for this. We found it condescending, but to be safe, we spread on some goo, too.

Without really thinking, we ran helter-skelter toward a picture of idealized parents that we believed every birth mother craved. We got high on a sugar rush of pop-culture stereotypes, the sweetness of achieving something to overpower the bitter taste of reproductive failure. We would do whatever it took. We could succeed. We would succeed. We must succeed. We . . . stopped. And took a deep breath.

We began again. We set out to communicate something authentic, some measure of essential truth about how we are in the world and what we might bring to the life of a child. We tried to put into words our love and longing, our deep, primal desire to raise a family, to witness the growth and flowering of a person and share in his or her life. We embraced anew this imperfect process and struggled to say simply what we desperately felt. We wrote the truth as best we could. In this way, we felt, we would connect with the child we were meant to have. If we weren't perfect people, well then, so be it. Some openhearted woman would see us for who we are, and entrust her child's care to our strong circle of love.

After finishing the letter, we paid a fee to have it listed, among hundreds of others, online in an Internet registry. It proved to be the right place for us. Our birth mother, who said she had read more than one hundred letters online before calling us, told us she liked our sense of humor, our quirky unconventionalism, and our honesty. As we got to know her, we grew to love the same things about her. Our son, Charlie, was born on May 8. We were there for the birth, and there were lots of smiles, hugs, laughter, and just a few tears to welcome him into the world.

Arabella, United States

> **TRIED AND TRUE:** Be authentic. If a birth
> mother chooses you, you may be spending
> plenty of time together over the next months.
> If your letter wasn't truthful, she will find out
> and may be put off.

What role does the baby's father play?

The legal rights of birth fathers are one of the most
complicated areas of adoption law. Each state has its
own laws, often conflicting with those of other states.
(Ordinarily, the laws of the state where the baby is
born or the laws of the state where the adoption will
be completed are followed.) The variables of each
situation—Are the father's identity and whereabouts
known? Does he know about the pregnancy? Is he married to the birth mother? Has he taken any action indi-
cating that he wants custody of the child?—determine
which laws will come into play and how they will affect
the adoption. For the security of your adoption, you
must work with an adoption attorney or an experienced
social worker to make sure that the baby's father—
or any man who might think he is the father—agrees
to the adoption, or at least knows about the pregnancy
and birth and has had the chance to object.

Placing my daughter for adoption gave her the potential for security and love. There's never been any question about me caring for Laura. I placed her because I wanted to be a good father.
—WARREN

Adoption 101: What Is a Birth Father?

- Biological father: **the man who actually contributed the DNA to the child's conception.**
- Alleged father: **the man named by the expectant mother.**
- Presumed father: **a man who was married to the expectant mother at some point during the pregnancy, even if they were separated or divorced by the time of the birth, or a man who took the child home, supported it, and claimed it as his own.**
- Putative father: **a man who has registered with the state's "putative father" or "paternity" registry to say he believes he is the father of a child.**

Do the baby's grandparents have rights?

Even if the birth parents are minors, the birth grandparents have no legal right to either approve or contest an adoption.

TRIED AND TRUE: Even though birth grandparents have no legal rights, our adoptive families—and experienced adoption professionals—say that adoptions go smoothly when the expectant mother's own mother supports her plan, even if the relationship between the two is poor.

How close should I be to the birth mother?

In about half of today's private adoptions, the expectant mother and adoptive parents have contact during the pregnancy. Only you can decide how much contact you want to have after the adoption is completed, but our parents caution against becoming too close to a mother before she relinquishes the baby. More contact doesn't always lead to more affection, our families say. In fact, it can bring differences to the surface.

Can I be present for the birth?

If it's important to you to be present at the baby's birth, ask the birth mother and check with the hospital where she plans to give birth. Most hospitals are more than cooperative and require nothing other than the birth mother's permission.

> TRIED AND TRUE: If the birth mother says she doesn't want you at the birth, or says yes and then changes her mind, don't get upset. You and this baby will have the rest of your lives together.

Zachary, United States

How do I know the birth mother isn't running a scam?

In the thirty-year history of *Adoptive Families,* we have occasionally come across "birth mothers" who were pretending to be pregnant, or pretending to be interested in adoption, in order to extract cash from prospective adoptive parents. While such scams used to be rare, the Internet has made them more common. This, if for no other reason, is why you should engage a good adoption professional. In our experience, the families who get scammed are the ones attempting to adopt on their own.

> STRAIGHT TALK: Mark McDermott, an adoption attorney and legislative director of the American Academy of Adoption Attorneys (and himself an adoptive father), says there are three signs that a birth mother doesn't plan to follow through with the adoption:
> - She doesn't want to be represented by an attorney of her own.

- She wants to speak immediately to the parents' attorney, not to the parents.
- She discusses money at first contact.

How many expectant mothers change their plans?

About half of the women who start out investigating adoption for their babies choose to parent instead. One third of our adoptive families doing private adoptions report at least one "false start" before completing an adoption.

Can we make a contract with the birth mother?

No state allows a mother to give up her parental rights *before* the baby's birth; even if she signs such a contract, it can't be enforced. You have to wait until after the baby is born. (Likewise, nothing can force prospective adoptive parents to accept a child, either.)

Canon, United States

REALITY CHECKLIST
Expectant Mothers

A mother who changes her plans about adoption usually has at least one of the following factors:

❑ She is under eighteen.

❑ Her parents do not support the adoption plan.

❑ She has picked out a name for her baby.

❑ She has unrealistic expectations about post-adoption contact—wanting to visit the baby every week, for example.

❑ She does not have independent counseling or legal advice.

❑ She continues to have contact with the birth father but does not identify him.

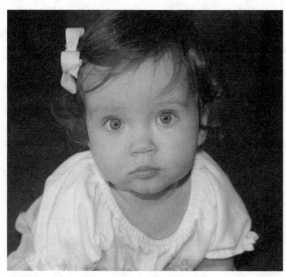

Katie, Russia

From Heartbreak to Hope
Susan Dodge

I BEGAN RESEARCHING ADOPTION AFTER OUR FIRST IN VITRO attempt failed. We weren't going to let agonizing fertility problems keep us from the joy of raising children. For a number of reasons, including our desire for a newborn, we decided on a domestic adoption. Our research of adoption agencies led us to one that emphasized open adoption, in which birth parents and adoptive parents stay in touch after the baby is placed. John and I felt it would be best for our child to know about his birth parents as he got older.

After a litany of questions, much soul searching, fingerprinting and background checks, endless paperwork, and a home study, we at last placed a newspaper ad and set up a toll-free number, so birth mothers could call us. One of the first calls we got was from a seventeen-year-old girl, who said she was very nervous but sure that adoption was the best plan for her baby: "We're just too young to raise a child." Her eighteen-year-old boyfriend agreed.

We met them shortly afterward, and we all bonded immediately. We talked about the girl's pregnancy and the baby's future with us. We all cried when she said she wanted us to be the parents of her baby.

Then, on a beautiful morning in June, we got the call that she was in labor. We rushed to the hospital, because she wanted us with her during the delivery. From ultrasounds, we knew the baby would be a girl, and we had already picked her name, Isabelle Celia. I was struck with amazement when her little head peeked through at the delivery. We had a few wonderful moments of holding her, looking into her bright blue eyes, and marveling at how tiny and perfect she was. Two days later, we were allowed to bring her home.

Three days after we brought Isabelle home, we got the heart-stopping call: Our adoption-agency counselor said that the baby's mother had changed her mind and wanted her back. We were in shock. We had known this could happen, but we thought that if it did, it would happen in the hospital right after the baby's birth—not now. But the baby's grandfather had arrived from out of state and promised to help raise the baby.

Although the baby's grandmother tried to reason with her, our birth mother had made up her mind. She wanted to keep the baby. Amidst tears, we took some pictures of baby Isabelle and told her we would always love her. We wanted her to have a good, happy life.

Nine months after our first adoption fell through, our son, Ben, was born. Not long before, we had met his birth parents. Instantly, it was as if they were old friends, and we sat in their kitchen talking and laughing for hours. They had three children through previous marriages and wanted to help a childless couple by placing their baby for adoption.

We eventually decided to tell them of our previous experience, because we wanted them to know that if we seemed hesitant, it was because our hearts had been broken. They went out of their way to create a positive experience for us, even though it was painful for them to say good-bye to their newborn son. I will never forget the words of Ben's birth mother as she held him in her hospital bed. She looked at me and said, "Let's let his mommy hold him now." And then she gave him to me.

Can I adopt from foster care?

There are half a million children in U.S. foster care. About 100,000 of them are already free for adoption, and 50,000 are adopted every year. Forty percent are white, 30 percent are African American, 20 percent are Hispanic, and the rest are "other." The average age of children in foster care who are eligible for adoption is eight and a half.

Seth, United States

What's the difference between adoption and foster care?

An adopted child belongs to her parents forever, just as if they had conceived, carried, and given birth. A foster child is a ward of the state, which can decide where he should live, go to school, and so on.

We had wanted to adopt internationally, but we worried about how a new child would fit in with our three biological children. We chose foster-care adoption, so the children could get to know one another before the adoption was finalized. We had increasingly longer visits with our foster girls, ages ten and twelve, and once we all felt comfortable, they moved in permanently. We didn't need the incentives, but the low fees, monthly stipends, and medical insurance we got by adopting from foster care let us put extra money toward the children's college funds.

—KATHRYN

Adoption 101: Adopting from Foster Care

- You can adopt directly from foster care. In this case, the children are likely to be older (they are rarely under two), and the birth parents' rights have already been terminated.
- You can foster a child, fall in love, and later apply to adopt. Your application will be considered along with those of other would-be parents.
- You can apply to a fost-adopt program, in which you foster a child with intent to adopt. In this situation, the child has not been freed for adoption, but social workers believe that there is a good chance that the birth parents will lose their rights, and will preapprove you to adopt should that happen.

How do children end up in foster care?

Half the children in foster care have been removed from their birth parents because of abuse or neglect; a quarter were relinquished by birth parents who are ill, incarcerated, or otherwise unable to care for a child. The rest are in foster care because of a handicap, delinquency, or a prior failed adoption.

STRAIGHT TALK: Your first encounter with a foster child may be through a photo listing, on the Web, or in an adoption-agency album. You should be able to read a brief description of each child, but the information will be very limited to protect the child's privacy. Experienced foster parents know how to look for clues: "Active" may suggest an attention disorder; recommendation for placement in a home without other children might suggest a history of severe abuse. If you plan to adopt from foster care, you must find out why a particular child is in the system. A child who was removed after parental abuse will need very different support from a child whose loving birth parent placed her for her own good.

Can I adopt a newborn from foster care?

Before a child can be adopted from foster care, social workers must first try to reunite him with his birth family. After it's decided that reunification isn't possible, terminating the birth parents' rights usually takes a little over a year. As a result, tiny babies are rarely adopted directly from foster care. If you want to adopt a baby from foster care, you should apply to a fost-adopt program or become a foster parent with the hope of adopting later.

What are the advantages of adopting a foster child?

Adopting from foster care gets relatively little attention, yet it is by far the most common type of adoption in the United States. It has one huge drawback: Until the adoption is finalized, your foster child can be removed to be reunited with her birth family or placed with another family. But there are also major advantages: You and the child get to know each other before the adoption; you can foster a newborn; and there are lots of financial supports for foster parents, some of which continue after adoption.

We had three birth children and wanted to expand our family. Initially, we wanted a little girl, but we ended up with Max, who was almost five. He was the one for us; if you saw him now, you'd think he'd always been part of our family. He gets speech therapy (free, through our school system) and is improving every day. Everybody tells us how lucky he is to have been placed in such a good family. We see it just the opposite. We feel blessed, for he makes us appreciate life's simple pleasures every day.
—TRACY AND JIMMY

Fostering Love
Rosemary Shulman

WHEN I MENTIONED MY DESIRE TO ADOPT TO A COLLEAGUE, she told me that she was pursuing adoption through a different route—fost-adopt. I learned that in Los Angeles, four thousand children in foster care become available for adoption each year. And with fost-adopt, I didn't need to own a home or have thirty thousand dollars in the bank to become a parent. I decided to give it a try, and within three weeks, I was attending MAPP (Model Approach to Partnerships in Parenting) classes with other prospective parents. The themes of attachment, abuse, neglect, and the loss a child feels when placed in foster care were daunting at first, but toward the end of the training, my group agreed that every parent should be required to attend classes like this. I concluded that I could handle the possibility of giving a child back—though I hoped I would never be faced with that.

I completed my application and home study straightaway and was officially placed on the "open homes" list. My house has one bedroom, so I was certified for one child, aged newborn through six months. Three weeks later, I was Renée's mom.

She arrived dressed in a hospital-issue undershirt and diaper, tightly bundled in an infant carrier. As I took her out of the carrier and held her, three of my friends stood beside me. I kept thinking, "Oh my God, I'm a mom. Now what do I do?" After everyone left, I fed her and changed her into her first pair of pink teddy bear pajamas. I admired her ten perfect fingers and ten perfect toes. We spent the next two weeks visiting our pediatrician, interviewing day-care providers, and coping with sleepless nights. I'd never been happier.

Three days after I returned to work, I received the call: Renée's great-aunt had been granted custody. My heart was in pieces when I went home that night to pack her little undershirts and sleepers. I wrote a letter to her family, explaining that she liked to fall asleep on her side, that she was a good burper after two ounces of formula, and that tickling her toes made her smile. The next day, I drove Renée to the agency. Her family hugged me and thanked me for taking good care of her, and I said good-bye to my little girl.

I had just begun to heal after the loss of Renée when I received a call from my social worker. A baby boy was waiting. He had been born nine weeks premature and was now ready for discharge from the hospital. The social worker didn't know whether he would be a permanent adoption placement. For me, the overwhelming desire to be a mom outweighed the uncertainty.

Justin was three weeks old and barely tipped the scale at four pounds, yet he was surprisingly healthy, with no obvious special needs. He needed to be fed every two hours, and he spit up every time he ate. I constantly worried that he wasn't receiving enough calories. Sleep deprivation became a way of life. At one point, as he lay in my lap sucking his bottle, newborn Pampers up to his armpits, I fell asleep. I woke to a screaming baby, soaked with formula. I couldn't tell if he was madder about being wet or about having missed dinner. I learned that Justin was a fighter. If he was willing, so was I. In two months, he gained six pounds, and we became a team—mother and son. Then, once again, the dreaded call came. A great-aunt had been found who was willing to take custody. Another great-aunt? It wasn't any easier to let go this time.

Even before Justin was gone, the agency called again. They had another baby boy. He was healthy and weighed over eight pounds—huge, after Justin!—and had no family members willing or qualified to take him. He would likely be placed for adoption. I had wanted a few weeks' break before I went back on the open-homes list . . . but before the social worker had finished giving me the details, I knew I would say yes.

Today, at three years, Matthew's bright eyes, beautiful smile, and curious nature make my life a wonderful adventure. We love each other beyond reason. Some nights I find myself standing beside his bed just to listen to him breathe. And he is here to stay; our adoption ceremony was held on June 19.

There are more than 100,000 children in foster care in this country who are legally free for adoption right now. There is minimal or no cost involved in adopting through the foster system. Single parents are welcomed. For families who have their hearts set on a newborn—well, I had three placed with me in a matter of months. Adopting through the foster-care system wasn't easy; then again, neither are the other ways of adopting. I had several court continuances over the same issue—incomplete paperwork. Yet, despite the aggravating delays—and the initial uncertainty—I will do it again. I treasure my memories of the time, however brief, I spent with my first two babies. I was there for Renée's first smile, Justin's first splashes in his bubble bath. Matthew took his first steps into my arms, and he is waiting for me with a big smile at the end of each day.

A key factor in our decision-making process was the predictable time line of an adoption from China—I didn't have the emotional strength to wait for an undetermined amount of time hoping to be chosen by a birth mother. Adoption has shown us the perfect way to complete our family and to find the person I always knew was missing. We just had to look a little harder.
—LEIGH

WISE WORDS: *Sarah Gerstenzang, associate director of the Collaboration to AdoptUsKids, a federally funded initiative to promote and facilitate the adoption of children in foster care (and herself an adoptive parent), says: "Even if the child goes back to the birth family, you have made a difference in a human life, and that is very powerful."*

ADOPTING FROM ANOTHER COUNTRY

Where do international adoptees come from? International adoption began after World War II, when small groups of war orphans from Europe and Japan were brought to the United States. Numbers grew after the Korean War, with the adoptions of Korean orphans and Korean American babies (children of Korean mothers and American soldiers). The Vietnam War brought another bump (including more than three thousand children brought out in Operation Babylift as the war came to an end). In 1992 the Chinese government authorized international adoption; China became the top "sending country" for the United States. In recent years, adoptions from Latin America and the former Soviet Union have also increased.

Most countries in the Middle East, Africa, and Western Europe forbid international adoption of their children, as do Canada and Australia. Other countries that don't specifically forbid adoption can make it next to impossible, either by requiring long residence by the adoptive parents or simply by not having an organized adoption system.

STRAIGHT TALK: No foreign country has official rules about the race of adoptive parents, but some Asian and Eastern European countries actively discourage adoption of their children by African American parents.

TRIED AND TRUE: If this is your first adoption, choose a country with a long-standing, stable adoption process and work with an agency licensed by both the United States and the sending country. International adoption can be complicated enough; don't add extra uncertainty to the process.

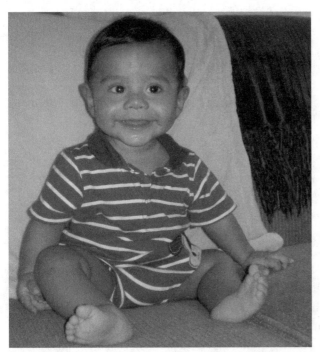

Alex, Guatemala

After eliminating the countries whose criteria we did not meet, we considered our feelings about race, color, and maintaining cultural practices for an internationally adopted child. We looked at the prevalence of alcohol use by birth mothers in certain parts of the world, quality of orphanage care versus foster care, and the ages of children available for adoption. We chose Guatemala because our child would likely share our Catholic heritage, we were comfortable with Hispanic culture, the risk of fetal alcohol syndrome is low, we liked the foster care system there, and we would be able to adopt a relatively young infant.

—MARCY

A Boy Like Him
Deirdre Levinson

THE AGENCY SENT A SOCIAL WORKER TO LOOK AT OUR HOME, and she urged us to start "Vietnamizing" the household. I had visions of water buffalo and hordes of U.S. conscripts milling around our apartment. It was just as well that we didn't work overtime at Vietnamization, because it wasn't a Vietnamese that we got. We got a Cambodian—one of sixty starvelings airlifted from an orphanage in Phnom Penh and flown, one wintry morning, to Montreal, where we hastened to claim him.

The airport was crowded with prospective parents. Never, the agency representative said, addressing us all, never in her experience had she encountered a batch so beautiful. Every blessed one of them a dazzler, she said.

I scanned the procession of ill-favored kids as one by one, amid flashing cameras, they passed down the ramp to their enraptured, evidently purblind new parents. I reminded myself that looks weren't everything. But when our name was called, I saw at a glance that this one—running sores, running nose, rotting baby teeth regardless—was not only far and away the pick of the bunch, he was a spectacular beauty by any criterion. "Beautiful?" said the pediatrician we rushed him to, letting out a snort as he scrutinized our scantling couched in the palm of his hand. "Then find me some beautiful flesh on his bottom to give him a shot."

We named him Malachi, after the last of the Hebrew prophets, and sent out our announcement of his adoption, inscribed with the words of his namesake: "Have we not all one father? Hath not one God created us?" As soon as he was strong enough, we had him circumcised, making him officially as Jewish as any Jew on this earth. Malachi himself was concerned with even more basic matters. Though of walking age when we got him, he was too weak to crawl, let alone walk. But that was all that was weak about him. He knew from scratch what he wanted, which was a family—father, mother, sibling rival, and all—and he set out single-mindedly to establish his claim. He sounded the charge against our five-year-old, Miranda, contesting her right to the merest kiss in his presence. He made himself one of us fast enough, and he could occasionally pass as ours by blood. (An interested passenger looking the four of us over on a bus once observed that the girl was her father all over again, the boy the image of me.) My own mother pronounced him conclusively, in the matter of character, far more my child than Miranda, bless her, with her refined little ways. Malachi contrived at the same time to use his otherness to unfair advantage. "I'll go back to Cambodia," he would threaten when crossed, and when we said we'd just follow him there if he did, he would parry triumphantly, "You can't. You don't know where it is."

It wasn't until nursery school that Malachi learned that being what he called "adocted" wasn't all beer and skittles. One summer afternoon, at going-home time, I found him on the steps there, the disconsolate subject of the speculation of three Lilliputian companions. He wasn't, they asked me, really mine, was he? I wasn't his real mother, was I? Rising to their challenge, fronting each in turn, I picked them off one by one. "Did your parents search the wide world for you? Did yours, for you? And how many steps further than the hospital did yours go to get you? We searched the wide world to get this boy."

That, he and I agreed as we stalked off together, should settle their hash once and for all. But there was more to it than that. "You wanted to get me?" he took to asking, unprefaced, sitting at the kitchen table, staring hard at the wall. Or in the elevator, apparently addressing the push button, "You wanted to get me?" Then, at last, point-blank, "You wanted a brown boy, Dad? Ma, you wanted a boy like me?"

A boy like him? Search the corners of this earth for his like, where breathes the half-American, half-English, Jewish, Cambodian boy who can match his speed in the hundred-yard dash, who can play the recorder so melodiously, throw a fishing line as dexterously, make friends as firmly, belch as resoundingly as our boy can? Show us the boy with an eye as sharp as his for finding money in the street. (Once he found twenty dollars on the sidewalk. He asked me to make special mention of that.) We should all have such a son.

My husband and I looked at international adoption because we had heard that we were too old to adopt domestically (we were thirty-seven at the time) and that adopting an infant could take a long time. As we set out to choose a country, we examined our and our families' beliefs. Would our families accept a child who looked Asian or Hispanic? Did we want a child who looked like us? Were we willing to help a child of another culture learn about his or her culture? Did we want an infant or a toddler who might struggle with a new language? We decided to adopt from Russia. We felt that being Caucasian would allow our son to keep his adoption private if he chose to, because it wouldn't be obvious that he was adopted.
—MICHELLE

How do children become available for adoption in other countries?

We think of orphans as children whose parents have died, but in fact the law (international and U.S.) defines an orphan more broadly: one who has lost his parents through death, abandonment, or surrender. Most of the children in foreign orphanages have been brought in by parents who are ill or desperately poor; others have been abandoned and are brought in by members of the extended family, neighbors, or the police. In countries where there is no formal process for surrender, parents may "abandon" a baby, or even fake their own deaths, in order to gain the child a safe home in an orphanage.

STRAIGHT TALK: The United States Citizenship and Immigration Service (USCIS) has very specific (if confusing) definitions of an orphan. Basically, a child can be considered an orphan if:

- both parents have died or disappeared or have abandoned the child;
- one parent has died or disappeared, and the remaining parent has released the child for adoption and emigration;
- both parents are living and identified but cannot care for the child, *and* they have released the child for adoption and emigration.

If a child does not meet these criteria, she might not be allowed to immigrate to the United States—even after being adopted abroad by American parents.

In some countries, concern about unethical practices has led the U.S. embassy or the local government to require DNA tests to prove that the person relinquishing the child for adoption is really the birth parent; at least one country tests twice, once at referral and again just before the visa is granted, to ensure that the child has not been switched.

What countries should I consider?

While your child will become a U.S. citizen with adoption, his birth country will also become a part of your life. You will want to learn about the country so that you can answer your child's questions; you may visit—to adopt, and perhaps later, with your child. So it's sensible to pick a country to which you have some connection.

Zoey, China

REALITY CHECKLIST
How to Choose a Country

❑ Do you have friends or family from a sending country?

❑ Do you speak the language of a sending country?

❑ Have you ever visited a sending country?

Which countries have healthy children?

The country of a child's birth is far less important than the circumstances: A perfectly healthy baby can be born into appalling poverty and chaos. However, in choosing a country, it's worth finding out as much as you can about its most common health problems and about the kind of medical records provided for adoptees. Some children (from South Korea, for example) arrive with detailed, accurate histories; others come with one unreliable sentence. If more information will make you more comfortable, factor this into your choice of country.

Which country has the easiest process?

One of the reasons China was long the most popular sending country was its process, notably organized,

Nathan, Russia

"We were all blessed to have found each other" is a far different concept from "You were lucky that we saved you." Adoption has allowed our family to find happiness in the face of sorrow. I don't know if we're lucky, but I do know that we have been blessed in our mutual need—and our mutual joy.

—JULIE

transparent, and predictable. In general, countries that control adoptions through a centralized government department (such as China's Center of Adoption Affairs or Ethiopia's Ministry of Women's Affairs) have more predictable time lines. In countries where adoption runs through local attorneys or disparate agencies, it's much harder to predict your wait time.

TRIED AND TRUE: Countries sometimes close or suspend their adoption programs. When you choose an adoption agency, pick one that works in more than one country; it will make it easier for you to switch, if necessary.

How do I bring a child into the United States?

A child who fits the legal definition of an orphan will qualify for an "orphan visa" and, depending on your sending country, will automatically become a U.S. citizen upon entering the United States, or when the adoption is finalized in a U.S. court.

Can I adopt a child from a war zone or a natural disaster?

Whenever a foreign war or natural disaster is in the news, would-be parents want to open their homes to affected children. However, United Nations policy (followed by the U.S. government) does not permit adoption from countries in a state of war or disaster. Families who have been torn apart need every chance to reunite.

WISE WORDS: *Merrily Ripley, founder and director of Adoption Advocates International, in Port Angeles, Washington, and adoptive mother to seventeen children, says: "Parents shouldn't adopt only to save a child from a life of poverty, but for most folks, there are multiple reasons they adopt. Concern for others can be one of them."*

Adrianne, Armenia

Adoption 101

The Hague Adoption Convention (formally the Convention on Protection of Children and Co-operation in Respect of Intercountry Adoption) is an international treaty to improve accountability, safeguards, and cooperation in intercountry adoption. Since it came into effect in the United States in 2008, its terms govern any adoption from any of the seventy-five or so signing countries. The convention safeguards include: mandated home studies for adoptive parents, prohibitions on inducements to birth parents, and prior approval for children to emigrate to their new countries before their adoptions are finalized.

How do I make sure my adoption is ethical? Periodically, there are media stories about baby selling, child abduction, and other adoption scandals. Sometimes countries close down adoptions because of corruption. In other cases, the United States stops processing orphan visas from individual countries because there is evidence that children were bought or stolen from their birth families.

As in a domestic adoption, parents adopting internationally have a responsibility to ensure that the birth family's rights are respected. For everyone's sake, you will want to confirm that the child was surrendered knowingly and voluntarily by the birth family.

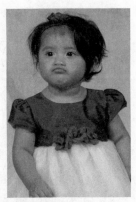

Betsy, Guatemala

TRIED AND TRUE: Someday your child will want to know the details of the adoption. You will want to be able to tell the story with pride.

Did I Steal My Daughter?

Elizabeth Larsen

WALTER AND I HAD TRIED TO DO EVERYTHING RIGHT. WE'D heard of corrupt adoption lawyers, fly-by-night operators who use online photo listings to lure parents, of baby stealing and baby selling, and of the myriad agencies that offer, for hefty fees, to help Americans bring home a child from some of the world's poorest countries. We chose one of the largest and most respected agencies, and faithfully attended all the counseling appointments it offered. "I just need to know that the child we adopt has no other options," Walter finally told our social worker. I can't remember her exact answer, but it was something along the lines of "All these children need families."

A week later, in Guatemala City, I stepped out onto rose-marble floors to face Flora's foster mother, Maria, a stout woman with a six-month-old girl riding at her hip in a woven sling. They cuddled and laughed—later I'd look at photos of this moment to remind myself that Flora could laugh. For weeks, her eyes grazed her new home with a dull blankness, and my heart sank.

When I asked Maria if she knew Beatriz, Flora's birth mother, she smiled. *"Muy linda,"* she said. *"Muy cariñosa."*

"Would she want to meet us?" I asked. Maria shook her head. I think she said that it would be too painful for Beatriz. I looked at Flora gumming a French fry. Maria had styled her hair so that two tiny ponytails stuck out atop her head, like miniature oil geysers. Somewhere, a woman was coming to terms with the fact that she would never see her baby again.

Maria, our daughter's foster mother, called on Flora's first birthday to say that Beatriz, her mother, wanted us to know she felt she had made the right decision. A few weeks later our social worker told us that Beatriz had visited the lawyer and wanted to see photos of her daughter. Several months later Maria called again. The lawyer had threatened to fire her if she continued to contact us.

By the time we returned to Guatemala City, Flora was two and a half. Walter and I had decided it would be easier for her to meet Beatriz this young. As she grew up, she and Beatriz would figure out what they wanted from their relationship. But it was an uneasy compromise. Unlike our domestic counterparts, we didn't have the benefit of longitudinal studies and books detailing best practices. We didn't even really have an open adoption. There was no legal document to set out the terms of contact, only a tendril of trust spun from the fact that Beatriz, Walter, and I all loved the same child.

When you meet your daughter's mother, you don't waste time with small talk. And at first, there was no need for talking, because Beatriz could not take her eyes off Flora.

"Hola, mi amor," she said as she bent down.

Flora frowned and turned away. "I want Daddy," she said.

Walter picked her up and kissed her cheek. "Sweetie," he said, "this is Beatriz. She's your Guatemalan mommy." Flora buried her face in his shoulder. Nervously, we tried to draw her out. But Beatriz told us not to worry.

Beatriz told us that she was deeply depressed for a year after the adoption was finalized. She got through her pain by turning to God. She'd loved being in the hospital with Flora and had demanded, as a condition of the adoption, that she be able to visit her in foster care. She'd assumed that she would never see Flora again, and now she was in shock that she had. She took obvious delight in how healthy and happy Flora was. She told us the names of all of Flora's relatives and explained that Flora gets her dimples from her uncle.

Many adoptive parents describe their connection with their children as something that was destined by a larger force. "God brought us to each other," they'll say. "We were meant to be a family." I understand why we want to think that, but the reality is, Flora is my child because something went wrong. To believe otherwise would mean that God intended for Beatriz to suffer because she couldn't afford to raise her child, that we were meant to have the option of adding a girl to our family because we could afford the price.

At the end of our third hour together, all of us—save Flora—looked shell-shocked, but no one wanted to leave. Beatriz asked if I worked. I said I was a journalist and that one day I hoped to write about women in Guatemala and other countries who place their children for adoption. I told her that we don't hear much about these mothers.

Beatriz nodded. "Please write about me," she said. "Please tell the Americans how much I love my daughter."

Loving an adopted child is easy. In fact, Flora's adoption was, in some astonishing way, more powerful than giving birth to my sons. To fall so deeply for a daughter who has no genetic link to me made me realize that we are simply hardwired to love the children we are given to raise.

Raising an adopted child is, however, a complicated privilege. Walter and I could not turn our backs on Beatriz's poverty. After trying unsuccessfully to find a nonprofit that would help us sponsor her somehow, we finally decided to just send her money, so she could finish her education. Might this encourage women in her neighborhood to place a child for adoption? Could we possibly not do it?

What I do know is that I have never felt more like Flora's "real" mother than when Beatriz and I were holding each other next to Ronald McDonald. And that's not because Flora so obviously saw me as her mommy. It's because I now understand I'm not her only one.

WHAT DO I DO NEXT?

Wait. Don't make any decisions yet. This is the time to explore all your options.

Lurk. Join as many online adoption-support groups as you can stand, and see what the parents are saying about their experiences.

Stretch. If you have assumed you will adopt domestically, join at least one international adoption-support group. If you have (even unconsciously) ruled out adopting from foster care, visit the AdoptUsKids website and look at the children (adoptivefamilies.com/foster). If you have decided on international adoption and have picked one country, explore others as well.

Can I Choose a Child?

How to Think About Race, Age, and Gender

How do I begin to think about choosing a child?

For many adoptive parents, the hardest part of the process is the choice. Some have an instant, clear vision of their child—a toddler from China, an infant who looks just like them, a teen from the local community. For others, the process raises uncomfortable questions about race, age, and gender.

The first and most important decision concerns age. Many of our families want to experience their child's "firsts"—the first days, first smile, first steps. Take time to think this through. If you want to adopt a newborn baby, you are ruling out international adoption, and you may be ruling out the ability to choose a boy or a girl.

above: Andrew, Russia

After several years of fertility treatments and a failed IVF, my husband and I took a five-month break, went on a cruise, got ourselves together, and started the adoption process. There was no question of the type of adoption we wanted. We, mainly I, wanted a newborn. I wanted the 0–3 month clothes and the night feedings; I didn't want to miss a thing. We met our miracle when she was five days old, and she is all I have ever wanted. Good luck to all of you going through this process of becoming a parent. It is everything you dream it will be.

—TINA

STRAIGHT TALK: Few adoption professionals will say this, but choosing to adopt a newborn makes it very hard to choose gender. If you want a newborn, you are limited to private adoption or fost-adopt, where opportunities to pick a boy or a girl will be very limited. If you are happy to adopt a child who's one year or older—domestic or international—many agencies will let you specify gender.

There are so many older children to adopt. Is it unreasonable to want a baby?

As with all the other choices, *your* responsibility is to adopt the child you can parent best. If raising a child from infancy is very important to you, then that's what you should do.

Adison, United States

Special Delivery
Kate McKee Robertson

WE THOUGHT WE WANTED A BABY. A TINY FIST WRAPPED AROUND our fingers. The smell of talcum powder. A coo, a cry, a cuddle. But after trying, unsuccessfully, to conceive—including an attempt at in vitro fertilization—my husband, Kevin, and I decided to explore adoption.

Overwhelmed by the prospects of international adoption and the costs and risks of independent domestic adoption, Kevin and I decided to sign up to be foster parents. We could help a child, we reasoned, while trying to decide the best way to get one of our own. We imagined a toddler, delivered to our door, longing to be loved and nurtured.

That's not what happened.

The faces of waiting children look much the same in every state. They are six and ten and twelve. They are children with difficult histories. They are not infants or toddlers. They are not blank slates. Some have emotional problems and learning disabilities and even serious health concerns. But like all children, they need permanent families. A place to call home, a place of safety and guidance today, a place to bring the grandkids for Christmas tomorrow.

Kevin and I looked through photos of Louisiana's waiting children. The faces haunted us. They were smiling for the camera, like puppies in a petstore window, wagging for a home. We were overwhelmed with sorrow and regret. Regret that we couldn't adopt them all. The question of *whether* to adopt one of the children in these photos became How do we adopt *one*?

A social worker helped narrow our search. Would we consider a sibling group? We had two extra bedrooms, Kevin pointed out. With bunk beds, we could easily take three.

Special needs? Here we hesitated. Older children in the foster-care system would likely have emotional problems, we reasoned. Could we handle learning disabilities, as well?

Medical conditions? We decided that we could handle "moderate" disabilities but that, as first-time parents, we did not have the skills or confidence to handle severe problems. And so we continued with our classes and waited for a call. It didn't take long for our children to find us. A friend was the temporary foster mother of a sister and brother, eight and ten, who were on their sixth foster placement. They were not yet available for adoption but were expected to be shortly. We saw their pictures, talked to their foster mother, and arranged for a visit. Three weeks later, our family grew by two.

Those first few days were a bit uncomfortable for us all. Kevin and I tried to help the children settle in. They were polite houseguests, busy with a new school and picking out new clothes and toys. The process of becoming a true family unfolded in the months to come.

Couples who consider adopting older children often worry that they will mourn having missed the firsts: first step, first word, first grade. But parents of older adopted children have their own set of firsts. The first time my son, Derek, stopped calling me Miss Kate and called me Mom. And how he liked the sound of it! For the next few days, he liberally sprinkled every sentence with it.

"Mom, what's for dinner, Mom? Mom, can I go outside to play, Mom?"

Or the first time my daughter, Arielle, blurted out "I love you" as she ran off to catch the school bus.

Or the first time my son felt safe enough to whisper in my ear a painful secret—a hurt he'd never told anyone—trusting that I would help him heal.

Or the first time someone passed my desk at work, noticed the photographs of the children, and asked, "Are those your kids?" And I said, "Yes, yes they are."

Derek and Arielle now have a home. As I hold my children's small hands in mine, and breathe in their smell of strawberry shampoo and SweeTarts, I know I have the babies I was meant to have. And so, as the adoption moves forward, we wait for a judge to say what we already know: We are a family.

What's the toughest age to adopt?

Many adoption professionals say that toddlers (children aged one to three years) have the hardest transition to adoption. They are old enough to feel the loss of familiar people and surroundings but too young to understand what's happening to them.

WISE WORDS: *Karen Schulz, an adoption specialist at the Center for Adoption Support and Education in Silver Spring, Maryland, says: "Parents experience adoption as the most joyous occasion. But for a toddler, it can feel like being kidnapped."*

Lukas, Russia

We brought Fisseha home two years ago, at age ten, and it was the easiest transition of any of our children. Everyone should start their families with ten-year-old Ethiopian boys! I tell other parents who are looking into adopting older kids that the start-up is like that with a newborn—it is all-consuming and exhausting. But after three months, instead of having a three-month-old, you've got a child who can be recruited for the soccer team, or who's started piano lessons, or who's in Brownies. It's intense at the beginning, but you get a child who can become part of your life faster than a baby can.
—MELISSA

Four years ago, my husband and I do-mestically adopted a sibling group of three. At the time, the youngest was twenty-one months, the middle was four years old, and the oldest about to turn six. It was quite the learning experience—to say the least—especially figuring out how to handle their differ-ent levels of "memo-ries" prior to the adoption. The bond-ing with each child occurred at a differ-ent rate, but we never allowed that to frighten us. Par-ents should remem-ber that it will be a matter of when— not if—the relation-ship fully develops. There are so many benefits to adopting "older" children that shouldn't be over-looked when consid-ering adoption.

—BETH

REALITY CHECKLIST
Are You Ready for a Toddler?

❏ What are your expectations? Be honest. Do you envision a youngster who is toilet-trained and sleeps through the night? A newly adopted two- or three-year-old may behave like a much younger child as a result of grief, neglect, or institutional care.

❏ Are you in good physical shape? Many toddlers need the security of being frequently held and carried. Others keep incredibly busy, exploring the wonders of their new life. Either way, you'll need strength and stamina to keep up.

❏ Can you tolerate extreme behavior? Some newly adopted toddlers rage for hours, cry inconsolably, or act out aggressively.

❏ Do you have a support network? The demands can be overwhelming. Do you have friends or family who can step in? Does your agency offer post-adoption support?

Small Wonders
Rochelle Green

MY LONG JOURNEY'S END WAS ON A DIRT ROAD IN DA NANG, IN the slender midsection of the sinewy dragon that gives shape to Vietnam. It came sixteen months after we opened the envelope containing a photo of our tiny baby boy, and three days after I pushed a suitcase and stroller toward airport security. Finally on my way to meet our new son, I had given a jubilant thumbs-up to my husband and daughter and waved good-bye.

The van pulled up to the orphanage just as a dozen toddlers streamed through the front door. I scanned their faces to find the one that matched the photo on my bedroom dresser. I spotted him in the arms of a young girl, who thrust him toward me. "Mama," she said excitedly to the boy. "This is your mama."

But the little boy for whom I'd waited so long had clearly not been waiting for me. He twisted his body away from me and hid his face in the girl's shoulder. He was a few days shy of eighteen months, old enough to know that something was up but too young to understand what it was. That day and the next, he warily allowed me to hold him, but his small chest heaved with deep, quiet sobs. In the passport photo taken just before the ceremony that made him my son, I saw the saddest, most frightened little boy in the world.

Some families, like mine, sign on for an infant but run into procedural delays, while others choose a country in which the process takes a year or more. Some prospective parents request a toddler, because of their own ages or the ages of their other children. Some simply relish the toddler years, typically defined as one to three. With their boundless curiosity and budding communication skills, toddlers radiate a sense of joy and wonder that shows us the world in a new way. But this crucial stage in development makes it a difficult time for a child to be taken from all he knows. Lacking the cognitive and linguistic skills to understand the often abrupt transition, most toddlers join their new families in a state of anger, fright, or grief.

By the time a child enters toddlerhood, he has already amassed an impressive résumé and is ready to explore his world. He has begun walking and can manipulate objects. He understands what's said to him and answers with sounds, body language, and a few words. Still securely attached to his caregiver, he is becoming aware of himself as a separate person and is making his first stabs at independence. Over the next two years, he'll master motor skills, string together words to express increasingly complex thoughts, and emerge as an individual. For a toddler who is just beginning to make sense of his world, adoption changes everything. Familiar routines disappear. The strangers who take him look and smell different. His abilities to trust and feel secure, along with his sense of control, are severely tested.

It's hard to predict how a toddler will adjust to his new home. Some children rebound quickly—within a week, my son, Julian, was gleefully running through hotel hallways and snuggling in for story time. But for many others, the adjustment takes time, attention, and parents who understand the challenge of adopting a child at this age.

Zachary, Guatemala

What does *older* mean in adoption?

When adoption professionals talk about older children, they generally mean older than five years. Some of our families have adopted both infants and older children; they say that while the experiences are different and require different skills, the eventual bonds and love are the same.

Contrary to popular belief, older children are not more likely to have attachment disorders than children adopted under the age of five. A child who has formed a strong attachment at some point in her life (to a parent or a caregiver) has the framework to form healthy bonds later. However, an older child will certainly have experienced some form of loss and, possibly, some neglect and abuse as well. Parents should be prepared with extra support (for the child and for themselves).

There can be great advantages to adopting an older child: speed, low cost, the ability to choose gender.

Some of our families have wanted older children from the beginning; others came to the decision after carefully weighing their options. All of them have become advocates for the adoption of older kids.

Can we adopt an infant now and an older child later?

Some adoption agencies will not let you adopt out of birth order; they want your adopted child to be the youngest in the family. If you want to adopt out of birth order, make sure you ask this question when you research agencies.

> **STRAIGHT TALK:** If you are adopting from a developing country, bear in mind that estimates of age may not be accurate. Babies may be months younger or older than expected, and we know families whose "four-year-old" turned out to be seven, or whose "eleven-year-old" was really fifteen. If you are adopting an older child and age is very important to you, talk to a pediatrician who specializes in international adoption *before* you accept your referral.

Can I adopt a child of another race?

In the United States, for many years social workers practiced "race matching" and denied adoptions of black children by white parents. A law passed in 1996 encourages race-blind adoption; agencies that receive federal funds—and almost all of them do—cannot deny or delay your adoption because you and the child are of different races. (The only exception: Native American children, whose adoptions must be approved by their own tribes.)

> **TRIED AND TRUE:** African American and multiracial children are overrepresented in the U.S. adoption system. Many social workers and birth mothers faced with a choice of

Our Belarussian daughter was twelve when she arrived, so teendom was very near. She'd spent only a couple of years in an institution, having had almost ten years in a loving family before she lost her mom. We met in a summer camp in Belarus, and, as she says, "we fell in love." She so much wanted a family, and that is what we try to give. We were attached before the adoption. Language was a little tough at first, but I had learned some Russian and she was fast learning conversational English. She is a beginning high-schooler this year—an honor-roll student and athlete, enjoying life to the fullest.

—JIM

Sitting in a restaurant not long after we adopted our sibling group (Marina is of Mongolian descent; Chris and Tori are African American), our son wanted to know why the people next to our table kept staring at us. I replied, "Those people think you and your sisters are the most beautiful kids they have ever seen." If you could have seen the smile on his face! Priceless.
—SUE

adoptive parents still prefer to place children in same-race families, so if you or your partner is black, or if you already have a black child, you can probably adopt very quickly.

How do I know if I can parent a child of another race?

While we would love to tell you that race doesn't matter, after a combined half-century of raising children transracially ourselves, we can assure you that it does. Raising children of another race demands extra support for both parent and child.

REALITY CHECKLIST
Can I Parent a Child of Another Race?

❑ Test yourself: Of course you don't think of yourself as racist, but almost all of us have been raised in a race-conscious society. Before you choose to adopt a child of another race, test yourself for what's called "implicit bias"—unconscious racism. Go to adoptivefamilies.com/transracial.

❑ Test your family: Think carefully about the relatives who will be spending time with your child. If they have made racist remarks, can you protect your child, or are you prepared to cut off contact?

❑ Test your community: Will your child feel alone in the school system? Are there adult role models? Can you find hair salons and dermatologists who can care for your child?

An Unmatched Set
Jana Wolff

AT OUR WEDDING, FRIENDS ASSURED MY HUSBAND AND ME that we would create good-looking children. And we believed them. It's that cloning fantasy: Our children would be miniature versions of ourselves, inheriting only our best features. I pictured a child with my green eyes and his thick, black hair. My dreams left out our worst features: big nose, freckles, a long second toe, and a proclivity to indigestion. So many of our dreams (and fears) were shattered along the way. All that talk about how pretty our children would be . . . and it turned out we couldn't even have any. When we started considering adoption, I wondered if I could feel like a mother to a child who didn't resemble me or my husband.

Much as we all like to think of ourselves as consumed with thoughts more lofty than the issue of appearances, looks play into the emotional process before and after an adoption takes place. Adoption is like a blind date in some ways—a permanent one. Early in the process, birth parent and child are faceless to potential adoptive parents. Adoptive parents worry that their child will be ugly or a dud or both. They care about looks, not because they are hopelessly superficial but because they want to fall in love with the stranger who will become their child.

Whether or not you like your own looks, they are familiar, and there is something safe about that. It's almost as if looking alike will ensure a degree of cohesiveness. Look-alike families are assumed to belong together, but families like ours—who don't match—are seen as curious groupings of individuals. A white woman holding the hand of a little black boy prompts guessing: His social worker? His babysitter? His black father's white girlfriend? His mother? (No, that couldn't be.)

Once adoptive parents decide that they can parent a child of a different race, they've got a more brutal decision to make—one so distasteful, it's often avoided. They must engage in a shameless discussion about skin pigmentation: How dark is too dark? Many who cross the color line are willing to do so on a continuum of palatability that often reveals an unspoken (and unspeakable) preference for yellow over brown, brown over black, light over dark.

I felt like a bigot when I first laid eyes on my son. "He's so dark," I thought, and felt ashamed for thinking it. My gut reaction was fueled by gut fear. I was pretty sure I had taken on more than I could handle. Adoption of a white kid would have been enough of a stretch, but we had to go for a baby that came not only out of someone else's body but out of someone else's culture. What kind of pseudo–Peace Corps types were we pretending to be? All I could think was that we were too white to be the parents of someone this black.

Since that rocky start, our lives as a transracial family have grown to feel exactly right. Though no one will mistake the boy sitting next to me for my offspring, he certainly feels like my son. A brown child has become familial, so brown children are now familiar. Pink kids look bland to me, compared with the beautiful mixtures we see in children of color, adopted and not. Is it possible that mixed-race children, like our son, are more beautiful than the population at large? Or does it just seem that way? Perhaps a kind of reverse preference evolves in transracial families, but it is not very different from the old idea of brunettes liking brunettes. If we perceive our family as a beautiful blend, we see the beauty in others' blends. Put simply, we are attracted to ourselves.

In the first stages of being a family created by transracial adoption, we were aware of how different from our son we looked. As time has progressed, and the emotional cement of family has hardened, we feel unified (even though the world does not always see us as belonging together). Looking nothing like my child causes questions and looks, but it holds no charge as a threat. We are family. Having said that, it is also true that we take great delight in discovering the ways we resemble each other. When people say that my son and I have the same smile, my smile gets even bigger.

Even though I was a closet pro-cloner when I first married, custom-designing the image of my offspring, I ended up with a child who is more beautiful than the one his father and I would have made. When I think back to my pre-adoption fear—"Could I love a kid who doesn't look like me?"—I know the answer now. I know that you can love a child who doesn't match, and that that child will be nothing short of beautiful to you. I also know that you will sometimes forget that you don't look alike.

Am I wrong to want a child who looks like me?

Transracial parenting means that you must face not only issues of race but issues of privacy: When families don't "match," they draw more attention. Your only responsibility is to choose the child you can parent best. Make the choice that feels right to you.

Can I specify gender?

This is one of the most controversial issues in adoption. Many of our families feel strongly that adoption should mimic biology and that parents should accept a child of either gender. Other parents—particularly those who have experienced infertility—feel they should be allowed this measure of control. Interestingly, about 80 percent of parents who choose want a girl. No one knows exactly why, but since single adoptive parents are predominantly women who want girls, this skews the overall numbers.

Many U.S. agencies and attorneys working in private adoption will not work with parents who want to specify gender. For some, it is an ethical issue. For others, it's just practical: It's hard to recruit birth mothers by saying, "We'll take the baby only if it's a girl/boy." If the choice is important to you, you have several options.

STRAIGHT TALK: A few countries bar single men from adopting girls.

In the United States, social workers are sometimes biased toward gender matching and will encourage single women to adopt girls and single men to adopt boys.

We did make a change of plan when our social worker stated that, given the fact that the community we were living in was not well integrated, she had some misgivings about our adopting a child of color. (We had been looking at adopting from India.) We readjusted, to looking at countries in which the children were primarily Caucasian, which led us to Russia.

—GAYLE

Allowing parents to choose the child that best fits their family situation is best for everyone—child and family. Biology didn't allow us to bear children, so why shouldn't we get a choice that bio-parents lack, to kind of even the score?
—SAMANTHA

For us, stating a gender preference gave us back a small sense of control that was lost as we endured years of infertility. After grieving the losses of our pregnancies, it was healing to build a new dream for a family, and to fulfill it with children who matched our mental images.
—AF READER

Adoption 101: Choosing Boy or Girl

- You can choose private adoption and work with an agency or attorney who will match you with birth mothers *after* the baby has been born. About one quarter of placing birth mothers don't make an adoption plan until after the birth, so you are eliminating three quarters of potential birth mothers. It may take longer for a match.
- You can search for a birth mother who has already had an ultrasound or other prenatal test to determine sex. They are rare—few birth mothers are old enough for routine ultrasounds, and even fewer have the resources for nonessential tests.
- You can search for a birth mother and offer to pay for prenatal screening before you commit to the adoption.
- You can find an adoption attorney who prescreens birth mothers and covers their prenatal testing before matching with parents.
- You can adopt from foster care. Foster agencies almost always let you specify gender—though some will do it only if you are fostering or adopting an older child.
- You can adopt internationally, choosing an agency and country that will allow you to specify gender. You'll need to do some searching. Some will allow it only if you are adopting older children; others only if you already have children and want to balance the family.
- If you want a girl, you can adopt from China. Parents are not formally permitted

to specify gender, but <u>more than 90 percent of Chinese adoptees are girls</u>.
- You can work with an agency that specializes in "waiting children" and "special-needs" children, either domestic or international.

STRAIGHT TALK: No prenatal test of gender is foolproof. Ultrasounds have a misdiagnosis rate of about 20 percent in the second trimester and 5 percent in the third. If you are pursuing a private adoption and are concerned about the baby's gender, you and the birth mother should plan for the possibility of a baby who doesn't come out as predicted.

Should I adopt a child with special needs?

Social workers use the terms "special needs," "hard to place," and "waiting" interchangeably. The meaning depends on the worker, the agency, and the pool of children they have available.

In general, "special needs" refers to children with physical or psychological issues along a spectrum, from a risk of ADHD to a missing limb. But it can also mean a perfectly healthy toddler (at an agency where parents are looking for infants), a healthy baby boy (when parents are requesting girls), or a child who's not white (at an agency with mostly white adoptive families). Children can move into the special-needs category if it is taking longer to find families for them than their agency's average. The child didn't change, the waiting list did.

If you hear any of these terms in the course of your adoption, make sure you know exactly what the speaker means. A reputable agency or attorney will send you a list of all the possible complications a child can suffer, from minor and correctable to lifelong. No

Our adoption took less than a year, because we were open to any race/ethnicity.

—AF READER

When I got the agency checklist, asking about all the complications I would be willing to deal with, I started by checking "none, none," no, no cleft palate, no missing limbs, no learning disabilities. . . . I wanted perfection. Halfway through, I burst into tears. Why can't we take a child who needs help? What kind of horrible people are we? I called my best friend, an adoptive parent, who said, "Don't be silly. Smart, healthy kids need parents, too. Ask for perfection, and if you get it, give thanks by giving that child the best education possible!"

—AF READER

When in public with our four children, we receive numerous smiles, greetings, and compliments from people of all races. In fact, I have noticed that we are more warmly received in public when accompanied by all four of our children than with just our Caucasian child. The number of doors opened, literally and figuratively, is multiplied by the diversity of our family.

—ANGELA

Caitlin, United States

one should pressure you to accept a child with needs you can't meet.

WISE WORDS: *Peg Studaker, supervisor of the Waiting International Child Program at the Children's Home Society & Family Services in Minnesota, says: "Parenting children with special needs should be a family's first choice. Adopting a special-needs child should never be a second choice because the family could not get the child they really wanted to parent."*

All's Fair
Corey Halls

MY HUSBAND, ERIK, AND I ARE BACK TO BATTLING. WHEN WE were going through infertility, it's all we did. He wanted to try in vitro fertilization. I wanted to be done with anything medical. (I won that battle.) Then, when we first turned our thoughts to adoption, I pictured a baby girl from China. He wanted a child who would "look like us," so we wouldn't be a "walking ad for adoption." (He won that battle.) We finally agreed on the Republic of Georgia, because we'd be able to adopt a baby from there as young as four months old. But then they had a revolution and stopped international adoptions. (We both lost.)

Then Erik wanted to adopt from Russia, because he liked the culture. I waged a strong campaign for Kazakhstan, because I liked its standard of care. (I won.) There were even battles during our six-week stay in Kazakhstan. I wanted to ask the caregivers if we could dress our baby in one of the cute outfits we'd brought with us, instead of the little blue sweater they put her in almost every day. He thought that request would be weird, uncomfortable, and hard to communicate. (He won.) I wanted to walk around the city and explore, so I could tell my daughter about the beautiful place where she was born. He wanted us to stay safely in our rented apartment. (I won.)

But when we finally returned home with our daughter, Siena, we agreed. We agreed that if we had changed anything—a medical procedure, the timing of our paperwork, our choice of agency, anything—we wouldn't have our daughter. We agreed to spend the money to feed our baby the "best" formula, since her early nutrition had been questionable. We agreed to put her to bed promptly at 7 P.M., following the advice in a book I read. Our daughter is two now, and all three of us still agree that we're addicted to her pacifiers and aren't ready to give them up just yet.

So now we're talking about a second adoption. We agree that we can't spend another six weeks in Kazakhstan, that we'll adopt domestically. But there the agreement ends. Will all this battling make our marriage stronger? Possibly. Will we get a perfect child in the end, no matter who wins which battles? Definitely.

Was I sitting down? Yes. . . . The tears began. It's a boy! More tears. His name is Xiao Ming. A boy from China? That was a surprise! But "Katie" became "Will" in less than a nanosecond, and I became a mom. I immediately called my mother to tell her that her new granddaughter would be a grandson, and he would be named after her dad, who had died when she was only six months old. Will and I will be celebrating our eighth "Will Day" in June. He continues to fill that hole in my heart that I didn't know was there.

—GINNY

Does being "picky" put my adoption at risk?
If you are open to a child of any age, race, or gender, your adoption will be fast and certain. With each restriction, you add time to the process. You will want to think hard about the issues that matter most and weigh them against the length of time you want to wait for a child. Given the greater demand for girls, for example, requesting a girl can double your waiting time.

WISE WORDS: *Lois Melina, an internationally recognized authority on adoptive parenting, says: "Prospective adoptive parents have more choices than biological parents do. We can choose the child's birth culture, sex, race, and physical and mental health conditions. Even if human cloning one day does become a viable option, the cloned child will inherit the entire genetic package of her nuclear parent—the acne will accompany the academic ability.*

"This choice places a huge burden on us—not to justify it but to be clear in our own hearts about why we value the choice, and what it will mean to us if, somehow, it leads to a different outcome than we imagined. We must be very careful, during the months or years that we wait to become parents, that we do not allow our imaginings to become fixed, to become expectations.

"We can't control whether our children interpret a choice we make about them as a gift or an obligation. However, we are responsible for checking in with our own hearts, to be sure that we recognize what is important—helping our children learn how to find true north, even though they will choose their own journeys to that point. And as long as our children are pointed in the right direction, we have done our jobs as parents."

WHAT DO I DO NEXT?

Think. Consider your lifestyle and what age child you can parent best. Talk to family members about race and look around your community. Is it a welcoming, nurturing environment for a child of a different race? Figure out how much you care about gender: If you have your heart set on adopting a girl, make peace with the fact that this may slow your adoption.

Decide. Take a deep breath, and choose your path to adoption.

Originally, I wanted a girl more than anything. Halfway through the adoption process, we changed agencies, and the new agency didn't allow us to specify. The second I saw the picture of my son, my heart was forever changed. Suddenly I didn't care about lace and bows—all I cared about was my beautiful boy.
—MICHELLE

I believe that when we are called to adopt, God knows whom we're being called to parent. When we adopt our second child, I trust that He will again match us with the perfect child for us, and I will not specify gender—unless, of course, I still live in a two-bedroom house!
—CHRISTY

PART II

Working on an Adoption

above: Sarah, United States

Where Do I Start?

Choosing Your Adoption Team

Who can help me adopt?

Once you have decided what kind of adoption you want, you need to choose the people who will bring your child home. Your team should include the professionals who will handle the logistics and legalities, a doctor who can help you understand medical issues, if necessary, and other adoptive families who can advise you when it is time to make decisions.

top: Ryan, United States   *bottom:* Daniel, Russia

Once we decided to go the domestic adoption route, we chose to use an agency, so that we could have more assistance with the entire process, would be assured of expectant/birth mother counseling, and could look for lower fee ranges. We worked with a local faith-based agency, and its fees were more than reasonable. We liked the fact that they worked only in our state, not the entire country. It gave everything a "small-town" feel. We felt an immediate connection with one particular employee we met at the beginning, and our caseworker ended up doing our home study and counseling our son's birth mother.

—AMY

Adoption 101: What to Do First?

- Private adoption: **The first thing to do is find out if you *must* work through an adoption agency to find a birth mother or if you can use an attorney; it depends on your state. Go to adoptivefamilies.com/domestic_adoption. Then you can start looking at agencies or attorneys; go to adoptivefamilies.com/search/agencies or adoptivefamilies.com/search/attorneys.**
- International adoption: **Start by looking for an agency with deep experience in the country you want to adopt from. Expertise is more important than location; if the best sending agency is not in your home state, it will partner with a local agency to complete the adoption. You should consider an agency with programs in more than one country so that if, for any reason, you need to change country midstream, the transition can go smoothly. Go to adoptivefamilies.com/search/agencies.**
- Foster-care adoption: **Your state's department of social services has legal responsibility for foster children, but states almost always delegate care, and the adoption process, to private agencies. You can start by contacting your local social services agency or foster agencies, but they will be limited to placing children from your own state. A better first step is to contact AdoptUsKids, a federally funded national program to place foster children, which has teams in every state and will work to place children across state lines. Go to adoptivefamilies.com/foster.**

What are the pluses and minuses of agencies and attorneys?

If you have decided to adopt an infant in the United States by being matched with a birth mother, you need to choose whether your primary resource will be an attorney or an adoption agency. Our families make arguments for both. Those who worked with an attorney say they enjoyed the sense of control and privacy. Those who worked with an agency liked having the support of a team, with all services (search, counseling, post-placement resources) in one place.

> **STRAIGHT TALK:** There is no such thing as a truly "private" or "independent" adoption. Even if you find a birth mother through personal contacts and choose to represent yourself in court, you must still be examined and approved by a social worker licensed by the state.

TRIED AND TRUE: If you think you want to adopt through an attorney instead of an adoption agency, research agencies anyway. You are looking for the perfect match. Likewise, if you have decided on an agency adoption, you should locate an adoption attorney you like. If something goes wrong later, you'll have someone on tap to answer questions— you don't want to be looking through the phone book in the middle of a crisis. To get started with both, go to our searchable database at adoptivefamilies.com/search/agencies and adoptivefamilies.com/search/attorneys.

What is an adoption facilitator or an adoption consultant?

An adoption facilitator is someone who matches prospective adoptive parents to birth mothers and/or children. An adoption consultant advises you on your path and helps you choose an agency or attorney.

We had unsatisfactory experiences with two private adoptions; we spent a lot of money but did not receive the services promised. Then we checked out the county social services agency and were impressed. It is important to trust your gut. We'd had anxieties about the private agency and found them to be justified. But the county played straight with us; they were thorough and realistic. It took about two and a half years after the first paperwork was filed to get our son. Other people we know have gotten children sooner. In our case, Michael (now four and a half) was definitely worth the wait!

—ED AND KAREN

Testimonials and technology made all the difference in our choice of adoption agency. We heard other adoptive families' rave reviews about the agency and talked with them privately. The other important advantage to our agency was its vast online resource center, with a step-by-step guide to the paperwork, fees, links to immigration forms, and so on. Whenever we had a question after hours or needed to know what came next, we could look it up online and get the most accurate information. It was a huge help as we waded through the piles of paperwork.
—ROBYN

In the United States, facilitators don't have to have any kind of license or training and aren't subject to professional regulations or codes of conduct. Many states restrict what facilitators can do. If your state permits them but the birth mother's or birth father's state doesn't, you'll run into trouble. Based on our families' experience, we would recommend against using a facilitator, unless he is also licensed as an attorney or works in partnership with an adoption attorney.

If you are doing an international adoption, your agency may have to use facilitators in the sending country. Most of the complaints the U.S. State Department receives about adoptions gone wrong involve facilitators. If your agency does use them, ask for a list of parents who adopted recently using the same facilitator, and talk to them about their experiences.

Adoption 101: Agencies

- A "sending" agency has custody of the child and the legal right to decide where the child will go.
- A "placing" agency is the matchmaker between the child and the parents.
- The "home study" agency approves potential adoptive parents.

Depending on the kind of adoption you're doing, you may work with one, two, or three agencies; if you're lucky, your sending agency can also be your placing and home-study agency.

Which agency do I choose first?

When you set out to find an agency, it's smart to choose the sending agency first; you want your principal contact to be the one that knows most about the child. If the sending agency is in another state and can't do your home study, ask it to recommend a home-study agency or a social worker whom it's worked with before.

What's the difference between public or state agencies and private agencies? Who regulates agencies?

Public agencies are part of your state or county government. They deal mostly with foster children. Private agencies are licensed by your state's department of social services and must submit to regular inspections—usually one a year.

STRAIGHT TALK: Many adoption agencies with religious-sounding names have no religious restrictions ("Christian" or "Jewish" in the name doesn't mean they work only with Christian or Jewish families); some agencies with secular-sounding names actually have a religious mission. When you start looking for agencies, don't rule anyone in or out based on the name, but do ask up front about religious preferences.

How can I tell if an agency or attorney is any good?

Before you sign up with an agency or an attorney, take a deep breath, remind yourself that this may be the most important decision of your life, and do some independent checking. Go to an online site where parents post comments about their adoptions, or join a local adoption-support group and ask parents who have completed an adoption about their experience.

We began our journey to our children with limited information. We simply opened the yellow pages of our phone book and looked under "adoption." In retrospect, we should have begun by opening our minds to the special issues in adoption—and how they affect all parties to an adoption—as well as to the many options available to families. The more we read and talked with others, the more we recognized the myths and misinformation about adoption pervasive in society, and the more empowered we felt to make the right decisions for ourselves and for our prospective children.
—DIANE

We knew what type of adoption we wanted but chose the wrong agency without knowing it. Only after we were halfway through our home study did we learn that the agency we chose didn't do local, domestic adoptions at all! In the future, we would work with the local agency that actually found our son, but I don't think we could have anticipated the mistakes that we made before they happened.

—AF READER

REALITY CHECKLIST
Testing Your Team

Agency basics

❏ Is the agency's license up-to-date? Check with the social services department in the agency's state.

❏ Is the agency in good financial shape? If it's a nonprofit, you're in luck; you can check its financials at one of the charity-oversight websites, such as guidestar.org.

❏ Have there been unresolved complaints against the agency? Check with the Better Business Bureau at bbb.org.

❏ Is the agency a member of one of the voluntary professional adoption organizations (the Joint Council of International Children's Services—jcics.org—or the Council on Accreditation—coanet.org)?

❏ If you are interested in adopting from a country that is a member of the Hague Adoption Convention (see adoptivefamilies.com/hague), has the agency been accredited to process Hague adoptions?

Attorney basics

❏ Is the attorney licensed to practice in the state where you live?

❏ Is the attorney a member of your state's bar association?

❏ Is the attorney a member of a voluntary professional organization (the American Academy of Adoption Attorneys)?

STRAIGHT TALK: We can't say this often enough: Look for an agency or attorney that has completed lots of adoptions just like yours—same kind of child, same kind of parents.

Who can help gay families to adopt?

While gays and lesbians have always adopted, they may face extra hurdles because of a state's adoption law, an agency's philosophy, or the attitude of an individual social worker. Even an agency that welcomes gay parents can subtly (or overtly) steer applicants toward hard-to-place children, and social workers who are uncomfortable with homosexuality may invent "reasons" to find the parents unacceptable.

Before starting a private adoption, gay parents must decide if they're comfortable being out to potential birth mothers during the search and screening process. Those who want to preserve a bit more privacy can work with an attorney or agency who will screen to find expectant mothers who are happy to place their child with gay parents. (Our gay families say this is easier than you might think, since many expectant women have been let down by their heterosexual partners.)

While 60 percent of adoption agencies in the United States welcome applications from gays, agencies that place children from foster care are the most likely to actually facilitate gay adoptions. (Watch out, though, for the small number of agencies and states that permit gays to foster but not to adopt.)

International adoption adds another wrinkle, as many foreign countries allow singles to adopt but don't officially accept gay adults as prospective parents. Gay prospective adopters wrestle with the question of whether to disclose their sexual orientation to an agency. Advocates for gay adoption encourage gays to be open about their sexuality and to find a social worker and agency that will work with them.

Since most adoptions must be finalized by judges at

We knew we wanted international adoption. We went to three different agency meetings before we chose our agency. It was clear from the meetings that each agency had certain international programs that it "majored" in. We vacillated between countries, but once we decided on international adoption, we did not consider domestic.

—JENNIFER

As a lesbian couple, we did not have international adoption available to us, and private was too expensive. However, we were committed to domestic adoption, as we knew how many children were in care waiting for families. We adopted from foster care and brought our son home at age four and a half months.

—AF READER

Paige, United States

Facilitators are illegal in the state we lived in. Nevertheless, we encountered two who were eager to tell us how to "get around" the law! Yikes! Talk about not having our best interest in mind!

—STEVE AND
   REGINA

the county level, adoption for openly gay and lesbian couples is influenced by the community in which they live. The court's decision hinges on the "best interests" of the child, a concept interpreted differently by different judges. Gay-adoption advocates recommend that, to be on the safe side, gay adopters have an attorney who has completed several local adoptions by gay parents represent them at their finalization.

TRIED AND TRUE: Many of our families report being turned away by several agencies (too old, too single, too gay, too atheist . . .). If this happens to you, don't get discouraged, just keep looking. Your child is out there, and there is an agency that will help you.

Do adoption agencies make money?

Adoption is a multimillion-dollar business in the United States. Even public agencies need fees to support their programs. Private agencies can be for-profit (like any other business) or nonprofit (a charity). Some of our families find that the idea of people profiting from an adoption makes them queasy. If you're like them, you may be more comfortable going through a nonprofit agency with humanitarian programs as well as adoption services.

What happens if my adoption agency goes out of business?

If the agency is licensed, state law requires it to transfer your records to another licensed agency, so that you don't have to start your application, home study, and so on, all over again.

What happens to your fees, though, depends on the agency's management or board of trustees. Some of our families in this situation have had all their fees refunded. Others have been left high and dry—yet another reason to choose a large nonprofit agency with a long track record and deep roots in the community.

When should I look for a pediatrician?

Our most experienced adoptive families recommend that you consult a pediatrician early on—even before you choose your path to adoption. The American Academy of Pediatrics has a section devoted to adoption medicine, with a directory of members who understand issues common to domestic, international, and foster-care adoptees. Get a telephone consultation with one of these doctors at the beginning of your adoption journey; they have a wealth of wisdom and a real commitment to the well-being of adoptees.

 TECH SUPPORT: To find a pediatrician specializing in adoption, go to adoptivefamilies.com/medical.

Who else should I add to my team?

Even the smoothest adoption is an emotional journey. Make sure you have a support group: family and friends who are enthusiastic about your plans, other adoptive parents (many agencies maintain Web-based groups), and at least one person who has recently completed an adoption like yours.

For a database of support groups, go to adoptivefamilies.com/support_group.

We adopted through fost-adopt. It took two very emotional, difficult years to finalize, but we persevered. The only things that made us successful were the support network we had—especially from workers with the county—the prayers of friends and family, and the determination to see it through.
—AF READER

Kenlee, United States

From the Bottom of My Heart
Deborah C. Joy

TOO OFTEN WHEN PARENTS TALK ABOUT THEIR ADOPTION EX-
periences, they focus on the pitfalls, setbacks, and insensitive or unkind remarks. On the other hand, I've experienced many wonderful things related
to the adoptions of my children, and I've received support in many forms
from many sources. I'd like to take this opportunity to thank those people.

My daughter's pediatrician was very supportive of my initial inquiries
about intercountry adoption. An anxious potential adoptive mother, I was
worried about the implications of developmental delays, hepatitis B, and
many other complications. This doctor simplified matters considerably
when he looked at me and said, "Let's give this baby a chance." Suddenly,
all of my fears about possible problems became secondary to the insight
that this was a baby we were talking about. Thank you, Dr. McGovern.

The doctor in Honduras who immediately affirmed my status as my
ten-day-old daughter's mother will never know how much he helped me
feel entitled to parent her. My daughter had a small broken blood vessel
in her eye, and through a translator, I was asking the doctor about it. The
doctor said something that made the translator smile and ask me if I knew
what he had said. When I replied no (being language-impaired), he said
the doctor had proclaimed me a good mother for this baby. Thank you, Dr.
Whatever-your-name-is.

My adoption social worker in Cincinnati remains calm and thoughtful,
no matter what idea I propose to her. She listens patiently and gives good
advice. She promoted my attachment to the second child I adopted.
When I called her to discuss the possibility of adopting a baby boy, she immediately began referring to this yet-unborn child as "your son in
Guatemala." Thank you, Joan Thomas.

Members of my support group took me in sight unseen, sharing their
stories and their lives. How do you express what thirteen years of monthly
potluck dinners, tears, laughter, games, and support have meant? Just
having a place to go with the kids on a Saturday night, where you don't
have to worry about them not having fun, and you don't have to hire a
babysitter, has been a blessing. Thanks, guys, for everything.

My sister traveled twice to Guatemala with me to help me adopt my last two children. On the last trip, she wore a very short skirt that caused a bit of a stir as we got off the plane, but we won't talk about that now. Thank you, Denise, for taking time out of your life to provide moral and physical support during stressful times.

My parents taught me much of what I know about parenting and about what it means to be a family. They love all of their grandchildren for who they are, not where they came from, and they are an important part of each of my kids' lives. Thanks, Mom and Dad.

My oldest daughter, Sarah, graciously accepted new siblings after she had been an only child for nine years. She's helped me a great deal with her brothers and sister and has given them a wonderful role model. Thank you, Sarah.

My children have traveled thousands of miles to become part of my family. Thanks, you guys. I love you.

A stranger in the park perhaps summed it up best. Who would think that a stranger might understand the implications of all of this? While watching the kids play on the jungle gym, she noticed there were differences in our family and asked questions about the children's adoptions. After I briefly told their stories, she said, "How wonderful." Here it comes, I thought. How wonderful you are for adopting these children. All adoptive parents know how inappropriate that feels. But she didn't say that at all. "How wonderful," she said again, adding, "that you all found each other." Thank you, stranger, for expressing it so well.

Jack, United States

If I were to give tips for finding the right adoption agency/ professional, I'd say, start by meeting other parents who have gone through the type of adoption you're seeking. They have stories to share and often give great advice. Decide what is important to you and write down all of your questions (and the agencies' answers). You and your spouse should both meet with them in person, if you can, then go home and review together privately before you decide.

—LARA

To print multiple copies of the following checklists, with space for answers, go to adoptivefamilies.com/planner.

REALITY CHECKLIST
Questions for an Agency

❑ How long have you been in business?

❑ How many children did you place last year?

❑ How many children from each of the programs I'm interested in did you place?

❑ How many children did you place with a parent just like me?

❑ How soon after I apply will my home study begin? How long will it take? When will I know if I've been approved?

❑ If I am not approved, can I find out why? Is there an appeal process?

❑ How long will it take from home study or dossier approval to the match with a birth mother/referral of a child?

❑ How much time do I have to decide on a referral/match?

❑ What happens if I don't accept the referral/match?

❑ What is the total cost of adopting through each program? Can I get a written breakdown of fees and a payment schedule?

❑ Does the fee cover the home study, all post-placement visits, fees to the placing agency? What does it not cover?

❏ Do you produce an annual report that shows your financial resources?

❏ Do you give clients a copy of their rights with the application form?

❏ Do you provide a contract that spells out my responsibilities toward the adoption, as well as what you are responsible for?

❏ Is there a written policy of quality assurance that will address my concerns during the process?

❏ What are the post-placement requirements, and what support services do you offer before, during, and after placement?

❏ What happens if I find I can't parent the child I adopted?

Hope, China

❏ What percentage of your adoptions have been disrupted or dissolved? (This is the $64,000 question. Any agency that has processed more than a few hundred adoptions will have had some that failed; an agency that claims a perfect score is either very small, very new, or not entirely truthful.)

Additional questions for international adoption

❏ Is intercountry adoption stable in my country of choice? Do you have programs in other countries I could switch to if regulations change or if a moratorium is declared?

❏ Are you licensed in the sending country as well as the United States? If not, are the agencies you work with licensed in sending countries?

Danielle, United States

❑ Do you use facilitators or private attorneys in the sending country? If so, how are they compensated?

❑ What information do we receive about a referral before we travel? How thorough and accurate is the medical information?

❑ What are the travel requirements? Do you help with travel arrangements?

❑ Do you have bilingual representatives, respected by the authorities in each foreign country, to obtain or assist with the referral of a child? Will they be there to assist me when I arrive? What is their experience and tenure with the agency? Do they work exclusively for you and exclusively in adoption?

❑ Are there country fees or mandatory orphanage donations separate from your fees?

❑ Does your fee cover the child's transport, visa processing, and medical exams?

❑ Do you prepare my dossier and obtain the various stamps and approvals it will need? Do you arrange for translation?

❑ Are we expected to support the child between referral and the homecoming?

❑ Do you financially support the orphanages from which you place children? How often do your representatives visit these orphanages?

STRAIGHT TALK: If you're doing an international adoption, check the requirements of the sending country (who's allowed to place children? what kind of parents are accepted?) and make sure they match what the agency tells you. The U.S. State Department maintains good information on each country. Go to adoptivefamilies.com/internationaladoption.

REALITY CHECKLIST
Questions for an Attorney

☐ How long have you worked in adoption?

☐ How many nonrelative adoptions did you complete last year? (The answer should be at least ten.)

☐ What percentage of your total practice is devoted to adoption? (A rate of 50 to 100 percent suggests adoption expertise.)

☐ Do you handle open adoptions, confidential adoptions, or both? Do you have strong feelings about openness?

☐ What services do you provide? Will you actively assist me in finding a birth mother, as well as handle the necessary legal work?

☐ If the birth parents do not have their own attorney, can you help them find one, and if so, how do you make that referral?

☐ What is the average cost of the adoptions you've handled?

☐ How do you bill—an hourly rate or a flat fee? (Experienced attorneys may have a higher hourly rate but charge less overall, because they spend less time than a less experienced attorney would.)

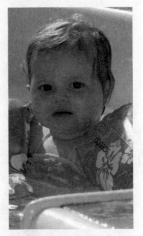
Ellie, United States

Elizabeth, United States

❏ Do you require a retainer fee in advance? If so, how much? What happens to my retainer fee if the birth mother changes her mind?

❏ Do you see counseling for birth parents as helpful? Why or why not?

❏ Will you accept collect calls from birth parents? Do you have a toll-free number?

❏ When you're away from the office, is another knowledgeable attorney available?

❏ In your experience, what percentage of birth mothers change their plans before placement, or before finalization? (An experienced, ethical attorney will tell you that some expectant women choose to keep their babies. An attorney who says she has never had a failure has done too few adoptions—or is not candid.)

WISE WORDS: *Steven M. Kirsh, past president of the American Academy of Adoption Attorneys, says: "Niceness is not typically a concern when you are looking for an attorney to litigate a case, but in an adoption, when the attorney is going to have direct contact with the birth parents, you need your legal representative to be a likeable person!"*

What happens if my agency or attorney screws up?

If your adoption drags on and on, or if you keep getting birth-mother matches or child referrals that don't come close to your requirements, you'll have to think about making a change.

An adoption agency or attorney should be willing to refund at least part of your fee if you make the case that it hasn't been earned. Generally, procedures are in place to settle fee disputes. If no other avenue is successful, consider a lawsuit, bearing in mind the high expense (and aggravation) of litigation.

The first step is to look at the contract governing your relationship. Under what circumstances are fees refundable? Has the professional performed the services agreed upon? What does the agreement say will be done if an adoption doesn't happen? How will fee disputes be handled?

If your adoption professional is an attorney, rules of professional conduct govern his or her practice. Each state has rules similar or identical to the American Bar Association's Model Rules of Professional Conduct. Model Rule 1.5 prohibits a lawyer from collecting an "unreasonable fee." Factors that determine whether the fee is reasonable include time, labor, and expenses involved—and results obtained. A fee can't be reasonable if nothing's been done to earn it. This common-sense proposition should hold true no matter who is being paid to handle an adoption. Each state has a grievance commission that investigates complaints filed against attorneys and a mechanism to impose disciplinary measures if violations are found. Contact your state bar association or state supreme court to find out where to file a complaint or request an investigation of an attorney's behavior.

Brody, United States

Similarly, an adoption agency is regulated by its licensing entity, which investigates and processes complaints and has the ability to suspend or revoke the agency's license to do business. In most states social workers are licensed, too. The licensing entity may be the state's department of social services, department of consumers and industry, or some other board or department.

If you've been working with an adoption facilitator, you will have to negotiate a mutual agreement. They are unlicensed and unregulated, and you have no recourse if things go wrong.

Libby, United States

WHAT DO I DO NEXT?

Search. Start looking at agencies and attorneys that specialize in the kind of adoption you have chosen. Go to adoptivefamilies.com/search/agencies and adoptivefamilies.com/search/attorneys to get started; make a list of "possibles."

Research. Go to the online support groups you joined after chapter 2; post a request for families resembling yours (same age parents, in the same state) who have recently completed adoptions like the one you want to pursue. Ask them—in depth—about their experiences with their agencies and attorneys. (Don't worry; recent adopters are usually very happy to share.)

Interview. Call the agencies and attorneys left on your list. Keep careful note not just of answers but of efficiency and attitude.

Stop. No matter how charming your chosen agency or attorney, no matter how glowing their references, check their licensing status and Better Business Bureau entries.

Carson, United States

How Much Will This Cost?

Real Expenses and Real Solutions

How do costs vary among different kinds of adoptions?

Every adoption has unique factors that affect cost, but as a general rule, <u>foster-care adoptions are the least expensive</u>; international adoptions are more expensive but generally predictable; private infant adoptions range widely, depending on the birth mother's situation.

No matter what kind of adoption you're doing, the child's own circumstances can profoundly affect the cost. Adoption agencies often offer incentives to parents who will adopt children who are older, not white, have any kind of disability, or come in a sibling group.

STRAIGHT TALK: The practice of discounting fees for the adoption of African American and biracial children is offensive to African Americans and to white families who have adopted transracially; it is being phased out at most agencies.

above: Julia, United States

Deep in my son's adoption files, I have hidden the fee schedule from our agency. It has two columns: the cost of adopting a white child and the cost for a multiracial or African American child. Fifteen years later, I am still trying to wrap my head around the fact that, because my beautiful, brilliant boy is not 100 percent Caucasian, he was half-price.

—AF READER

Occasionally, we were bitter because to have a family we had to pay for it, while others get to have a roll in the hay, so to speak. But we understood that the approval process for adoption has to be in place to assure the safety of children. We did a lot of homework and worked only with professionals whose fees seemed reasonable and completely transparent. When people inquire about the "high cost" of adoption, we point out that no one wants babies "given" to families without some sort of background check.
—CYNTHIA AND
　TONY

Why should adoption cost money, anyway?

Many of our families come to adoption after years of expensive infertility treatment and feel it's unfair that they now have to pay to adopt a child who needs a family. Among the strategies they recommend are understanding every component of the fees, so you feel more in control; taking advantage of every possible form of grant and reimbursement to get the costs down; working through a nonprofit agency with humanitarian programs—you can take comfort in the fact that your money is doing good.

Where does the money go?

Fee schedules vary among agencies, attorneys, and countries, but understanding all the possible components of the costs will help you avoid surprises later. Before you sign a contract with anyone, get a complete breakdown of their expected fees; check the breakdown against the lists below, and ask about any missing items so you can calculate potential extras.

REALITY CHECKLIST
Your Adoption Budget

All adoptions, wherever from and via whatever method, include a home study, the process where a social worker checks that you are eligible to adopt. After that, budget items vary.

Home study

❑ Social worker (one or more visits)

❑ Certified marriage and birth certificates

❑ Criminal-records check

❑ Physical exams and vaccinations

☐ Notarization of documents

☐ Postage (certified mail or courier) and phone

Private infant adoption via agency

Home-study costs *plus*

☐ Application fee

☐ Agency fee

☐ Pre-adoption education for adoptive parents

☐ Birth mother's medical expenses

☐ Birth mother's living expenses

☐ Birth-family counseling

☐ Travel, food, and lodging for adoptive family

☐ Court filing fees for finalization

Private infant adoption with an attorney

Home-study costs *plus*

☐ Attorney's fees

☐ Attorney's office expenses

☐ Advertising and networking

☐ Birth mother's medical expenses

☐ Birth mother's living expenses

☐ Birth family's attorney

☐ Birth-family counseling

☐ Travel, food, and lodging for adoptive family

☐ Court filing fees for finalization

The agency I adopted our daughter through helps pregnant moms in crisis. I see my fees as a donation that allows them to help other women in crisis and "save" babies that might otherwise be aborted.
—AF READER

My husband was always uncomfortable with the cost of adoption in general. We adopted from Russia, and he pondered the high cost and wondered where it all went. By the time they placed our daughter into our arms, he didn't care where the money went or what the amount. His heart melted, and whatever we needed to do to bring her home is what mattered to him.
—CARA AND JOSHUA

We used an agency with humanitarian programs here and abroad. One year after we adopted our son, our nineteen-year-old daughter went to work as a volunteer in his orphanage and saw exactly where our fees went: to feed, clothe, and vaccinate other children as they waited to be adopted, and to support children who were unlikely to find families.

—ISOLDE

People love to ask how much. I tell them my children are priceless, and I don't have a dollar sign on them.

—JUDI

Nathan, United States

International adoption via agency

Home-study costs *plus*

❑ Agency application

❑ Agency program fee

❑ Country fee

❑ Certification of documents

❑ Translation of documents

❑ Fingerprinting

❑ Court fees in sending country

❑ Medical exams for child

❑ Orphanage donation

❑ Foster care between referral and travel

❑ Passport for child

❑ U.S. visa fee for child

❑ Passports for adoptive family

❑ Visas for adoptive family

❑ Travel to meet child

❑ Travel to bring child home

❑ Escort fee to bring child home

❑ Court filing fees for finalization or readoption

Adoption from foster care

Depending on whether you are adopting directly from foster care, doing fost-adopt (applying to foster a child you plan to adopt), or fostering with the possibility of adoption later, you may have the following costs:

- ❏ Home-study costs
- ❏ Court filing fees for finalization
- ❏ Agency application
- ❏ Foster-parent orientation and training
- ❏ Foster-parent license fee

But bear in mind, all of these may be waived or subsidized, depending on your circumstances and the child's situation.

TECH SUPPORT: To see real, current adoption budgets for recently completed adoptions and to download worksheets for your own budget, go to adoptivefamilies.com/cost.

How much do I pay a birth mother in a private adoption?

The expenses that prospective parents pay in connection with an adoption are regulated by state law. In many states, adoptive parents can pay a birth family's medical, legal, and counseling expenses during the pregnancy and for a short time afterward. Many states also permit some assistance with living expenses (check your state's guidelines for limits).

STRAIGHT TALK: State regulations on birth-family expenses are complicated and ever-changing; in addition, judges have some discretion in deciding

Since we adopted through the Texas foster-care system, there were no fees to us. Our girls lived short distances from where we were, so there were no big travel expenses. The state offers a great subsidy package that paid adoption fees, as well as pays us each month to help with their care. And when they are ready for college, that's paid for, too! What a deal, and two beautiful kids as well!

—CATHIE

Aiden, United States

We didn't have to finance our adoptions. Our son, now four, joined our family at four months, and our daughter, now three, came to us at birth, through the state foster-care system. Yes, for two years we had to contend with visits and the possibility that they would return home. Getting to know their birth mom, however, and having her blessing for the adoption when she finally realized she could not and should not parent her children, was an experience I now cherish and can share with my children. Thanks to adoption support programs, finances do not have to be a barrier to opening your heart and home to another child, and another, and another!

—MAEVE

what's reasonable. To safeguard your money and your adoption, never, ever pay a birth family directly—even to reimburse them for expenses. Always pay via an attorney or agency.

If she backs out, can I get my money back?

In some states, expenses paid on behalf of a birth mother are considered to be a gift and can't be recovered. In others a reimbursement agreement with a birth mother is legal and enforceable. Yet, even when adoptive parents have the option of suing, the reality is that most mothers won't be able to repay them. Adoptive parents hoping to recoup their money will only end up having spent more in legal fees, with little chance of success.

At big adoption agencies, with deeper pockets, families who have suffered through a birth family's change in plans can request a reduction in agency fees and assistance in applying for adoption grants.

STRAIGHT TALK: Instead of hoping to recover money spent on expectant-mother expenses, take steps to minimize your financial risk in the event of a failed adoption. Put money into escrow to repay the birth mother for expenses after the adoption has been finalized, and ensure that the birth mother has counseling through her pregnancy and afterward.

What kind of payments are illegal?

While states vary in specific rules on reimbursing a birth parent, the underlying principle everywhere is that no one can profit from giving up a child. Payments or gifts to a birth family that are more than reimbursement for "reasonable and customary expenses" could be grounds for overturning an adoption. Your agency or attorney should have guidelines; follow them carefully, and make sure they are explained to the expectant mother and her family.

In some U.S. states, payments to facilitators or consultants are illegal.

In international adoption, practices vary from country to country, but the Hague Adoption Convention has two simple rules: No one can give money to a child's birth parents, or to anyone else, as an inducement to relinquish a child, and no one should receive an incentive for locating or placing a child. Even if the country you're adopting from has not joined the Hague Convention, you'd be wise to follow the guidelines. They are just common sense.

What are common hidden costs?

Adoptive families sometimes find themselves surprised by expenses that crop up when they're well into the process: attorney or agency mailing and copying expenses, notaries' fees, doctors' bills for physicals. Before you sign a contract with an agency or attorney, ask for a complete, written breakdown of costs, including an estimate of expenses the agency or attorney will pass along to you, and compare notes with other parents who have adopted by the same route.

> **STRAIGHT TALK:** In our experience, most of the "surprises" are in the cost of travel. Even if you are adopting within the United States, you may well end up paying for the birth mother and her family to travel closer to you, or you (and your family) may travel to her. Either way, you are likely paying airfares and hotel costs for several people.

What kind of financial help is available?

There are enough sources of financial support for adoption so that you can, in all likelihood, get your costs down to a manageable figure. Don't hesitate to ask for help everywhere. If you feel embarrassed, remember that every penny you save will be spent on the child later. Be diligent about getting and keeping receipts—you'll need them.

We adopted Max from the Pennsylvania foster-care system, and it did not cost us anything, except for the finalization legal expenses, which amounted to a few hundred dollars.
        —*TRACY AND JIMMY*

Abby, United States

My co-workers organized the biggest shower ever given. There were eighty people, and enough gifts to fill my living room. The best gift was a check for a thousand dollars to pay for my plane fare. I started to cry, and I am not one who cries easily. Everyone was so interested and excited. It was an amazing outpouring of love.
—DEBBIE

Kyra, United States

REALITY CHECKLIST
Where to Go for Financial Help

❏ Adoption agencies: Many nonprofit adoption agencies base their fees on the adoptive parents' incomes—the less you make, the less you'll pay. Some agencies also offer adoption grants and/or low-cost loans.

❏ Federal government: The U.S. government offers a tax credit for parents whose gross incomes fall below a certain limit (it changes every year). The credit can even be applied to domestic adoptions that fall through, as long as the attempts have been documented.

❏ State governments: Several states have tax credits for adoptive families, sometimes restricted to those adopting from that state's foster-care system. States may also continue to subsidize ongoing treatment for a child with special needs. If you are adopting a child who qualifies for such financial assistance, be sure to apply and receive approval *before* the adoption is finalized.

❏ Your employer: Many private companies and the U.S. military reimburse adoption expenses. Go to adoptivefamilies.com/topcompanies (and while you're there, read "How to Lobby Your Employer for Adoption Benefits").

❏ Airlines and hotels: Whether you're doing a domestic or an international adoption, if it involves travel, ask airlines and hotels about adoption rates. Even if the rate isn't any lower than normal discounts, reservations agents are human and will often lift restrictions or make special concessions for an adoption trip.

❑ Friends and family: You can request donations in lieu of shower gifts; if you're not comfortable asking yourself, enlist a family member to make the suggestion for you.

Should I borrow money for an adoption?

Many of our adoptive families have gone into debt to finance their adoptions. Some, especially those who were already stretched by payments for infertility treatment, continue to struggle with financial issues for years after the adoption is completed. We have never heard a parent say it wasn't worth it.

TRIED AND TRUE: If you plan to borrow to finance your adoption, let your agency or attorney know at the beginning of the process, and ask if this will cause a problem in your home study. If you have a realistic repayment plan, social workers are usually happy to approve parents working on credit.

Will my health insurance cover the child?

Under U.S. law, insurers must treat your adopted child exactly as if you had just given birth (even if the child is a teenager). They cannot ask you to wait until reenrollment, they cannot deny treatment for existing conditions, and coverage must begin on the day you became responsible for the child, even if the adoption hasn't been finalized yet.

Can I get leave from work to adopt a child?

Under the federal Family and Medical Leave Act (FMLA), large companies must allow up to twelve

We financed the adoptions of both of our children by taking out home-equity loans. In addition, my husband's employer offers an adoption reimbursement. Luckily for us, the reimbursement grew from five thousand dollars for the first adoption to ten thousand for the second! We would never have known that this benefit was available to us if a co-worker had not brought it to our attention, so do your homework! For those who voice their unsolicited opinions to us regarding the expense of adoption, we say this: "Most people pay/borrow more money to purchase a car than it cost us to go through the adoption process and build an amazing family!"

—LISA

Someone told us, when we were starting this journey, "You can buy a car for this amount that you'll only have for, if you're lucky, ten years, or you can spend this money on helping a life and adding a life to your family, which you'll have forever."

—TINA AND MARK

Anders, United States

weeks' leave for specified circumstances, including the adoption of a child. However, FMLA leave is unpaid, and employers can require employees to use any accumulated vacation, sick leave, or other paid time off during the leave. Some employers offer paid adoption leave in addition to the FMLA leave. Our families say it's a good idea to find an adoptive parent in your company's management or human-resources department and ask for guidance, to make sure you get every benefit possible.

WISE WORDS: *Lillian Thogersen, who has worked for more than thirty years with the adoption agency World Association for Children and Parents, in Seattle, and has adopted eight children internationally herself, says: "I have never seen a family who wanted to adopt let money stop them."*

WHAT DO I DO NEXT?

Estimate. Ask your agency or attorney for a detailed breakdown of everything that could possibly come up. Check with your support group: Is anything missing?

Budget. Figure out how you're going to pay for this. Talk to your accountant, if you have one. If you are coming up short, line up any grants and loans you may need.

File. Set up a system for all your receipts.

Can I Adopt a Healthy Child?

Understanding the Medical Issues

Can I be sure I'll get a healthy child?

All parents, biological or adoptive, want perfect children, and all realistic parents understand that there is some risk in having children by any method. If you were pregnant, you would learn about nutrition, take your vitamins, and find a good doctor to deliver your baby. As a prospective adoptive parent, you will learn about different adoption options and pick a good agency or attorney to help you bring your child home. In either case, the overwhelming odds are that you'll have a healthy child, but doing your research and choosing the right professionals will make your odds even better.

How do I discuss health with an agency or attorney?

Most agencies' and attorneys' applications will ask if you can accept a child with medical or psychological problems. Often you are sent a chart showing possible issues ranked by severity, from lifelong to treatable,

above: Harry, Russia

*After we had ac-
cepted the referral
of a little boy, the
agency's pediatri-
cian became con-
cerned about some
test results. Even
though we hadn't
met him yet, we had
become attached to
the idea of this baby
and told the agency
we would take him,
no matter how the
next round of tests
—brain scans—
came out. Our
social worker said,
"No. When you
were thinking
clearly, you asked
for a healthy child,
because that was
best for your family.
There are other
families who asked
for a child with
challenges, and
they'll be better
equipped to care for
him."*

—AF READER

and you check off the problems you would accept in a child. You will also be asked to sign a disclaimer, acknowledging that no one can guarantee that the child will, in fact, be healthy as promised, but reputable agencies and attorneys do their best to disclose any health issues; no good comes of sending a sick child to an unprepared family.

TRIED AND TRUE: Many of our families say they thought about saying they'd accept a child with "some" medical issues in order to speed up their adoption. Adoption professionals say it's not worth shaving a couple of months off your process to end up with a child you're not ready to parent. If you want a healthy child, say so.

Are there health issues common to all adoptees?

The one concern shared by all adoptees is the lack of reliable information about hereditary illnesses. Even in the best possible situation—a private infant adoption, with both birth parents supplying information—adoptive families may not get a full medical history for their child.

WISE WORDS: *Dr. Deborah Borchers, an adoption specialist and adoptive mother of three, says: "An adopted person's life is a jigsaw puzzle. There are pieces he'll never find, but you do your best to find what you can."*

TRIED AND TRUE: Even in an open adoption, with both sets of parents committed to ongoing interaction, contact is likely to diminish over time. Our families recommend that you get as much information about the birth families' histories as you can before and immediately after the baby's birth.

What can I do to make sure my child is as healthy as possible?

Medical issues vary enormously, depending on where and when a child is adopted. A preteen foster child from Kansas, a toddler from Guatemala, and a newborn from California will be at risk for different illnesses. However, the factors that affect the child's long-term health are the same all over the world: the birth mother's health while pregnant, the birth itself, and the environment where the child lived between birth and adoption. Before you choose your route to adoption, investigate different countries and communities, talk to adoptive parents whose children have been home for several years, and consult with an adoption pediatrician. You can't eliminate risks, but you can lower them by choosing your child's environment wisely.

Samuel, United States

Our son came to us at nine months old, and we had a detailed checklist self-reported by his birth mother. Over the years, we have found that there were omissions: Our son was in early-intervention programs for developmental delays while with his birth mother. She never told us, and it was another full year before we realized he was missing benchmarks and we had to start his intervention programs over. This was a big disservice to our child.
—AF READER

We had good information—in fact, we attended two doctor's visits (one was for the ultrasound) with our son's birth mother. We received information regularly from the social worker who works with our lawyers.
—AF READER

Facing the Unknown
Theresa Reid

I WAS LOOKING OVER THE PROGRAM FOR AN ADOPTION CONFER-
ence recently. "Parenting the Child Affected by Fetal Alcohol Syndrome,"
I read. "The Attachment-Disordered Child: Paths to Hope." "Syndromes
Affecting the Post-Institutionalized Child." If we had encountered dire
subjects like this before we adopted, I'm not sure we would have gone
through with it.

We were scared enough as it was. The first time, we were afraid that we
wouldn't love the child. ("I admire you," a friend told us. She was the biological mother of two, a social worker famed for her work with abused
children. "I don't think I could love a baby that wasn't mine.") We were
afraid that our child's earliest environments—intra- and extrauterine—
would hurt her irreparably—afflict her with AIDS, hepatitis B, fetal alcohol syndrome, ADHD, attachment disorder. All of these were reasonable
fears that we had to face down so we could give ourselves permission to
parent a child.

Boy, did we get lucky. Our first daughter came to us at thirteen months,
in the ninety-fifth percentile for height and weight, developmentally exactly on target, perfectly healthy. And, of course, adorable. We were
quickly, passionately in love with her. Our dearest dream—and none of
our fears—had come true.

Still, the second time around, we were even more fearful. We no longer
doubted that we could love a child not born to us, but we were pretty sure
we couldn't possibly love another child as much as we loved our first.

And this time many of our fears proved true. Our younger daughter
came home at thirty-two months, weighing only eighteen pounds. Her in-
trauterine environment had clearly been hostile; she had medical complications; she was indiscriminate in her attachments, so the bonding process
was much slower than with our first child. But with considerable effort on
both sides, attachment grew, and now we love each other to pieces. She
has enriched our lives beyond our wildest imaginings.

Most adoption stories have such happy endings. But we were not
wrong to be afraid; some endings are not so happy. A child can be deathly

ill, physically or emotionally, or unable to attach. Some adoptions don't work out.

Some people chastise prospective adopters for being "choosy." All children available for adoption are in desperate need of love, they say. How could we presume to reject any one of them? We should love them all. But fear is a normal and important part of the process. Our fears gather where we think the limits of our ability to love might lie. We are right to want to know those limits, to try to estimate what we can cope with and what we can't.

The hard part is that the labels we commonly use—"special needs," "developmental delays"—are not helpful. We don't use the phrases that would help: "cleft palate, but a beautiful spirit and great potential," or "will need some speech therapy, but this child will fill your heart with joy."

Key lessons for people considering adoption and grappling with the unknown: Let yourself have fears. Listen to them. Take them seriously. Do not be shamed by them. Know that your love will run even deeper than your fears.

How much damage do prenatal drugs and alcohol do?

Experienced adoption pediatricians say they assume that any child placed for adoption may have been exposed to drugs, alcohol, and tobacco. Long-term effects depend on which substance, the degree and timing of the exposure, and the mother's own health. Before you choose your adoption path, talk to an adoption pediatrician about risk factors and complications.

We were reminded that the info given to the agency is only as good as what each woman reported, but we have no reason to think they left anything out. We believe each birth mom had the baby's best interest in mind.
—AF READER

REALITY CHECKLIST
Drugs, Alcohol, Tobacco, and More

❏ Alcohol: Drinking during pregnancy results in a spectrum of results from fetal alcohol syndrome (FAS, which, in its most severe form, results in lifelong physical and mental

Our birth mother gave us a full medical history freely. We were also able to talk openly with her doctor, which was quite wonderful. We had an amazing and inspiring experience with our adoption.
        —MARLENE

We received the information directly from the birth mother. We had a bit of info, but as for smoke and alcohol exposure, her answers changed once he was in our custody. It turned out that she had smoked and drunk more than was thought initially.
        —AF READER

Because our daughter was a "safe surrender," we received little to zero info.
        —JENNIFER

handicaps) to fetal alcohol effect (FAE, which has implications for behavior and learning disabilities) to no discernible damage at all.

❏ Marijuana: Heavy use is correlated with attention deficit disorders and learning disabilities.

❏ Heroin: Babies exposed to heroin during pregnancy may need treatment for withdrawal, but there don't seem to be long-term consequences.

❏ Cocaine: Twenty-odd years ago, when crack cocaine was epidemic in U.S. inner cities, sociologists predicted a "lost generation" of crack babies with permanent, devastating brain damage. In fact, while cocaine is far from harmless, long-term studies of exposed children show very mild, if any, effects on behavior and learning.

❏ Ecstasy (MDMA): Early research suggests that Ecstasy used in the third trimester of pregnancy may produce learning disabilities, but no definite link has been made.

❏ Methamphetamines: Researchers are still accumulating data on the long-term effects of meth use, but indications are that use in any stage of pregnancy may cause behavioral disorders and learning disabilities.

❏ Tobacco: Whether the birth mother smokes herself or is exposed to secondhand smoke, the risk is of low birth weight, with its attendant complications.

☐ Prescription drugs: Adoptive parents focus on illegal drug use but should be alert to use and abuse of prescription drugs as well. Some commonly used medications (such as the acne drug Accutane) do more damage to a fetus than cocaine or heroin.

☐ Environmental toxins: In international adoption, parents should learn about the environment where the birth mother lived during pregnancy, and where the child lived before adoption. In countries with no environmental protections (that is, virtually all sending countries), both may have been exposed to chemicals (through industrial pollution, for example) or other toxins at levels no longer seen in the United States.

WISE WORDS: *Dr. Jerri Jenista, a pediatrician and adoptive mother of four Indian-born daughters, says: "Early in your adoption process, think about the worst case you can accept. Then, when you are faced with a birth-mother match or a child referral, remember—and stick to—your original decision."*

STRAIGHT TALK: Drugs and alcohol can have a direct effect on the fetus, but they can also have the indirect effects of premature birth and low birth weight—the two most significant indicators for long-term problems. The most important bits of information to get are: How long was the pregnancy, and what did the baby weigh?

Since our child was removed from the birth mother at birth, we did not know about the birth mother's health ahead of time during pregnancy. We were told that she used drugs, and our child was considered a drug-exposed infant. Due to this, we had to monitor our child closely for potential complications through the first year of life. We are blessed that our child is now a healthy, joyous toddler, who is thriving and developmentally on target.
　　—ALISON AND
　　　CHARLES

Derek, United States

The state our son was born in required a pretty extensive family medical history from his birth family, and they took great pains to fill it out. It helps, though, that we have ongoing contact. For instance, our son was recently screened for vision problems. We knew many in his birth family wore glasses but not why. Out came the cell phone, and we had that history in ten minutes.
        —STEVE AND
          REGINA

Can I find a birth mother who definitely hasn't used drugs or alcohol?

Some of our families have chosen to adopt from countries or communities with lower rates of drug and alcohol use. China, for example, was favored because young women, especially in rural areas, didn't have easy access to alcohol. It's certainly worth factoring this into your choice of country or community. (The Centers for Disease Control publishes state-by-state reports on the prevalence of drinking before and during pregnancy in the United States. The World Health Organization publishes country-by-country reports on alcohol use in general. Go to adoptivefamilies.com/medical.) However, statistics are always out of date (as China has become wealthier and more urban, alcohol use has risen dramatically), and, more important, they can't tell you anything about an individual child.

Can't we just test the birth mother—or the baby?

In private infant adoption, if the expectant mother is getting prenatal care, her doctor will order a panel of tests that may or may not include tests for substance abuse. (This will depend on state requirements and the doctor's own practice.) Your social worker or attorney is required to tell you the results of those tests, if they're available—and to tell you if the birth mother refused testing. However, tests are of very limited use. Alcohol, for example, appears to do its greatest damage in the first eight weeks of pregnancy, when the mother may not even realize she is expecting. Testing a newborn will tell you only about drug or alcohol exposure during the past seventy-two hours, so while a positive result would be cause for alarm, a negative isn't particularly useful.

In international adoption, you are unlikely to know much about the birth mother's drug and alcohol use. Before you get a referral, find an adoption pediatrician experienced in evaluating signs of fetal alcohol syndrome, and make sure your agency knows how to get photographs and videos (full face, straight on, no distortion) for diagnosis. To see the photo standards, go to adoptivefamilies.com/medical.

Can the baby or birth parents be tested for hereditary diseases?

Would-be parents sometimes ask if the baby, birth mother, and even the birth father can undergo genetic testing. The American Society of Human Genetics and the American College of Medical Genetics state jointly that "the principal objective of genetic testing should be promoting the child's well-being." In other words, geneticists can test for a disease that would appear in childhood, and could be cured by early treatment. They cannot (or should not) test for an untreatable disease, or one that will only emerge in adulthood; they cannot test to rule a child out for adoption. (The only situation in which doctors will test to eliminate a child from adoption is when the adoptive parents have lost biological children to a genetic disorder and are adopting to avoid repeating the tragedy.)

STRAIGHT TALK: Experienced social workers, doctors, and adoptive families rely not on tests but on counseling for the expectant mother. A birth mother whose counselor is clearly working for her benefit, not for the adoptive parents, is far more likely to make an honest disclosure of her own history— and to follow her counselor's advice for a healthy pregnancy. For this reason alone, adoptive parents should insist that a birth mother have independent counseling.

Is a child whose birth parents abused drugs and alcohol more likely to grow up to be an alcoholic or drug addict?

Not enough is known about the heredity of risk factors to make any assumptions. Psychologists warn,

We were told that the birth mother had had prenatal care and that the baby was perfect. We received this information through the agency. However, during the days we were in the hospital waiting for the baby to be born, we learned that, in fact, she hadn't had any prenatal care until she was six months pregnant. That correct information came from members of the birth mother's family, who were waiting with us. We got lucky, though, and our son was and is absolutely, perfectly healthy, so in the end it didn't matter. But it might have been a deal breaker if we had known that ahead of time.

—AF READER

*Our adoption at-
torney arranged a
meeting with a
young prospective
birth mother and
her mother (whom
I'll call Jane). Jane
mentioned that she
had grown up in an
acrimonious house-
hold with an alco-
holic father. After
we left the meeting,
I said to my hus-
band, "We can't
adopt this child.
There's alcoholism
in the family!" My
husband shot me a
curious look and
said, "Uh, what
about your brother?
My sister?" "Oh
right," I thought. In
my enthusiasm for
screening the ge-
netic problems of
the child that would
join our family, I
had allowed the
skeletons in my own
family closet—and
there were many—
to somehow drop
from my conscious-
ness.
—AF READER*

however, against creating a self-fulfilling prophecy.
Parents and professionals should discuss drug abuse
with adolescents, without suggesting that the child is
more likely to abuse drugs because her birth parent
did so. As an adolescent develops an identity, such
suggestions may, in fact, increase a child's interest in
exploring illegal substances, rather than curtail the
behavior. In open adoptions, adoptive parents need to
promote abstinence but not offer criticism of the birth
parents.

When should I look for a pediatrician?

No matter what kind of adoption you're doing, it's
smart to enlist a pediatrician before you make any
other decisions. The American Academy of Pediatrics
has a section for specialists in adoption and foster
care. Several of them offer general pre-adoption con-
sultations by phone for a fairly low fee. They can also
help you evaluate a referral and can refer you to a local
pediatrician with a special interest in adoption, who
can examine your child when he comes home.

TECH SUPPORT: For a list of pediatricians
with a practice in adoption medicine, go to
adoptivefamilies.com/medical.

What are the health issues with private in-
fant adoption?

The advantages to private infant adoption are that you
are likely to have at least some medical history from
the birth mother (if she wants to be anonymous, you
will get non-identifying medical records), and the
baby will undergo standard state-mandated newborn
tests for infectious diseases and a variety of genetic
disorders. Even if you are not matched with a mother
until after the birth, you can probably get some prenatal history, and you have the right to see the baby's test
results.

What's different about foster children?

One of the several advantages of adopting from foster care is the opportunity to fully evaluate a child's health over time, with your own pediatrician, before you commit to an adoption.

> **STRAIGHT TALK:** Children in foster care may have seen multiple providers—possibly in different states—or visited doctors only for emergency care. Without routine checkups, a child could have missed multiple recommended immunizations. Your pediatrician should run blood tests to check for antibodies (titers) to common childhood diseases. If antibodies can be verified, a child simply receives booster shots as needed. If the levels don't correspond to the vaccination record, the child can be reimmunized.

What are the health issues in international adoption?

Experts in international-adoption medicine stress that the child's country of origin is less important than the individual child's circumstances. Children with disastrous, lifelong problems can be born to healthy couples in wealthy countries; perfectly healthy babies can emerge from chaos and poverty. However, our adoptive families recommend that while you are deciding on a sending country you investigate the most common problems among its adoptees. The Centers for Disease Control is a good source of information about diseases in sending countries. For information more specific to adoptees, join the online support groups for each country you are considering, and search the message archives for references to medical issues. TB? Attachment disorders? Intestinal parasites? Fetal alcohol syndrome? If any medical problem appears common there, find out as much about it as you can, and think hard about how you would cope if your child came home with that problem.

They showed me a five-minute video that had been filmed at the agency, and I immediately fell in love with a gorgeous twenty-month-old baby boy. I was allowed to review his file that day. It described medical complications that weren't in the video. I asked to meet him, and a visit was arranged for two days later. The foster mother brought him into the room and set him down. She told me not to expect much from him, as he didn't talk, didn't walk well, and didn't respond to people he didn't know. He pulled up to the chair I was sitting on, stuck his finger into my tummy, made direct eye contact, and said, very clearly, "Mommy," a word he'd never said before. Done deal!
—BARB

The social worker told me a baby girl had been born at one pound, twelve ounces, and that the mother planned to relinquish rights. Were we interested? I said yes, and she gently reminded me that I should check with my husband. I could hear the shock in his voice. He asked me lots of questions and had a lot of reservations. I said, "This is the one." I didn't even know a baby could be alive at twenty-six weeks gestation. I was about to learn about the world of preemies! After three months in neonatal intensive care, our baby came home. Seventeen months later, she joined our family at the courthouse.

—SUE

How much will I know about the child's health at referral?

There is no standard set of tests for international adoptees. U.S. embassies mandate tests for HIV, TB, syphilis, and local infectious diseases before granting the child a visa, but these tests are minimal (and you won't see the results—you'll just be told if the child's visa is being denied). Depending on your country and agency, your referral can be scanty—height, weight, a note about general health—or it can be a detailed report, with medical evaluations, vaccination records, developmental information, even birth-family history of medical disorders. Photos or videos may be available and can be extremely helpful, particularly to a doctor who is familiar with children from the same situation.

Adoption 101: Why You Need an Adoption Pediatrician to Review a Referral

- Medical terminology from some countries may be unfamiliar, even confusing, to many U.S. physicians. In Russia, for instance, terms and phrases describing inherent maladies in children are sometimes based on assumptions rather than on diagnoses.
- Most physicians preparing pre-adoption referrals will pay careful attention to information about the size of a child's head. A small head (microcephaly) may suggest malnutrition, fetal alcohol exposure, or a birth defect, either genetic or resulting from the birth process. Adoption physicians agree that a child will typically lose one month of growth

CAN I ADOPT A HEALTHY CHILD? 119

for every three months in an orphanage. With mild malnutrition, the child may be smaller than his peers, but his head size should be normal.

- Developmental milestones should coincide with a child's growth, as recorded on a growth chart. For example, a one-year-old child the size of a nine-month-old should be at the nine-month level developmentally. Extreme delays may predict long-term challenges.
- Photos and/or videos of all children (not just those from Russia and Eastern Europe) should be assessed for signs of possible fetal alcohol syndrome. Signs of this disorder include facial abnormalities, growth delay, and developmental delay.
- Whenever possible (when videos are available, for example), language should be assessed, particularly to rule out hearing disorders. A child should also be assessed for unusual stiffness (increase in muscle tone) and/or asymmetry in the way she uses her body, which can indicate underlying disorders.
- Particular attention should be paid to a child's social interactions and language skills, especially if a video is available. A video reflects only moments in a child's life, but it may demonstrate how a child responds to familiar adults and children. Behaviors such as seeking affection, responding to verbal commands, and looking for solace when upset are important in assessing how a child may attach to a new family.

I remember sitting at my desk at the law firm I work for. The phone rang and the caseworker for the agency asked, "Are you sitting down?" Of course, I jumped up immediately! I was adopting from China, and the only information the caseworker had was the name the orphanage had given the baby, her date of birth, and her weight at the time of referral. I feverishly wrote everything down on a Post-it note and asked a ton of questions the caseworker couldn't answer at that time. After I hung up the phone, I ran around the office, telling everyone that I had a daughter and showing them the Post-it. It was so precious to me to have that little nugget of information— it was like my own sonogram. I still have that note taped in her memory book, and I look at it from time to time and smile.

—DONNA

My husband and I were in the process of adopting from Russia when we were notified by a friend of ours about an eighteen-month-old boy who had been adopted from Russia one month earlier. The adoptive family was going to disrupt because they had taken him to a doctor, who diagnosed him with fetal alcohol syndrome. A little boy needed a home, and most of all, he needed a forever family. We were excited, yet a little scared. Well, to be perfectly honest, terrified! That was two and a half years ago, and this little boy is now the light of our lives and doing very, very well!

—WENDA AND TREVOR

What do I do if I have questions about the referral?

Our adoptive families say this is the toughest step in the journey. The child is now real, with a name and a face, but the referral is incomplete or contains worrisome information. Now is the time to remind yourself of your original decisions about what kind of child was right for your family, and to lean heavily on your support group. Your agency should give you plenty of time to think—two or three days is common, with extensions if you need to take the referral to a specialist.

If, after looking at the referral, your pediatrician can't assure you of the child's health, you should request another examination in the sending country and ask that the results (in their original language and in translation) be sent directly to you or your doctor. Experienced adoption pediatricians say that their evaluations are best when they are based on separate exams over a period of time, so they can judge whether the child is developing. (You should also ask if there are any earlier data on the child—quite often the orphanage has measurements taken when the child enters the system.)

Can I refuse a referral because of health problems?

One of the most important questions to ask your agency or attorney *before* signing a contract is, Can I refuse a referral, and if so, for what reasons? A good agency/attorney will allow you to decline a referral for any reason and will continue to send you referrals without asking for more money. If you feel you are being pressured to accept a referral, this is the time to switch agencies.

Burden of Choice

Linda Claire

WHEN WE RECEIVED A REFERRAL FOR AN ELEVEN-MONTH-OLD girl, just six weeks after we sent our paperwork, I told my husband, "The hard part is over. Why would we ever turn down a referral?"

I spoke too soon.

Questions arose as soon as we began sifting through the file. Some of the medical information raised concerns, but test results that would address those concerns were due shortly. When they arrived, however, we learned that the child had undergone a simpler, less conclusive test, not the one that would provide the answers we sought.

We could decline the referral or wait for the more extensive test to be completed. In theory, it was a no-brainer. This child had medical needs beyond those we felt we could handle. But it was not simple. This was no longer a theoretical child. Here was a name, a face, a person whose life would change as a result of our decision.

I agonized, my gut telling me different things at different times. I made lists, weighing pros and cons. I tried to calculate the likelihood of every possible outcome. I spoke to very patient doctors, asking the same questions over and over. I went to bed thinking we should wait and woke up thinking we should decline. Finally, my husband and I decided to wait for the next round of test results. We both felt committed to this child, so why not see the process to the end? We began to think that we would accept the referral—unless the results revealed drastic medical problems.

We waited four weeks. Then we got the news that the conclusive test had been canceled; no further testing was planned. We had to make a decision with only the information at hand. Although the child's doctors said that there was little cause for concern, our international-adoption doctor believed that there was a possibility of a serious, lifelong medical problem.

By this point, we'd accepted the prospect of living with regular doctor visits, invasive procedures, and, perhaps, surgery. But we knew that we couldn't move forward without knowing the specifics of the child's medical condition. Without that information, it was too great a risk. Combined with the stress of first-time parenting, we knew it was more than we could handle.

We declined the referral.

It was as if we had suffered another miscarriage. But this time the loss had a face and, in many ways, was much more complex. A miscarriage was a misfortune, whereas declining this referral was an active choice. With that choice came responsibility. Most of our family, close friends, and adoption-agency staff were supportive, but a few slightly raised their eyebrows, a few looked at us as if our hearts were simply too small. And the loss was not ours alone. We had consigned a little girl to waiting weeks or months to be placed with a family. Finally, we were haunted by the lingering fear that we had declined to adopt a child whose needs we might have met, whom we certainly would have loved had we known her.

Still, I know we made the right decision. Every child deserves a family who will accept her without hesitation. Even now, when I read about the medical condition she most likely has, my muscles tense and my heart beats quicker. I realize that any child—adopted or biological—comes with risks. But when you adopt, you are asked to specify the characteristics of the children you could welcome into your life, to ensure the best possible match. You are asked to choose. So we chose. Just don't let anyone tell you that having choices makes it easier.

Ellie, United States

What tests should be done once we get back to the United States?

No matter how healthy your internationally adopted child appears, she should see your physician within the first few weeks after her arrival—or sooner, if there appear to be problems.

TRIED AND TRUE: The first doctor's visit in the United States can be scary and stressful for a newly adopted child, especially one who has seen death and disease up close. If you can, recruit someone who speaks the child's language to translate and reassure.

REALITY CHECKLIST
Testing the Internationally Adopted Child

The following tests are recommended by our adoption pediatricians and by the American Academy of Pediatrics. Many (such as the tests for HIV, TB, and syphilis) will probably have been done in the sending country to qualify for the orphan visa, but they should be repeated, so that your child's medical file is complete. Even if your child came with immunization records, they may be incomplete and/or inaccurate; vaccinations may have been given at too young an age to ensure immunity, or a child may have received out-of-date or unrefrigerated vaccines. Blood tests for antibodies (also known as titers) will determine the child's current immunity status and can be used in place of vaccination records for schools in the United States.

❏ Hepatitis B profile, to include HBsAg, anti-HBs, and anti-HBc

❏ Stool examination for ova and parasites

❏ Mantoux (intradermal PPD) skin test for TB with candida control

❏ HIV-1 and HIV-2 testing

❏ RPR or VDRL for syphilis

❏ A complete blood count, with erythrocyte (RBC) indices, and a dipstick urinalysis

❏ A developmental exam, especially for those who have been institutionalized

❏ Children from Eastern Europe, Russia, and China should have their lead level and antibodies to hepatitis C checked.

We had been attending a Chinese-culture group for over a year, in anticipation of our daughter's arrival. One evening we shared with the group the sad news that the girl who had been referred to us just two weeks earlier had become seriously ill. Perhaps even fatally so. We chose to accept a new referral, but our joy was tempered by the memory of so recent a loss and the realization that it could happen again.

Once in China, we met the daughter I am sure was always meant to be ours. We were also excited to discover, days after our arrival, that the daughter who will always be the first daughter of our hearts was alive, and had been placed as a special-needs child.

—NANCY

My husband looked at the picture and flatly stated, "She's the one. That's our girl." I lamented the possible problems noted in her medical evaluations and guarded against loss. When we went to Russia to meet her, I measured her head circumference and looked into her eyes, searching for some intangible sign of recognition. I gathered medical opinions and took more photographs. I still wasn't sure. But when we got her home, I knew immediately that he had been right all along. This little girl settled into our home, our family, and our hearts immediately. She never looked back. She, like her father, seemed to know that she was one of us, and that she had finally come home.

—KATHY

❑ If the child is from China, hypothyroidism screen, because of the high incidence of dietary iodine deficiency

❑ Vision and hearing screening

❑ Testing for antibodies to infectious diseases—polio, hepatitis A and B, measles/mumps/rubella (MMR), and diphtheria/tetanus/pertussis (DTaP)

Dr. Dana Johnson, director of the International Adoption Clinic at the University of Minnesota, warns that your regular pediatrician or family physician may be reluctant to perform all of the recommended tests. "Unfortunately, physicians tend to look at the parents, not the child," he says. "The parents come from a middle-class suburb; they don't have TB, therefore the child doesn't either. Physicians don't feel they need to do the screening tests. However, if the birth parents had walked in with the child, the physician would probably have ordered even more tests. So parents may have to remind their physician to consider the child's country of origin and the diseases that are endemic in that country that can't be diagnosed solely through a physical examination."

What is attachment disorder, and how can I tell if a child is at risk for it?

Child psychiatrists believe that children lay down emotional patterns beginning in infancy. A child who does not experience consistent affection may never learn to feel or express affection for others. This syndrome is called attachment disorder or reactive attachment disorder (RAD).

Psychiatrists generally say that attachment disorders cannot be caused by anything that happens before a child is five months old; if your baby is younger, he or she won't be at risk. Many psychiatrists also believe that a child who has been loved by a parent or caregiver in its first three years builds up "immunity" to attachment disorder; as a result, children who have lost parents after age three may be traumatized and grief-stricken but will generally be able to heal.

It's commonly assumed that only older children or internationally adopted children are at risk for attachment disorders, but this is untrue. Any child who lacked individual attention between about six months and three years is at risk. If your child was in an orphanage with a high ratio of children to caregivers, or in a series of short-term foster placements, you should assume that attachment disorder is a possibility.

True RAD is extremely rare and must be carefully diagnosed by a therapist. A child who consistently displays many of the following symptoms should be evaluated—but bear in mind that *all* children, including healthy children raised in their biological families, exhibit some of these symptoms some of the time.

Gunnar, United States

REALITY CHECKLIST
Symptoms of Reactive Attachment Disorder

❑ Superficially engaging and charming personality

❑ Lack of eye contact

❑ Tendency to be indiscriminately affectionate with strangers

❑ Lack of ability to give and receive affection on parents' terms—not cuddly

❑ Inappropriately demanding and clingy behavior

Siena, United States

❑ Persistent nonsense questions and incessant chatter

❑ Poor peer relationships

❑ Low self-esteem

❑ Extreme control problems—may attempt to control openly or in sneaky ways

❑ Difficulty learning from mistakes

❑ Learning problems—disabilities, delays

❑ Poor impulse control

❑ Abnormal speech patterns

❑ Abnormal eating patterns

❑ Chronic "crazy" lying

❑ Stealing

❑ Destructiveness to self, others, property

❑ Cruelty to animals

❑ Preoccupation with fire, blood, and gore

Obviously, most of these are symptoms that appear over time and may not be immediately apparent from a video or a first meeting. Adoptive parents should investigate their child's early history and learn as much as they can about his living situation. If the child is from an orphanage, talk to adoptive parents who visited previously: Were the children cuddled and loved? Were they held for feedings, or were bottles propped on their chests? Were the caregivers attached? Did they know individual children's names and personalities? There are good orphanages and bad ones; factor this into your decision.

Eli, United States

What happens if I discover a health problem after the child is home?

While almost all adoptees—even those coming from the most dire situations—turn out to be perfectly healthy, every once in a while families discover serious and unexpected health problems in their child. Most react exactly as they would had they given birth to such a child, that is, with love and commitment. When you are interviewing adoption agencies, ask about post-placement support, particularly for families faced with disability and illness. A good agency will have social workers on staff to help you navigate the medical and mental-health system for your child.

Logan, United States

Great Non-Expectations
I. D. Steinberg

WHEN IT BECAME OBVIOUS THAT I WAS NEVER GOING TO GET pregnant, I figured that I had dodged a bullet. Like many women approaching forty, I knew when I boarded the infertility roller-coaster that the chances of a pregnancy were slim. But I wanted to try, if only to avoid future regrets. After all, if the treatments didn't work, my husband and I would retire early and travel more.

And so, as my doctor broke the news to me after each failed IVF, I felt a kind of relief. I even wore workout clothes to the final procedure, planning to go straight to the gym and, afterward, to indulge in all the other pleasures I'd denied myself during treatment—wine, sushi, chocolate, sex. Sometimes I felt guilty. I knew women who were devastated by infertility. I thought I was being supportive when I pointed out how great their lives were—terrific husbands, beautiful homes, great friends. And I was equally fortunate. I could hardly complain about my inability to conceive.

My husband just nodded his head when I got on my soapbox. I'm sure he saw it as my way of dealing with the disappointment. It wasn't until the fifth (and final) IVF that he told me how much having a child meant to him.

We had discussed adoption in the past, but Eric hadn't wanted to open our lives to scrutiny. So, at the gym, after the last doctor's visit, I programmed the treadmill and began planning our future. If we saved our money, we could both retire by fifty-five and buy a little place on the beach, which would serve as home base when we weren't traveling the world.

Later, as I laid out my grand plans, my husband gently interrupted me and said he'd been reconsidering adoption. "WHAT???" Nothing could have surprised me more.

Pondering this plot twist, I rethought adoption as well. If we got a healthy, older kid, not a newborn, we would know that there weren't any defects. Harsh, maybe, but my husband's brother was born with conditions that will keep him in a group home for the rest of his life. The truth was that I didn't want a child badly enough to take on one with disabilities.

Reluctant but game to learn more, I joined my husband in a meeting with an adoption attorney recommended by several friends. The meeting is a blur now, but the conclusion was that we would stock up on diapers. Having been told that the process could take anywhere from nine months to two years, we went home to create a photo collage, write a heartwarming letter to potential birth mothers, and wait.

It was only days until I received a call at my office. A birth mother was ready to talk to me. She proved not to be the one, but by the time the next call came, I had my sea legs. I began the conversation by asking her if she agreed that this was a little weird. The ice broken, we got to know each other, and although I knew she had other couples to consider, I felt hopeful. I let myself think about being a mom. After we had a few more conversations, she called one day while I was out. There was no official, momentous pronouncement. She was just wondering what we needed to do next. I grilled my husband—What did she mean? Were we the ones?

Our attorney confirmed that we were. I felt relieved, fearful, and, surprisingly, joyous at what lay ahead. In the astonishing months that followed, I took her to doctors' appointments and coached her through labor. I was the first one to hold the baby she'd been carrying. My new son began cooing to me, and instinctively, I replied in kind. Many mothers had tried to convince me that my lack of interest in babies would change. "It's different when they're yours." I always nodded but never believed them. My apologies to them all.

Although my husband and I had agreed to take turns getting up with baby Jack, I found myself bounding out of bed to beat him to the bassinet. At the office, I spent the day waiting for the time when I could leave work and rush home. I even considered faking an illness to get out of the evening at the Emmy Awards, usually a highlight of my professional life.

I was out of control, and loving every minute of it.

Then, six months into parenthood, as we watched our son—and our love for him—grow by leaps and bounds, life handed us a script change. During a checkup, our pediatrician noticed that Jack's eyes weren't tracking normally. Tests showed that our beautiful boy has a rare, and potentially serious, condition called optic nerve hypoplasia (ONH), which can reduce vision or, in the extreme, cause blindness, hormone deficiencies, and decreased motor skills.

Rather than feeling burdened, I saw that everything made sense. The preeminent medical specialist for ONH is based near us. Had our son stayed with his birth mother, he might never have received the diagnosis and treatment he needs.

We won't know the extent of Jack's vision problem until he's older. We do know that his motor development is a bit delayed. But for now, things are going well. I often say that Jack's a typical Hollywood type, with three therapists and meetings all day long.

As hard as I tried to avoid having a child with "special needs," I'm a better parent because of it. I am determined to give as much joy to my boy as he's given to us.

WHAT DO I DO NEXT?

Learn. Find out as much as you can about medical issues in the environment your child is coming from. Talk to an adoption pediatrician.

Support. If you are doing a private adoption, work with your agency or attorney to make sure your child's birth mother is counseled and helped to take care of herself and her baby.

Record. Keep careful note of any medical information you can glean from the agency, social worker, or birth family.

7

Why Is There So Much Paperwork?

Preparing Your Home Study and Dossier

What is a home study?

It's a document that says you can be a parent. It contains the story of your life: your family and marital history, your health, your financial situation. It includes a description of your home and neighborhood, as well as personal references and discussion of any health concerns or criminal record. It also details your family relationships and your feelings about adoption, parenting, and infertility, if applicable. It ends with a social worker's recommendation that you be allowed to adopt; sometimes it specifies how many children, and of what ages.

TRIED AND TRUE: Some of our families recommend that if you are open to adopting more children (now or later), you ask the social worker to approve you for one more child than you plan to bring home, so that you can easily update the home study.

above: Zane, United States

We were not "trying"—see, it even happens with adoption! I was sitting at my desk at work when I had a call to say a biological sibling of our four-year-old had been born that morning. I stood up and said out loud, "I'm having a baby—I mean I had a baby—I mean I have a baby." I went in and told my boss I was taking maternity leave, starting right now. We brought him home two days later.
—KAREN

Heyden, United States

We cleaned and straightened every-thing in sight for our home-study visit. Our six-year-old son was so excited to show our social worker our home, he wanted to be the tour guide. When we got to his bedroom, he said, "Hey, who cleaned up my room?" Luckily, our social worker had a sense of humor and laughed aloud while our faces turned red.

—SHERRI

Does everyone have to have a home study?

Whether you use an agency or a private lawyer, whether your adoption is domestic or international, whatever state you live in, whether you are a celebrity or a regular person (yes, we promise you, even the biggest Hollywood stars go through this), you are legally required to complete a home study before you can adopt.

If the thought of opening up your life to a social worker makes you squeamish, you're not alone. People often worry that they'll be found ineligible to adopt. In our experience, it's extremely rare for a home study to end with a negative recommendation.

How can I help my partner/spouse put up with the home study?

Every adoptive parent we know has said, at some point during the home study, "This is unfair; they don't make people go through this before they get pregnant." For some initially reluctant spouses, the prospect of having their lives examined is too much to bear. Our families say the best way to deal with this is to turn the process around: Think of the home study as the chance to ask an expert—the social worker—everything you want to know about adoption.

We've Been There: Home-Study Homework

Your home study will not only assess your ability to parent a child through adoption, it will also help you understand more about adoption and parenting. You are likely to be asked about the topics below, so give some thought to these questions. Note your answers; if you are adopting with a partner, *do* compare your notes.

About yourself

- What is your experience with infertility, and how have you resolved your grief over infertility?

- What are your religious/ethical background and beliefs and your plans for your child's religious/ethical training?
- How were you parented in your family of origin, and how might your experiences growing up affect your own parenting?
- Is there any drug or alcohol dependency in your family of origin? How does this affect you?
- What is your relationship with your spouse/partner? How do you approach problem solving and handle conflict as a team? Give examples.

Wyatt, United States

- Have you ever been arrested? What for? Was this the result of "youthful indiscretion"? What changes have you made in your life to avoid a repetition?
- What role do alcohol and drugs currently play in your life? Have you ever been treated for drug dependency?
- Have you ever been seen by a therapist or counselor? What was the result? What is the current situation?
- What is your employment status? What are your plans after your child arrives?
- What is your financial situation? Are you able to live within your means and save for future expenses?

About parenting and adoption
- What is your motivation to adopt?
- What type of child are you interested in adopting, and why?
- Can you consider taking a child with prenatal drug/alcohol exposure? Any other disabilities?
- Are you open to an ongoing relationship with your child's birth parents?
- Are you open to parenting a child of another

Liesl, United States

My husband interviewed social workers and adoption agencies before we chose one. He asked how they would treat a prospective adoptive parent who had had a drunk-driving conviction fifteen years earlier but had not had any subsequent problems with alcohol. Once he had identified social workers who were comfortable with us, and vice versa, it was a painless process.

—AF READER

race? If so, what experiences do you have with children and adults of other races? How would you incorporate same-race experiences into your child's life?

- What efforts have you made to educate yourself about adoption (books you've read, conferences you've attended, and your impressions)?
- What are your expectations of parenthood? Of your child?
- What are your theories about parenting (particularly discipline)?
- What experiences have you had caring for children?
- How does your family feel about your plans to adopt?
- If single, what are your daily support systems, your plans to provide your child adult role models of the opposite sex, and your plans in case of your death or disability?

Who does the home study?

The home study must be written by a social worker licensed in the state you live in. Some states, and all Hague Convention countries, mandate that the social worker be attached to a licensed adoption agency. If you are adopting through an agency, the agency worker assigned to your case will probably do it. If your agency is in another state, it will recommend partner agencies in your state. If you are using an attorney, you can hire an agency to do the home study or, if your state allows, you can contract with an independent social worker.

Can I choose the social worker?

If you are in a situation where you are allowed to use an independent social worker, you can certainly shop around for a compatible person. If you're working through an agency, you will need to make it part of the process of choosing the agency. When you are first interviewing agencies, ask who is likely to do your home study, and request a quick, informal chat.

If you are adopting internationally, make sure your social worker has done home studies for your sending country. Every culture has different biases; you don't want to find out *after* your home study is in that you should have emphasized churchgoing.

> **STRAIGHT TALK:** The reality is, most adoption agencies are understaffed; once you sign up with an agency, you may not have a choice of social worker.

How much will the home study cost?

It will depend on what kind of adoption you are doing, where you live, and your agency's practice. If you live in a large, expensive city, and you're doing a private or international adoption, the home study can cost up to three thousand dollars. If you live in a less expensive area and are adopting from foster care, it can be less than five hundred dollars (which may be reimbursed after the adoption is completed). Sometimes the home-study fee is rolled into a larger agency fee. If you work with a private lawyer, attorney fees generally do not include the cost of a home study. When you choose your agency or attorney, ask them to clarify, in writing, whether the home-study fee is included.

How long will it take?

Our families report that their home studies generally took three to six months from the time they contacted the social worker to the time the report was written.

How can I speed it up?

When you're interviewing agencies or social workers, ask how long they expect each phase of the home study to take. Don't hesitate to ask your social worker about his workload; if he seems disorganized or takes

We knew that the home study wasn't about a white-glove cleaning inspection, but we did clean the house. We had been collecting kids' books on adoption and diversity, so we laid those out to share. The afternoon before the home visit was spent reviewing the paperwork we had already submitted, including our autobiographies. Having them fresh in our heads made it easier to answer the social worker's questions.

—JODANE

too long to return your calls, ask to be assigned to someone else. For your part, gather all your documents and make your medical and fingerprint appointments early in the process.

What are they looking for?

A home study is meant to explore what kind of life you can offer a child. It is not intended to get skeletons out of the closet. It is not meant to intimidate. Dust in your house is all right—social workers are not typically critiquing your housekeeping standards. A certain level of order is necessary, but some family clutter is expected. (Some agencies even believe that people living in a picture-perfect home would have a difficult time adjusting to the mess a child brings to a household.) You don't have to have toys or a decorated nursery. Social workers are just looking for people who will be sensible, loving parents.

Isabella, United States

It's Home-Study Day and I'm Not Perfect Yet

Jeanne Marie Laskas

THE SOCIAL WORKER IS DUE IN A FEW HOURS. WE'RE BASICALLY ready. I mean, we've cleaned this house like nobody's business. And we've put rock salt all over the driveway, so she won't slip. I was going to make applesauce, so the house would have the warm, welcoming smell of cinnamon. But now I'm thinking I should bake bread instead. Or how about a fire in the fireplace? The smell of a fire definitely says home. But what is the smell of parent? More specifically, what is the smell of good parent material? The social worker is coming to consider us. She's coming to our house today to do a "home study," step one in the adoption procedure.

Alex and I have decided to adopt a baby from China. Well, we haven't decided-decided. But we're deep into the decision process. The deeper you go, the more your heart pounds. There's a lot you can do before you commit. Lots of paperwork you can get behind you. So this is what we're doing. This is our way of deciding, of tiptoeing, of cracking open the door to the unknown.

"Do you think we should have the smell of baking bread wafting through the house?" I ask Alex.

"Might be a little contrived," he says. "We never bake bread."

"Okay, applesauce."

"We don't make that either," he says.

"I made it in seventh grade," I point out. "It was the first thing we cooked in home ec."

"All right," he says. He knows to surrender when I am driven by stress.

"But will the smell get all the way back to the family room?" I ask. "Should we bring a fan in here or something and aim the aroma toward the back of the house?"

"No," he says. "No, we should not." He knows to speak clearly, definitively, when I am losing my marbles.

I'm nervous. I've never had a home study before. I've never had to put my domestic self out for review. It is not my most developed self. My inner Martha Stewart is not what you'd call a fully actualized identity. It doesn't help that it's raining. That the ice outside is slowly giving way to a yard that looks like soup. "Welcome to the ugliest day on our farm," I imagine saying to her when she pulls up. But then she might think I mean it's ugly because she's here, so, no, I'd better not go there.

I'm nervous. I want this to go right. I'm peeling apples. I'm wiping the counters again and again, to show off what a good counter wiper I am. I'm sprinkling cinnamon on the apples, lots of it, to make sure the aroma of my domesticity, of my promise as a mother, is unmistakable.

I could, of course, be insulted. I mean, maybe that's the more empowering emotional direction to go in right now. The outrage! A home study? Why should I have to prove my parental potential to a complete stranger? Any wacko with the right plumbing can become a parent. No forms to fill out. No history to reveal. No how-do-you-handle-conflict essay questions to answer. Why me? Poor me. It's not fair. Life isn't fair. Which, of course, is only half the story. Life seems unfair only when it's throwing curves. But what about when it's sending out those equally rare perfect pitches: a good job, a good husband, a happy home, a supportive family, a baby who needs a mom? In China, we're told, that would be a girl.

Okay, here comes a car. A white car. Make that a muddy white car. Oh, dear. I should have prepared her. She pulls up the driveway, sits there for a few minutes. She's flipping through papers, writing things down. She's giving us bad marks for mud. I can just tell. I am biting my nails. I am pacing. "Just be yourself," Alex says. He has an umbrella. He is going outside to her.

"Brilliant idea!" I say. "Bring her an umbrella! Blind her with chivalry!"

"It's raining," he says.

When she is in the house, I begin my apologies. For the rain. For the gray sky. For the ruts on Wilson Road. For the way the kitchen is not yet renovated. For the lightbulb that is out on the porch. For the way the cat sleeps on the satellite dish, despite the fact that I have provided him with a perfectly good cat bed.

"You seem nervous," she says, smiling. "Please don't be. This is not an investigation. This is a . . . warm-and-fuzzy. You know? I'm just here to help you bring your daughter home."

My . . . what? Excuse me? This is the first time I have ever heard that word used that way. That is one big word. *Daughter. My daughter. Our daughter.* That has a ring to it, all right. Alex looks at me. He is smiling. I am smiling. The social worker is smiling. Three people enjoying the same music. Decisions are like music. New songs you try out. The more beautiful the sound, the more your heart starts pounding.

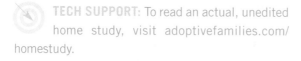 TECH SUPPORT: To read an actual, unedited home study, visit adoptivefamilies.com/homestudy.

Who gets approved?

Well over 90 percent of the people who apply for a home study are approved by their social worker. The social worker *wants* to approve you—she is in the business of finding families for children. Enlist her help, and be absolutely honest about your situation and any concerns.

What should I worry about?

If you have a medical, financial, or criminal record that you fear might result in an unfavorable home study, don't wait to mention it. If you plan to adopt internationally, your social worker can steer you to a country that is more likely to be accepting, and can address your situation in the home study in a way that's consistent with the country's cultural values and requirements.

Gracie, United States

Adoption 101: Home-Study Problems

■ Conviction record: **Misdemeanors stemming from youthful indiscretions usually aren't held against prospective adopters in the United States, although a social worker will want to know if your past behavior is truly past. If you have a DUI on**

I had been a big partier when I was younger and had gotten a DUI fifteen years earlier. I couldn't shake the thought that because of my record we would fail the home study and destroy our chances of having a family. The social worker looked at us under a microscope. Though my party days were long over, he had to dispel the possibility that I was an addict before he could endorse us. In the end, a social worker will not punish a responsible adult for mistakes he made as a college student. The most important thing is to demonstrate who you are today. Just be honest. It is far worse to get caught in a lie than it is to confront the past.
—AF READER

your record, for instance, she'll ask if you went through a rehabilitation program and what your current drinking habits are. If you have committed a felony, the U.S. government won't approve you to adopt internationally, and you will have trouble finding a domestic agency that will accept you.

- Health problems or disabilities: **An agency will want to know that you can care for a child long-term. If you're in the middle of medical treatment or have a condition that threatens your life expectancy, you might be prevented from adopting. If you have a medical condition that is under control (for instance, high blood pressure or diabetes that is managed by diet and medication), you may still be approved as an adoptive family. If your family has sought counseling or treatment for a mental-health condition in the past, you may be asked to provide reports from those visits.**
- Financial problems: **A history of bankruptcy, high debt, or failure to pay child support could be cause for denial. But you don't have to be rich to adopt; you just have to show that you can manage your finances responsibly and adequately. If you're adopting internationally, some countries have specific income requirements.**

Motherhood in the Balance
Emalee Gruss Gillis

I SAT AT THE KITCHEN TABLE, HOLDING THE PHONE RECEIVER as I waited for Nancy, our social worker at the adoption agency, to come on the line. How could I tell her that I had just been diagnosed with bipolar disorder? How could I not? In my mind's eye, I could see myself as I was in the hospital, just days earlier, so inwardly focused that I lost my ability to speak coherently. I had recovered within a day, but the diagnosis would surely change our future. I was terrified that what I was about to say would end our dream of having a child. I had never longed for anything so in my life.

As Nancy and I began to talk, I was deeply sad. I fully expected her to tell me that the agency could no longer present our family profile to birth mothers. But Nancy took her time and kept asking questions. At the end of our conversation, she asked for a letter from my psychiatrist, explaining the diagnosis and what it meant for my future. The letter said that bipolar disorder—formerly known as manic depression—is a treatable illness, that he was confident I would respond successfully to treatment, and that I would make a good parent.

Nancy allowed us to proceed with our adoption. I was tremendously relieved, but I doubted that a birth parent would choose an adoptive parent with a mental-health disorder, even a treatable one. Amazingly, during the year after that conversation, several sets of birth parents selected my husband and me for consideration. Ultimately, each birth mother chose another couple, but in no case was the decision due to my diagnosis.

Finally, we were selected again. Before we met the birth parents, Nancy told them about my diagnosis. She advised us to follow their lead in discussing it. As the four of us chatted awkwardly over lunch that first time, we talked of many things, but neither of them brought up my health situation. We learned later that they had done their own research and had concluded that bipolar disorder was a treatable illness.

Just after our child was born, the birth father invited us into the birthing room. Our son was beautiful. He opened one eye and looked at me. Then his tiny mouth opened into a yawn. What bliss when our son was finally placed in my arms a week later!

I know that mental illness is still feared and stigmatized, and I am deeply appreciative of the people who looked beyond my diagnosis and recognized my potential to be a good parent. After doubting I would be a mother, I savor parenting even more. I'm thrilled by my son's first attempts to read and at watching my daughter (adopted later, from Korea) do a cartwheel. And what sweet joy to kiss them both good night.

Kamron, United States

Our first agency rejected us because we had lost a biological child and they wanted us to wait longer before adopting. We knew we had grieved enough and were ready. We applied to, and were accepted by, another agency.

—AF READER

What if I'm rejected?

In the unlikely event that your social worker doesn't approve you, the first thing to do is appeal to the head of her agency to make sure it's not a matter of personal chemistry or just a quirk of your worker (it's been known to happen). Next, check with your online support group: Have other people in your situation been approved? If so, by whom? If there's no absolutely objective reason for your rejection, apply to another agency.

Who sees the home study?

Given how sensitive the information in your home study is likely to be, you should ask your social worker about confidentiality. You should also ask whether you will be allowed to read it yourself. It will likely be shared with other social workers and other agencies, to help in matching the most appropriate child with your family. In some cases, the information might also be shared with birth parents.

We've Been There: Home Study Step-by-Step

There's no set format for home studies, but most include the following steps:

1. Training: Many agencies require prospective adoptive parents to attend parental training prior to or during the home-study process. These sessions are meant to help you under-

stand the needs of children waiting for families and decide what type of child or children you could parent.

2. Interviews: You will probably be interviewed several times by the social worker. You will be asked to explain how you handle stress and describe past experiences of crisis or loss. In the case of couples, some agency workers conduct all of the interviews jointly, with both prospective parents together. Others will conduct both joint and individual interviews. If you already have children, the social worker will want to chat with them—even if they are adults and are living away from home.

Ann Marie, United States

3. Home visit: Home visits primarily serve to ensure that your home meets state licensing standards (e.g., working smoke alarms, safe storage of firearms, safe water, adequate space for each child). Some states require an inspection from the local health and fire departments, in addition to the visit by the social worker. The social worker will generally want to see all areas of the house or apartment, including where the children will sleep, the basement, and the backyard. She will be looking to see how you plan to accommodate a new family member or members.

4. Medical exam: Most home studies require prospective parents to have some form of physical exam. You can almost always choose to have this done by your own physician. Some agencies have specific requirements— for example, agencies that place infants only with infertile couples might require a physician to confirm the infertility. Other agencies just want to know that the prospective parents are healthy, have a normal life expectancy, and

Marcus, United States

are physically and mentally able to handle the care of a child.

5. Background checks: Most states require criminal and child-abuse record clearances for all adults (including children over eighteen, relatives, and household help) living in the home. In many states, local, state, and federal clearances are required. Your social worker will give you blank cards to bring to your local police station to get your fingerprints taken. You then send the completed cards, with accompanying forms, to your state clearance agency.

6. References: The social worker will probably ask you for the names, addresses, and telephone numbers of three or four people to serve as references for you. If possible, references should be people who have known you for several years, who have observed you in many situations, and who have visited your home and know of your interest in and involvement with children. Most agencies require that references be people unrelated to you. Good choices might include close friends, an employer, a former teacher, a coworker, a neighbor, or your pastor, rabbi, or leader of your faith community.

7. Autobiographical statement: Many social workers ask prospective parents to write an autobiographical statement. You're not being graded on the quality of your writing; they just want to know a bit about your own childhood and life, why you want to adopt, and what kind of parent you expect to be.

For sample reference letters and autobiographies, go to adoptivefamilies.com/homestudy.

REALITY CHECKLIST
Documents

The list of documents looks daunting; just take them one by one. You can make the process easier if you get the correct documents on the first try—nothing is more frustrating than having your home study held up because you have to chase yet another bit of paper. Before you start, ask your social worker exactly what version of each document you need, and whether they must be originals, certified, notarized, or apostilled. Make photocopies of every document before sending it anywhere, and *always* use registered mail, FedEx, or some other trackable system.

Grace, United States

❑ Multiply. If you're planning an international adoption, get *three* originals of every document on this list. You'll need one set later for the dossier that will be submitted to the foreign government and another when you petition the U.S. government for the child's visa. If you will be readopting your child later in the United States, get *four*; you'll need a set to submit to your local court.

❑ Notarize. To notarize means to certify that the document and any signatures on it are true. Notaries are licensed by the state; you can find one at notarypublic.com, but our families recommend that when you're starting your home study, you locate a friendly notary at a local institution (try your town hall, bank, library, and doctor's office), introduce yourself, and explain your needs. Many will offer to notarize all your adoption documents for one nominal fee.

Ava, United States

Christopher, United States

❑ Apostille. For an international adoption, many documents will need to be apostilled, a kind of super-notarization that must be done by a secretary of state and involves fancy gold stamps and seals. If you're working through an adoption agency, it will likely take care of the apostille process. If you need to do it yourself, call your local secretary of state and ask about the process.

❑ Birth certificates, for the adoptive parents and any existing children. Ask your social worker if you need long-form or short-form certificates. Long-form (also known as "certified photocopy" or "book copy" birth certificates) are exact photocopies of the original birth record that was prepared by the hospital or attending physician at the time of the child's birth and usually include parents' information (address of residence, race, birthplace, date of birth, etc.), additional information on the child's birthplace, and information about the doctors who assisted in the birth of the child. Short-form birth certificates (also known as computer certifications, certifications of birth, or certificates of birth registration) have more limited information. Baptismal certificates and hospital souvenir birth certificates (the cute ones with the little footprints) are not acceptable.

❑ Tax returns. Most agencies will want returns for at least the past two years. Some want just the front page.

❑ Marriage certificates. Ask your social worker whether you need a marriage certificate or the certified marriage license.

❑ Divorce decrees for either parent, if applicable.

Depending on your social worker or agency, you may also need:

❑ Paycheck stubs.

❑ W-2 forms.

❑ Bank statements.

❑ Copies of mortgage or lease.

❑ Life-insurance policies.

❑ Health-insurance policy. You may need to show that the adopted child will be insured. Just make a printout or a copy of the page that says dependents are covered; by law, insurance agencies in the United States must treat an adopted child exactly as they would a biological child.

Luke, United States

❑ A letter from your doctor. Ask your doctor to include the phrases "normal life expectancy" and "able to parent an adopted child."

❑ A letter from your existing children's pediatrician, if applicable. Ask the pediatrician to note that your children are up-to-date on their checkups and vaccinations.

❑ Letters of reference. Ask your social worker if your references should emphasize any particular aspect of your personality or life—church attendance, work habits, etc.

Our eldest child was applying to universities at the same time my husband and I were applying to adopt our youngest from Ethiopia. Sometimes the processes were weirdly similar: personal essays, interviews, reference letters, maps, physical exams. Now, when I counsel friends slogging through their home studies and dossiers, I say, "Think of it as practice for college application, which will be here in no time."

—ISOLDE

What happens if the child is born or lives in another state?

If you have to cross a state line to take your child home, you must comply with the Interstate Compact for the Placement of Children. Before the child can leave, you must ask permission from the sending state's ICPC office (your agency or attorney will take care of it). When permission is granted, your local ICPC office will contact you, and you can head home. The whole process usually takes just a few days. Some of our families doing private adoptions have avoided it altogether, by moving the expectant mother to their home state and having her deliver at a local hospital.

What is a dossier?

If you're doing an international adoption, you'll need to prepare a dossier, which is basically the home study dressed up to be sent to the government of the sending country. Most of our families waited until their home studies were complete before doing their dossiers, but you can start preparing it earlier—especially since you'll be putting the same documents in both files.

When will the adoption be final?

If you are doing a private adoption, you wait until the birth parents have signed their consent to the adoption, then wait some more until the consent is irrevocable, then apply to your local family, surrogate, or probate court for a finalization. The waiting time and kind of court depend on the state you live in. Go to adoptivefamilies.com/statelaws for details.

If you're adopting from foster care, your local social services department and adoption (or foster-care) agency will have its own rule on how long you have to have the child at home before you can apply to finalize.

In international adoptions, some sending countries grant the adoptive parents temporary guardianship or custody. These adoptions must be finalized in the United States, like domestic adoptions. (This is sometimes referred to as readoption, but it's not; technically, it's finalization.)

The court appearance itself is a simple and joyful ceremony. You and your child appear before a judge who will recognize you as a family and issue a new birth certificate showing you (and your spouse, if you have one) as the parent(s).

Olivia, United States

STRAIGHT TALK: Judges generally want a social worker to visit the family at least once after the child is at home before they'll approve a finalization. Some courts accept an agency or independent social worker's report (if you adopted through an agency, this should be part of your package). A few courts insist on sending their own social worker—or a probation officer. This is a formality, not a test of your parenting skills. Your child is not going to be taken away.

What is readoption and when is it necessary?

Readoption is when you completed a legal adoption in another country and then ask your local court system to recognize it. It's not always strictly necessary. If you adopted in a country that is party to the Hague Adoption Convention, or if you met your child before the foreign adoption took place and you live in a state that automatically recognizes foreign adoption, you don't *have* to readopt. But our families recommend that all internationally adopted children be readopted in the United States, as an extra measure of security. This way, your child's rights to citizenship and inheritance can never be questioned. (Hard to believe, but we know of two cases where parents' wills were contested by relatives who claimed that, since the children weren't adopted in the United States, they weren't entitled to inherit.)

Ava, United States

The Final Step

Eliza Newlin Carney

DURING THE LONG MONTHS MY HUSBAND, DAN, AND I WERE waiting to adopt a baby, I often wondered how I would react when I finally held this child of our dreams. Would I shed tears, like the weepy parents in media portrayals of hospital births? As it happened, I was grinning merrily on the day our beautiful daughter, Beth, just two days old, was put in my arms. I floated, giddy, as high as a kite; I did not cry. There was a day, however, when the joyful tears flowed freely. That was the day Dan and I drove to a Maryland courthouse to finalize Beth's adoption.

I had not expected this to be a banner day. If anything, I was cranky and jittery on the spring morning that we buckled Beth into her car seat and fought our way through rush-hour traffic to an unfamiliar part of Montgomery County. Would we find the courthouse? Would we arrive on time? Would my parents and my older brother know where to find us? Perhaps, too, there was a submerged fear: What if some sudden obstacle rose up at the last minute to impede this final, crucial step on our road to parenthood? Rationally, I knew this court appearance was routine, a mere formality. Yet I desperately wanted it to go well.

As it turned out, our finalization hearing before family-court judge James C. Chapin was one of the more memorable milestones in our adoption journey. Genial and gray-haired, Chapin endeared himself to us immediately by making a fuss over Beth, then eight months old. Admittedly, she was looking adorable in the little blue-and-white flowered dress, complete with matching hat, that I had selected for the occasion. "I can't take my eyes off her," he declared. "Adoptions are a judge's highlight," Chapin told us, following introductions by our lawyer, Mark McDermott. "Family court is typically a place where people hash out disputes," he continued, "but in adoption, everybody's happy."

Even the legalistic phase of the hearing was moving. It was surprisingly gratifying to hear Chapin intone authoritatively that the court "finds that it is in the best interests of this child that this adoption be granted," that "the child will now have the relationship of parent and child with Daniel and Elizabeth Carney." What Chapin said next left me wiping away those tears I had wondered about for so long. "It's almost a shame that Beth is so young that she can't really appreciate what's going on," he concluded, "because I always like to reflect on the fact that when we come into this world, we don't pick our parents and our parents don't pick us. It just happens. However, in adoption it's a little different. The adopting parents so love the child that they go to a great deal of trouble to seek out the child, to have that child become theirs. I'm sure there's nothing but wonderful family love ahead of you."

I had known that, once our adoption was finalized, Beth would be issued a new birth certificate with our names on it. Early in the process, I had found this odd, even strangely deceptive. I looked into obtaining a copy of her original birth certificate, so that her records would be complete. But amid the excitement of being a new mom, I never followed through. Fortunately, Maryland's recently enacted open records law ensures that Beth, should she ever wish to, will have access to this document. Funnily, though, I no longer regard her "altered" birth certificate with ambivalence. In its own way, it tells the real story: We are a family, and she is our daughter. I knew it in my heart the moment that I looked into her sweet face. Now I know it in my head. And now, the state of Maryland—even the U.S. government—recognizes it, too. It's a small victory, perhaps. But it's one that brings a quiet sigh of relief and maybe even a tear to the eye.

TRIED AND TRUE: In some states, readoption is a simpler process than finalization, and a few of our families have filed the court papers and represented themselves. Online support groups often have members who can walk you through the process.

Will anyone keep track of us after the adoption?

Emily, United States

The U.S. government does not generally monitor adoptive families after finalization. But many agencies do ask you to agree to send reports (it will be part of your contract), and some foreign countries have their own post-placement requirements.

Isaac, United States

STRAIGHT TALK: Adoption is often controversial within sending countries. Post-placement reports can be used to reassure critics that adoptees are not being used—to cite two common international fears—as organ donors or slaves. Several countries have stopped or slowed adoption to the United States because post-placement reports were not sent as promised. If you adopt internationally, you must comply with the sending country's wishes; if not, you can put an entire program at risk.

WHAT DO I DO NEXT?

Organize. Order appropriate copies of all the documents you'll need. Ask your local police station about fingerprinting; find a friendly notary; make appointments for your physicals. Start a filing system.

Warn. Call your references and let them know what's expected of them.

Prepare. Before your home study, compare notes with your partner on parenting philosophies. Walk around your house and imagine how a child will fit in. Don't bother polishing silver, but check for dangers—an unfenced pool, a snapping dog.

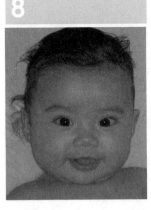

8

Why Does This Have to Take So Long?

Preparing for Your New Child

When should I tell friends and family?

Our adoptive families recommend that you share your plans in stages. While adoptions take, on average, less than two years from the date your home study is accepted, you won't be in control of the timing. And if yours drags on, the last thing you want is daily phone calls asking, "So, any news?"

When you're preparing your home study, tell your closest relatives and friends (who may be writing your letters of reference). When your home study has been approved, tell extended family and key co-workers. Put off making your news public until you accept a referral or a match with an expectant mother.

How should I tell them?

Bear in mind that some of the people who will hear your news won't have any personal connection to adoption. Use your announcement to educate them.

above: Joslyn, Guatemala

I had to wait eighteen months to bring my two children home from Guatemala. If I had known it would take that long, I would have set some ground rules for my family. My mother called every day to ask if we'd heard anything. It got pretty difficult, as I was trying hard not to think about the adoption every second!

—HOLLY

Our families were not aware that we were struggling with infertility, so I was anxious about the questions they might ask about our decision to adopt. We waited to share our plans with our extended families and friends until we had a referral for a child. This was a good decision for us. My husband told our parents and siblings personally, and they were all extremely supportive. I should have given them more credit and trusted in their support. However, there were a few who made—and, occasionally, still make—remarks that are unsettling. The comments are not intended to be hurtful; they are simply a result of a lack of understanding.
—AF READER

Provide as much general information as you can, making it clear that you have thought long and hard about this step.

How do I deal with hurtful comments and intrusive questions?

Every adoptive parent will tell you that after they announced their adoption plans, two things happened: First, friends and colleagues came up to say, "You know, I adopted, too," or "I'm adopted, too." Second, someone made a silly—or plain rude—remark. Welcome to parenthood. This is a chance to practice a skill you'll need for the rest of your life: defending your child from inappropriate comments. Resist the temptation to respond by explaining too much. Our families say it's good to share general information that will help others understand adoption, but your child's own story is his or hers to tell. Keep information about birth family and the reasons your child was available for adoption to yourself. If your child chooses to share them later, that is his choice.

Logan, United States

My So-Called Friends
Barb Reinhold

THE OTHER DAY, I MENTIONED TO A CO-WORKER THAT MY HUS-band and I were looking into international adoption. You'd have thought I said we were thinking of becoming terrorists. "What do you mean, you're going to adopt from Russia? What about all the kids in Milwaukee who need good homes?" she demanded indignantly.

I am, despite being a lawyer, an essentially polite person. I formulate nasty responses in my head but utter mild demurrals. What I said was: "Well, we really like Russian culture, and the conditions over there in the orphanages are really horrible. We think it's a good alternative, although we haven't decided for sure yet." What I wanted to say was: "Who are you, someone capable of producing three kids, who has never known the heartbreak of infertility, to judge? I just want a child who looks like me and fits into my family. Is that a crime?"

I am not unsympathetic to the plight of kids with special needs who move from one foster home to another. I know they need good homes and parents to love them. But is a child in a Russian orphanage any less worthy of a good home and loving parents, just because he or she had the misfortune to be born there instead of here?

Apparently so.

Everybody, everywhere, not just at work, has opinions on international adoption—few of them favorable. In the past six months, I've heard hateful and irrational opinions from people I used to think of as intelligent, rational adults. I've been accused of racism. I've been accused of favoring "communists" over "red-blooded Americans." I've even been accused of trying to "buy" a child.

Through it all, I've never heard anyone ask a pregnant woman why she chose to give birth rather than to adopt a special-needs minority child. I've never heard a father of six condemned for his "selfishness" in choosing to have so many children, rather than "give a home to a deserving Milwau-kee kid."

And while we're on the subject, why do people whose insurance companies pay thousands of dollars for them to give birth think that this doesn't constitute "buying a child," but that paying adoption expenses somehow does?

"If I couldn't have kids, I would take a special-needs child," said one acquaintance, a sanctimonious mother of six biological children.

"Oh," I said sweetly, "just because you can have biological children doesn't mean you can't adopt, too. And, as you've said, these are children who really need good homes so badly. Why don't you open up your heart and give one a good home?"

She stared at me with an expression that said, loud and clear, "I know you're not playing with a full set of ovaries or a full deck of cards." She spoke slowly and loudly, lest I miss her meaning: "I have children of my own. I don't need to adopt."

"Oh," I said, my tone only slightly less sweet. "I get it now—only defective people should adopt defective children. The truth is," I told this woman, "neither my husband nor I are equipped to raise a child with special needs."

I freely concede that this is selfish. I wish that I could be altruistic and have enough of everything—patience, confidence, skill—to give a child with special needs a special home. I wish that I were big enough not to care that the child wouldn't look like my husband or me. I wish it weren't so important to me that the child who joins my family be as perfect and bright and healthy as he or she possibly can be.

But like everyone who has chosen to have only biological children, instead of adopting a special-needs child, I do care and it does matter. In that way, I am like every parent who has ever given birth to a child. The only difference is that I am willing to tell the truth.

Benjamin, United States

When do I tell my other children?

If you already have children—biological or adopted—you'll need to think carefully about when and how to tell them about their new siblings.

We've Been There: Telling Your Other Children About Adoption

1. Resist the temptation to ask your children if they want a new sibling. Even if the answer is an enthusiastic yes, children shouldn't bear this kind of responsibility.

2. Tell your children as soon as you start your home study, if not before. Children can sense when something is being withheld. If you're worried that your home study will be declined (it almost never happens), then just tell them that the social worker is there to help you make the decision about adoption.

3. If you're doing a private infant adoption, prepare your child for the possibility that the birth mother will change her plan. If your first child came from a similar adoption, be very clear that, once an adoption is finalized, it is forever.

4. Involve your children in the adoption planning. They can help announce the news to friends and family, and can choose equipment, toys, and clothes.

5. Reassure your children about their own security. Children understand that adoption involves loss. For some, the new adoption may make them worry about what happens if you die or become ill. You should explain why and how you are different from the new child's birth family (better health, more resources, greater maturity). Depending on the child's

Around Christmastime my husband and I were ready to tell our families about our decision to adopt. We spoke to our parents, in person, ahead of time, but we told the rest of the family by way of the gifts we gave them. Each family received a copy of a book by Patricia Irwin Johnston, Adoption Is a Family Affair! What Relatives and Friends Must Know. *They were all excited!*

—ANGIA

When we received our referral, we sent out Godiva chocolates in little gold boxes, with pink ribbon and carriage charms attached. We attached miniature announcements with a wallet-sized referral photo. They were a huge hit. The wonder of adoption still amazes us. There hasn't been a day in the past six months with my treasured child that I have not cried and thanked God.

—TERRI

age, you might also explain your plans for guardianship, in the unlikely event that something does happen to you.

6. Help your children prepare for questions and remarks they're bound to hear about their new sibling, such as "Where's her real mother?" Let your children know that they needn't answer every query. Decide in advance what information should be public and what should be shared only with close family and friends, and talk to your children about privacy issues. In addition, think ahead about what to share with your older children about your new family member's history. There may be details that shouldn't be shared with anyone, even older siblings.

When do I tell my employer?

Our families recommend that, before you tell your boss or co-workers, you research your benefits. Is your company big enough to be covered by the Family and Medical Leave Act? If it is, you are entitled to the same unpaid leave given to your colleagues who give birth, and to get your job—or an equivalent one—back when you return to work. How much leave is offered? Is your employer one of the rare (and blessed) companies that offer *paid* adoption leave? Can you get adoption fees reimbursed? Keep an eye out for executives or human-resources staff who are themselves adoptive parents; they will likely be your best source of information. Once you've done your research, and your home study has been approved, tell your supervisor and your colleagues.

Allyson, United States

STRAIGHT TALK: It's important to understand the difference between disability leave and family leave. Women who give birth get *paid* short-term disability leave for six to twelve weeks. All new parents—adoptive, biological, fathers, mothers—are entitled to *unpaid* family leave if the company qualifies. For information about adoption benefits in the workplace, and for a sample letter lobbying your employer, go to adoptivefamilies.com/topcompanies and adoptivefamilies.com/cost.

When we received the referral of our daughter, we sent an announcement to family and friends with her picture, information about her, and the first verse of "With Arms Wide Open," by Creed. We wanted everyone to see her and share our joy. The framed announcement now hangs in her room. We want her to know how blessed and lucky we feel to have her!

—LISA

What supports can I line up before my child comes home?

The very best way to occupy your time while you wait for your child is to learn everything you can about raising adopted children, and to prepare for any eventuality. If your child is coming from another country, learn about the culture, memorize at least a few phrases in the language, and, if the child is more than a year old, find someone who can translate. If you are adopting transracially, build a network of caring adults of the same background who can serve as role models for your child, and learn about skin and hair care (yes, it's different, and it matters). If you have any reason to think your child may have medical or psychological problems, track down local experts.

Having Faith
Matt Forck

WE HAD REACHED A CROSSROAD IN OUR QUEST TO BECOME
parents. My wife, Stephanie, a teacher, and I, a utility worker, had to
choose between reaching for the top rung of the fertility ladder or taking
a different path, adoption. Stalling as best I could, I was able to defer the
choice until early summer, after a long-planned family vacation. June
came, the vacation went, and the period of contemplation left us both
thinking adoption was best. I left for work the next morning, happy with
our choice but wondering, where do we go from here?

When I returned home that evening, my question was answered. My
wife had every adoption book from our local library scattered on the living
room floor. We spent July reading and discussing, thinking, praying, and
hoping. We took notes and talked. We laughed and cried. Above all, we
learned.

Although it seems like yesterday, it was almost two years ago. As I write
this, our beautiful daughter, Natalie Faith, slumbers. I have a different
perspective on adoption now. I think the books had merit. They helped us
to understand the different types of adoption. They covered the laws,
what to expect from agencies, the average wait times for an infant, and the
average expenses. But for all they offered, some things weren't covered, so
I want to share my newfound expertise.

"It is better for people to think you an idiot than to open your mouth
and remove all doubt." Announcing that you are adopting spawns questions or comments that are somewhat reflective of this old saying.
Everyone knew we were in the process because we told them, via a mass
mailing. (We did this in case someone knew someone who could help
us.) But as we waited, we were asked many questions. "How is the adoption going?" "Have you heard anything?" "How much longer?" These are
sensitive probes in an emotional time. Books mentioned that there
would be such comments, but never talked about how they would make
us feel.

The pre-placement questions were discreet compared with the post-adoption comments we've heard. The one that wins the idiot prize referred to my daughter's darker-toned skin. We were asked, "Is she part something else?" My wife replied, "No, she is all human." I have become intensely protective of my daughter, so such statements yank my heartstrings. If books offered advice on coping with things people say, they should read, "Most people ask because they care or are trying to make conversation. Those not in this category are idiots."

Like it or not, each child comes with a birth mother. The books we read did nothing to prepare us for the reality of a birth mother. Books centered on how to find a birth mother and what to talk about once one was located. As we began a domestic independent adoption, I envisioned a sensible sixteen-year-old high school homecoming queen finding herself accidentally pregnant by the quarterback. She, of course, wants to place the child, so she can accept her scholarship to an Ivy League school as a premed major. This scenario is what I wanted. I was afraid of other, riskier situations.

I have had relationships with two birth mothers now (our first situation fell through), and there are remarkable similarities between them. Both were from abusive homes. Both had been through the court system as juveniles. Drug and alcohol problems affected their families. Both were from poor homes. I know I can't generalize too much, but I think these women were more typical than was the homecoming queen in my dream. These realities were hard to swallow; they scared me to death. I spent endless time worrying about genetics versus environment. I worried about the child's health. The burden was so heavy that I visited a counselor and a priest.

There is one more thing the mothers had in common, and that is love. Each birth mother loved her baby immeasurably. The first expressed her love by choosing to parent her child. The second, our birth mother, told us repeatedly that she did not want Natalie to think that she was "bad" for not raising her. She wanted her to know that she loved her and wanted to raise her. But she knew what kind of life that meant for a child, and she didn't want that for her baby.

There is no larger part to the adoption story than faith, and not one book talked about it. From the beginning of our road to parenthood, we have attended a local adoptive-parents group. Whether a couple is anguishing in the waiting stage or is raising three beautiful children, we often hear faith-filled statements. "God has a plan for us." "Our baby will be with us soon." "Our son was meant for our family."

I relied on faith through this process. I was often scared. I thought of stopping, but I kept telling myself, this will be all right. God wouldn't give me more than I could handle. As I struggled with the challenges, I was tested to an even greater degree. Four weeks prior to our daughter's birth, we received a call from an attorney saying that we had been matched with another birth mother. It was almost exactly my dream scenario—she was sixteen, pregnant by her high school sweetheart. It seemed so simple, and our current situation seemed so complicated. My first reaction was, "Thank God!" However, after thinking and praying about it, the next night we decided that our current situation was best for us. As scared as I was, and as risky as this seemed to be, I felt calm. So we passed up the "ideal" situation. I have never regretted our decision because it enabled me to meet my daughter. Faith—it is her middle name and the backbone of adoption.

If you save one life, you save the world over time. This Jewish proverb speaks to the last item not mentioned in the books, and that is the baby. The books talk about the means to get the infant, but not about him or her. The books never told me how soft my baby's cheeks would be and how warm they would feel when I press them to mine. Books never described the glow in her eyes as she smiles at me. No one ever said how much we would laugh and giggle with her over things like feeding her sweet potatoes. The books didn't tell us we would dash to her room in the evenings, just to watch her sleep. The books didn't talk about it, so I will.

I never imagined the joy of being a father. It is the best experience I have ever had, and I live it every day. "Adoption versus biological" doesn't cross my mind. She is my daughter, period. Many people have told my wife and I that our daughter is lucky to have us, that we are doing a good thing. Really, it is Natalie who has saved us. I think all parents with adopted children would say the same.

How far should I go in preparing a room?
First, you don't need to decorate a nursery for your home study; just show your social worker where you plan to put the new child. But many of our families did pass the time by painting and decorating; for those whose adoptions took longer than expected, the empty room became a constant reminder. However, once the child came home (and your child *will* come home), they were happy to have time to focus on parenting rather than decorating.

> TRIED AND TRUE: In some Jewish communities, parents traditionally don't bring any baby clothes or equipment into the home before the baby's birth. If you live anywhere with a sizeable Jewish population, local baby stores will store items you've purchased until you alert them to deliver and assemble everything.

I should have held off on shopping. Even at nine months old, fresh from a Chinese social welfare institute, my daughter had a clear sense of her own taste. She refused to put on or play with anything she didn't like!
—SUSAN

Tinsley, United States

Many people within our circles of family and friends wanted to give us baby showers before our daughter was born. But we didn't feel comfortable having them before the actual birth and signing of papers. Things worked out beautifully when our daughter came home—and was the guest of honor at many Welcome Home parties. We celebrated her birth and adoption, even as we introduced her to so many who had prayed and waited anxiously for her arrival.

—MAUREEN

When can I buy clothes and toys?

Our families recommend holding off on buying clothes and toys, except for the bare essentials—a couple of everyday outfits and underwear. Once your child comes home, you will be buried in gifts from family and friends.

If you are adopting internationally, bring the child comfortable clothes for the return plane trip—including a few changes that can fit into a carry-on bag, in case of an upset tummy.

TRIED AND TRUE: Internationally adopted children rarely match American size charts, and height and weight measurements from orphanages are notoriously unreliable; clothes brought from the United States can swamp your new child. It's best to bring pieces whose arms and legs can be easily rolled up—sweat suits with stretchy cuffs, for example. If you are adopting an older child—especially a girl—from another country, be sensitive to cultural concerns about modesty.

Is it appropriate to have a baby shower?

Most of our families waited until they had, at least, accepted their referral before agreeing to a shower. Many waited until the child came home and turned the event into a combination shower/welcome party. Bear in mind that for a baby older than five months, or for an older child, a party with lots of strangers can be overwhelming. If you are "cocooning" (keeping your new child close and limiting visitors), you might decide to wait to have your party until several months after homecoming.

Many of our families who had private infant adoptions opted not to have showers until the baby was born and the birth mother had relinquished her rights. They didn't want to "jinx" the relinquishment by celebrating too soon. As a result, we've been to lots of baby showers where the *baby* was the center of attention. Unconventional, perhaps, but enchanting.

When should I interview pediatricians?

Unless you're lucky enough to live near your adoption pediatrician, you'll want to find a "regular" pediatrician in your neighborhood. This is the doctor who'll take care of your child after the initial screening by the adoption pediatrician. (In the case of a private infant adoption, she may be the first doctor you see.) Most pediatricians offer free interviews to parents who are doctor shopping. You will want to ask all the questions a bio-parent would—and a few more.

From the day I told my manager and co-workers about my adoption plans, I felt a tremendous amount of support and understanding. When I visited my son in San Salvador, my teammates stepped in to cover my workload. And when I traveled to bring him home, they transferred their hard-earned vacation days, so that I could spend more paid time off with him. I could not imagine working for a more flexible, generous, and supportive employer.
—ALICIA

I wish I had taken baby-care classes. I didn't know about swaddling until a friend mentioned that babies love it.
—PAM

I wish I had spent more time getting to know other adoptive parents in my community. Even though our pediatrician has a number of internationally adopted kids in her practice, some of my questions went beyond her expertise.
—SHELLI

I should have gotten more involved in the local adoptive and Asian communities and started taking a Mandarin Chinese class. My husband and I are working on these things now, but it would have been nice to have had a jump start before our little one got home.
—KAREN

Lindsey, United States

We've Been There: Choosing a Pediatrician

Ask your insurance company for a list of pediatricians on its plan in your area. Then start calling, and note which doctors seem to have well-run offices. Even with the healthiest child, you'll be visiting several times a year—you want a practice where phones are answered promptly, where files are well organized, and where referrals to specialists are fast and smart. When you meet the doctor, ask the following questions:

1. What hospital do you admit to? Are you on staff/consulting there? (If your child is hospitalized, having a familiar doctor present makes things easier for everyone.)

2. Are you affiliated with a teaching hospital? (If your child needs specialists, the best will

likely be teaching at a medical school. If your pediatrician is part of their network, specialist referrals will be better informed.)

3. What is your philosophy on antibiotics? (More doctors are—sensibly—choosing to withhold antibiotics for common infections. Make sure you agree.)

4. What is your philosophy on vaccinations and immunizations? (If you are adopting internationally or from foster care, your child may have nonstandard records. You want a doctor who understands the issues and can support you when the child needs records for school.)

5. Do you have daily phone-in hours?

6. Who covers for you when you're on vacation?

7. What is the average wait for well-child appointments?

8. To whom do you refer children who are developmentally delayed?

9. What is your policy for a sick child—first come, first served, or must we make an appointment?

10. How much experience do you have with adopted children? (A doctor who thinks adoption makes no difference will not be sensitive to gaps in birth-family medical history.)

What can I do about child care?

Use this time to research child care, but unless you have to return to work right after homecoming, put off making firm arrangements. You don't know yet how much support your child will need—and you don't know how you're going to feel about being a parent.

If you know that your child has special needs, as we did, I'd urge you to read up on potential challenges. Then speak with specialists and line up recommended screening appointments in advance.

—SUSAN

Don't make a decision about child-care arrangements until you know what will be best for your child. The people who have the most difficulty with their children's adjustment are those with preconceived ideas about how things "should" work, who are unwilling to consider what would actually benefit their children.

—DIANE

I so appreciate the feeling of wondering if the wait will ever end. When we started the process, it was supposed to take six to eight months. We waited two years and one month. I remember the days when I felt like I was in the movie Groundhog Day—*a day playing out over and over again. I remember wondering whether I had the strength to continue to wait with no end in sight. For those still waiting, I would say, you are not alone. We do know that no one can understand exactly how you're feeling. Can you go on one more day? You can.*

—ALYSON

If I'm adopting a school-age child, when do I notify the school district?

As soon as your home study is accepted, visit your local school administration and explain your plans. Ask what kind of documents they will need to admit your child. Find out what resources they have to support your child: English-as-a-second-language tutoring? School psychologists familiar with adoption?

TRIED AND TRUE: Every school district in the United States has a special-education department. Even if you have no reason to believe your child has any learning disabilities, you should apply to the special-education committee for screening as soon as he enters the school system. If your child needs support, it will start sooner; if your child is fine, you will have a baseline evaluation, which can be useful for tracking development.

How do I keep from going crazy while I wait?

The only advantage to pregnancy is that you know, more or less, when it will be over. Adoption is unpredictable, and not knowing when your child will come home can be agony. As all of our families can tell you, you *will* be a parent—and then there will be days when you long for time to yourself, but that's another story.

Aidan, United States

Picturing Love
Barbara Sinsheimer

I PICKED UP THE PHONE AND HEARD A FAMILIAR VOICE. "YOU have a son," said our social worker. "He's fourteen months old and . . ." I never heard the rest of the sentence.

"Barb, are you there?" she asked.

"Oh, my God, oh, my God," was all I could say.

We had mailed our dossier only four weeks earlier and were told to expect a one- to three-month wait for our referral.

I settled down enough to finish the conversation, then I ran into the bedroom we were redecorating. After hours of hard work on it, the room was nearly ready to welcome a child of either gender. We'd refinished the wood floors and polished them until they shone, painted the walls sea green and sky blue, and stenciled sea-life figures onto the dresser and bed. I found my husband, Tom, in the closet, paintbrush in hand.

"What is it?" he asked, alarmed. "Who called?"

"Oh, just our agency, telling us we're the parents of a fourteen-month-old boy." I tried to sound nonchalant but ended up choking out the words. He took me into his arms and cried with me. I'd seen my husband cry only once before, when his father died.

Our adoption agency told us to expect to travel in eight to ten months. Naturally, we assumed the speedy match with our son meant we'd receive permission to travel sooner.

"He might be home for Christmas!" I exclaimed.

"I bet he's home for Easter, at least," Tom chimed in.

"At the latest, he should be home for his second birthday," I added, hedging our bets. That would mean June, almost ten months away. Surely we wouldn't have to wait that long.

Our agency was absolutely correct in its estimate, despite our high hopes. Nearly ten months to the day from receiving our referral, we got the go-ahead to travel. It was the longest ten months of my life.

Our well-meaning friends compared the wait to a "normal pregnancy."

"You have the anticipation of the child arriving, getting the room ready, and buying children's gear," I often heard.

Yes, I rushed out and bought every adorable little-boy outfit I found—sweat suits with tractors on them, slippers, pajamas, hiking boots, and baseball caps—despite warnings to hold off, since children grow quickly, and the wait is long (no kidding). And yes, we put the finishing touches on Tyler's sky-blue, sea-green bedroom.

And yet, the waiting was not the same. My child was already born, already past his first birthday. He had taken his first steps and cut his first teeth. He had spoken his first words, in a language I did not know. And with each day, he was growing more attached to a foster mother, a mother who was not me.

Six days after the phone call, Tom and I drove the two hours to our adoption agency. I can't remember the name of the social worker, but I'll never forget her handing me a short stack of photos. "Your son is beautiful," she said.

I struggled to focus through a blur of tears and looked into the most beautiful, serious little face I had ever seen. I saw my son at one month of age, at three, six, nine, and twelve months old. As I thumbed through the stack, he grew before my eyes. I tried to say something but couldn't find words to express how I felt. The social worker exclaimed, "Now you're making me cry!"

On the way home, Tom and I stopped to eat. After we sat down, I propped the five photos against the salt and pepper shakers on our table, so our new family could eat together. Daddy, Mommy, and Tyler. I couldn't take my eyes off him.

Every three months until we traveled, we received an updated medical report and photo. With each new picture and report, I would think, "Maybe this will be the last update before we travel." Then another three months would go by.

In the first update, we saw our son at fourteen months old. The photo was taken on the day we were notified of his existence. He's smiling in that photo. Was it because he knew we were out there somewhere, getting ready to come get him?

A few months later, we saw a photo of our son at eighteen months of age, standing alone in the middle of a dirt road, wearing mismatched clothing. He looked worried. Maybe he was wondering when we'd come, I thought.

Throughout our months of waiting, Tom and I wrote letters to our son. We told him about our jobs, our hobbies. We described the bedroom that was waiting for him, the sea-life decorations and the colors we'd painted the walls. We told him about our town and the people who lived in it. We sent him coloring books and crayons, picture books, stuffed animals, and a small photo album, so our faces would become familiar to him.

In the last photo we received, just weeks before we flew to Thailand, our son was twenty-one months old. He was sitting on the floor, holding a picture book we had sent to him. Other gifts, a stuffed animal and construction paper, lay on the floor in front of him. He was touching things we had touched. We were amazed to see evidence of our connection. It made everything seem real—and it made me even more anxious to bring this little boy home.

Our hoped-for milestones passed by. Christmas came and went. Easter was celebrated, with still no word of a travel date. Just as I began to get discouraged, the call came, in late spring. No, our son would not be home for his second birthday, but we were to travel shortly after, at the end of June. The day we would fly home was my mother's birthday. When I called her with the news, she exclaimed, "That will be the best birthday gift ever!" For Tom and me, it would be the gift of a lifetime.

Wesley, United States

We adopted domestically and thought the wait would be interminable. As it turned out, it was only four months! We had ten days to prepare before our beautiful son was born. In hindsight, I wish we had gone shopping before getting the call—we spent too much precious time in baby stores during the days following our son's birth!

—LIBBY

WHAT DO I DO NEXT?

Announce! Start telling family and friends about your plans.

Plan. Find a neighborhood pediatrician. If you have any reason to believe your child may have medical or psychological issues, line up support now. If you're adopting a school-age child, contact your local school system.

Shop. Start looking at nursery furniture, toys, and clothes—but don't overdo it; you'll be buried in gifts when your child comes home.

Relax. Take long baths. Watch R-rated movies. Eat in restaurants with candles and tablecloths. Go to concerts. Have massages. Read novels. You'll thank us later.

Tyler, United States

Is This My Child?

Choosing to Accept a Child Referral or Birth-Mother Match

How will I hear about my child?

Our families love to talk about "the call," the moment they learned about their child. Sometimes the call is actually "the e-mail." Either way, it seems to arrive when you least expect it. But the effect is always the same: relief, excitement, joy—and fear.

Whatever kind of adoption you are doing, our families say: Stay calm. Don't get too attached to *this* birth mother or *this* child just yet.

Adoption 101: The Call

- If you're making an independent search for a birth mother, your first contact with your child will be a phone call or an e-mail from the birth mother herself, a member of her family, or a friend.

---

above: Mia, China

We were in the security line at the Jacksonville airport, on our way to Saint Thomas, U.S. Virgin Islands, when the screener told us that my cell phone was ringing as it was being X-rayed! I picked up the bag containing my phone and glanced at the number showing on the missed-call screen. I grabbed my shoes with one hand and hit redial with the other. By the time I'd heard the news and hung up, everyone at the security checkpoint knew the whole story from my husband. We got lots of latex-gloved thumbs-ups from the TSA staff.

—CHESLEY

- If you're doing a private adoption through an agency or attorney, you will get a call or an e-mail with some details about the birth mother. If you're adopting from foster care, your social worker will contact you with details about the child.
- In an international adoption, you will get a formal referral: a document that identifies the child and provides some medical and social information. The referral usually includes a photograph, and sometimes a video, as well.
- In some sending countries the process is "blind referral." The adoptive parents travel to meet a group of children; the referral is made in-country. The parents go back to the United States and wait for paperwork to be completed, then return to bring their child home. Parents who have gone through this process say it is the hardest path to adoption. You meet and fall in love, then spend months knowing your child is living without the care you want to provide. If your agency has an online support group, this is the time to lean on it; other traveling parents may be able to take supplies to your child and can bring information back to you.

What do I say when I first talk to a birth mother?

When you speak to a potential birth parent, realize that you are encountering someone with a huge problem to manage. Treat her as you would any friend with such news. Let your first thoughts be not of your needs and concerns but of hers. There will be plenty of time later to discuss things like her medical history and your post-placement relationship. Don't get ahead of yourself. This is about human connection. Focus on what she needs most, and address yourself to those needs. Isn't that the kind of parent you would want, if you could choose?

Nothing can fully prepare you for the strangeness of this first encounter. But every day, people negotiate first contacts. And every day, people find a way past the awkwardness and come together for the sake of a child. You can, too.

We've Been There: Talking with a Birth Mother

1. Ask about the pregnancy: How's it going? Ask her whether she likes her doctor, how she's getting to her appointments, what foods she's craving.

2. Ask about the people in her life. Does she have friends or family she can talk to about what's going on?

3. Answer her questions simply and honestly. Be as open and vulnerable as you would like her to be. Let the conversation flow without an agenda. In a first meeting, it is less important what you talk about than that you talk—and, most important, that you listen. Remember that, although your biggest fear is that she won't like you, her biggest fear is that you won't like her.

What if I don't get matched until after the baby is born?

In about a quarter of domestic infant adoptions, the birth mother doesn't begin to plan the adoption until after the baby is born. The disadvantage: Would-be adoptive parents have to make decisions fast, and your interaction with the birth mother may be even more

We received our first call from our son's birth mother during a party we were throwing for friends. There were about fifty people in the house, and it was very noisy. I had to take the phone into a bathroom to be able to hear her. We talked for about twenty minutes and made arrangements to talk again. After the call, I had to host the party while acting like nothing had happened, despite the overwhelming emotions I was experiencing. My advice to waiting families would be to write down some of the items you would discuss with a birth mother during the first conversation, so that when the moment comes and your mind is in a whirl, you will have your wits about you.

—ANNETTE

We were very nervous to meet our baby's birth mother for the first time. She was about seven months pregnant, young, and had no family. We chose to meet for lunch at her favorite restaurant. We brought her a small gift, and I had purchased a card to let her know that I appreciated what she was doing for us and the sacrifice I knew she was making. Once we were seated, we started talking like we were friends. It was wonderful! She had also brought me a gift—it was a framed picture of our son's first sonogram.

—TRACEY

emotionally charged. The advantage: The baby is here and can be evaluated before you commit to anything.

TRIED AND TRUE: Some of our families suggest that you appoint a trusted family member or friend to be your "voice of reason." As you get to know your birth mother, your voice of reason can gently remind you to check off the essential questions.

Adoption 101: Birth Mother Basics

- Does the birth father support the adoption?
- Do the birth grandparents support the adoption?
- Did the birth mother receive prenatal care?
- Will she accept counseling?

Julia, United States

Hold On Tight
Michelle Farrell

HAVING JOSEPH HAS HELPED ME PUT EVERYTHING IN PERSPEC-
tive. But before the adoption was final, I had the ride of my life.

My husband, John, and I were at the farmer's market one ordinary Saturday when my cell phone rang. It was our agency, telling us our son had
been born last night. He was healthy, and, by the way, how soon could we
get there? Just like that, I was a mother, even if my son was two time zones
away.

Less than twenty-four hours later, we called our agency from bag-
gage claim at our destination. There, surrounded by an infant car seat,
a portable crib, and suitcases stuffed with toys and baby clothes, we heard
that we shouldn't go to the hospital. The baby's mother wanted more
time with the baby. The news sent me reeling. Was she changing her
mind?

I had never spoken to her. She had chosen us only a month before her
due date, and John was the one who was home when our agency placed
the conference call. I didn't even know this person who had such control
over our lives.

The next morning we heard that she was to be discharged and we were
to meet her at her house. We got there before she did. As each car drove
down the street, my stomach flipped as I thought, "This is her!" But they
all sailed past. No birth mother. No baby. I panicked.

Then she arrived, holding our dreams in an infant seat, covered with a
blue fleece blanket. We hugged on her front steps, then I lifted the blanket and gazed in wonder at this tiny, precious being.

She invited us inside and we sat down to talk, eager to get to know each
other. She was already struggling to raise three kids. If love was the only
thing the baby needed, she said . . . but she knew it wasn't. She wanted to
explain why she'd chosen us. John and I had selected the best pictures we
had of ourselves for our Dear Birth Mother profile, but what charmed her
was the one of us wearing funny wigs, a photo that we'd thrown in on a
whim. That's what cemented the connection for her.

All too soon, it was time to go. Her state requires a seventy-two-hour waiting period before a birth mother can sign the papers, so I spent another night worrying that she'd change her mind.

I needn't have. Early the next morning, we got word that she'd signed. My worries fell away in an instant, but I wasn't prepared for the sadness I felt as we drove to her house. It got worse when I saw how beautiful she looked holding our son. When I left with him, I felt like I was walking away with her heart in my hands. It was the hardest thing I've ever done.

Our life is so ordinary, so normal now, that I've been able to put those first anxious days into perspective. What felt so scary turned out to be nothing at all. Our wait on the birth mother's doorstep was caused by nothing more than her need to stop at the pharmacy. And her request for more time with her baby at the hospital? Since she had to wait to sign the papers anyway, she decided there was no reason to rush. I wouldn't trade that roller-coaster experience for anything. After all, it gave us Joseph.

What happens when I meet a foster child for the first time?

In foster adoptions, the agency will generally arrange a supervised meeting between you and the child. With older children, there may even be a series of meetings before placement, so that you can get to know one another. If the foster child is an infant, however, you may simply be asked to accept the placement immediately.

Charlotte, United States

STRAIGHT TALK: Once upon a time, state agencies regularly held "adoption fairs," also known as "meet and match," where foster children were gathered to meet would-be parents. Recognizing how stressful the experience is for the children, most agencies have turned adoption fairs into information-gathering sessions, where social workers explain adoption without the children present. If your state permits traditional adoption fairs, talk to a social worker about how to interact with the children.

What does a referral look like?

In international adoptions, your agency sends you a "referral" to an individual child; you may accept it or reject it. Depending on the sending country and agency, the referral may be skimpy or detailed, but it should at least contain a name, date of birth (which may be estimated), height, weight, and a photograph.

REALITY CHECKLIST
Responding to a Referral

Slow: Proceed with caution if

❏ You are not certain you can handle the child's medical condition.

❏ You can't get more information from those who cared for the child.

❏ Something about the placement doesn't feel right.

❏ Issues regarding legal situations, subsidies, or prognosis are unclear.

Stop: Turn down the referral if

❏ The child is beyond the limits you set for the type of child you can parent.

❏ You have little information and are under extreme pressure to decide.

❏ You and your partner disagree about whether to proceed with adoption.

❏ You feel overwhelmed with guilt and pity, as if you are the child's last chance.

❏ The child's prognosis is unclear, and you know that you could not handle the worst-case scenario.

I was with my mother, who was dying. I was torn about what to do. Should I stay with Mom or go to China? My gracious and generous mom said, "You must go get my granddaughter. There is no other decision." I still wavered, and she peacefully died the next morning. I was able to make my flight on time and still say a loving good-bye to my mother. I believe she, in some way, was determined that I would be able to do both.

—SUSAN

I know your nerves get on edge when you're put in an adoptive situation. No matter how hard it may be, relax, be yourself, and be as open and honest as possible. The right situation will arrive. When it does, you will realize the right situation for you (and for the other family or parent) is worth waiting for!
—CHANDOS

Connor, United States

Go: Accept the referral if

❑ You've seen all the child's pertinent files, records, and test results.

❑ You've talked to all significant professionals. The child and your family seem to be a good match.

❑ Everyone in your family is agreed on the adoption.

❑ Issues regarding travel, visitation, legalities, costs, and subsidies are clear.

❑ You are happy when you think about the placement.

Can I get a choice in international adoption? Some countries with large numbers of waiting children allow agencies to send lists of available children to would-be parents. You may also get a sheaf of photographs or a DVD. Families who have experienced this process talk about the stress of choosing a child—and, by definition, not choosing other children—but many talk about simply, and unexpectedly, falling in love.

Vital Signs
Victoria Moreland

FOR US, CONCEPTION HAPPENED WHEN OUR AGENCY SENT US an e-mail. Robert forwarded me the message and waited on the phone. We scrolled down the screen together, until a round-faced, twelve-month-old Russian girl stared back at us with blue-gray eyes. "She's beautiful," he said.

I found the words. "She looks just like you." The full face, the dimple in her chin.

"I swear I haven't been to Russia," he laughed.

For weeks, we were too nervous to tell anyone our news, afraid that some errant piece of red tape might cause us to lose her. But we'd steal secret glances at the pictures we'd slipped into our wallets. Robert kept one in his desk drawer at work. "I can't stop looking at it," he confided.

A video arrived a few days later, showing a toddler who had learned to stand, crawl, and feed herself, without parents to witness each milestone. Our daughter-to-be plucked an orange toy off a linoleum floor and watched as another little girl marched across the room. A lady in a kerchief folded children's clothes in the background.

We also received our daughter's translated medical records. We were told there might be "health issues," so I spent nights searching the Internet, reading about separation anxiety, language difficulties, and angry children who raged against their families.

Our agency recommended a pediatrician who specialized in adoption medicine, and we sent her the video and records. At our telephone appointment, Robert and I each sat with a receiver, straining to hear the doctor's soft voice. "She has good eye contact," she said. Good eye contact meant that she should be able to attach. "She doesn't look as though she has fetal alcohol syndrome." FAS can sometimes be detected by features such as thin upper lips and short noses. "She seems curious about her surroundings," which was an indication of her mental capabilities. "Your child is very adoptable," the doctor told us. Nevertheless, Robert and I went through our list of questions, checking off each one as we listened to her cautious but optimistic responses.

Looking back on that evening, I wonder how many parents-by-birth consult books about toddlers and behavior disorders before they conceive. Not many, I'm sure. Why do we inherently trust our own genetic makeup more than that of a stranger? Biological parents think nothing of the terrible twos, threes, and fours, but adoptive parents question each tantrum, fearful of the problems they've been warned about. My heart told me, biological children do not come with guarantees. Why should we expect adopted children to have them? How could we deny this child, who was waiting for someone to love her? How could we deny ourselves? Despite our limited knowledge and our uncertainty, we decided to make travel plans.

Robert and I held hands outside a closed door, the number 3 embossed on a metal plate at the top. Our escort, Yuri, rang the buzzer, and a woman opened the door. The noise of children reached us from down a hallway. I heard my daughter's name, mixed in with a stream of Russian words. Yuri turned to me and said, "It will be a minute. You can wait in the music room."

He escorted us to a quiet room, with a piano and several small black chairs. I walked around in circles, thumbed a key on the piano, and stopped at a window, with a view of a playground set encased in a layer of ice.

Several moments later the door creaked open and we saw our daughter. We stood up and walked to her. She stood right where the caretaker left her, belly poking out, a pout upon her pink lips, her eyes cast down to the floor, absolutely motionless. The caretaker said something to Yuri, who translated, "She is shy."

"No," I thought, "she is still."

She was also small. Her hands were much smaller than I'd expected, and she was so tiny that she barely reached my knees.

She played with the ball we had brought and turned the pages of a book, yet she didn't say a word. We saw her every day for the next two weeks, and her silence continued. She laughed only when the caretakers tickled her. I was uneasy about her cautious personality, but I also knew that it was good that she was wary of us. She had attached herself to the caretakers, which meant she could attach to us. And, sure enough, each day our little girl seemed a bit more secure. She began stretching her body around the woman who dressed her each morning, so she could see us watching her.

Before we left to file government paperwork, I gave her caretaker a teddy bear. "She should sleep with it," I said. I'd been sleeping with the bear for weeks, so it would smell like me. That night, I missed the bear's soft fur on my cheek, but I pictured it wrapped in my daughter's arms.

Then came the day of our court appearance. "Bundle her up," our agency had told us. "Even if it's warm." In Russia, they believe in coats and hats and gloves. So we swaddled her in layers of clothing for the thirty-second walk to the van.

After the orphanage had passed out of sight, we began unbuttoning and unsnapping. As our daughter emerged from the layers, she smiled and looked out the window with a curiosity I hadn't seen before. It was as if we were watching her enter the world for the first time. She played with everything—door locks, seat belts—and wiggled in my lap.

Later that day we heard her speak for the first time. Robert was sitting in the front seat of a taxi, while I sat with her in the back. She looked up at me and said, *"Da!"*—the Russian word for "yes." Robert turned around. "Did she just say something?"

I nodded, then looked back down at her and said, *"Da!"*

She giggled, long and sweet, and responded, *"Da!"* Our daughter was coming to life in a cab in Moscow.

Our adoption agency had told us to expect our child's transition to take six months. She'd probably have some separation issues, they warned. May not be able to sleep at night. May not like our food. Could take a while to attach. From the day we left the orphanage, she ate everything we put in front of her, slept soundly throughout the night, and cried whenever I left her side.

People are often surprised when they find out that we adopted, and ask why we did. Look at her, I want to say. How could we not have?

We have two children adopted from Latvia and one who was born to us. Getting "the call" is like that moment when you see the pregnancy test turn positive. You finally know it is true— you are going to have a child—yet you know you still have a time to go until you hold that baby in your arms. I can't remember much about the waiting; it all fades away (like the memory of childbirth pains!) once your child is with you.

—JULI

When can I take my child home?

In a private infant adoption, you will usually take your baby directly from the hospital (remember to bring an infant seat for the car or plane), even if the birth mother hasn't finally terminated her rights. If the baby was born in another state, you may have to stay in-state for a few days or weeks while the paperwork of the Interstate Compact on the Placement of Children is transferred to your home state.

In international adoptions, the process varies by country. If your country allows proxy adoptions, and you choose not to travel, you can have your child escorted to the United States by a representative of your adoption agency. In countries that require you to visit, you will apply for an orphan visa before you leave the United States, and will pick it up at the sending country's embassy, so that you can bring the child home with you.

Christopher, United States

TRIED AND TRUE: Some of our internationally adopting families choose to have their children escorted home so that they will be well rested when the child arrives. Families who have traveled instead say that the experience of seeing their child's first home is invaluable. There is no "right" choice here; parents should do what feels best.

WHAT DO I DO NEXT?

Stop. Don't agree to any match or referral on the spot. Go back to your original decisions about what kind of child, from what kind of situation, you're best able to parent. Does this situation match up?

Consult. Talk to your support group and to your adoption pediatrician.

Commit or move on. Never, ever, feel pressured into accepting a match or referral. If something about this birth mother, or this child's situation, just doesn't feel right, move on and try again; there will be a time when you'll say, "That's my child!"

I remember it like it was yesterday. It was early evening; I was at work (in the operating room) when my husband called to say we had a referral. Her picture was waiting to be opened in an e-mail. I was so excited, I couldn't wait to finish surgery and run to the nearest computer (and phone). My husband and I opened the e-mail together, and our daughter peered at us from the computer screen. What an incredible moment! We were seeing our daughter for the first time! We knew the moment we looked into her beautiful face that she was our daughter.

—LORI

What If It Doesn't Work Out?

How to Make Sure Your Adoption Succeeds

When do adoptions fail?

Adoptions fall apart at different stages (with different legal consequences), and there are different reasons for each kind of failure.

Adoption 101: Glossary of Grief

- Failed adoption: **one that falls through after referral or matching but before the birth parents have terminated their rights**
- Disruption: **when an adoption falls through between placement and finalization**
- Dissolution: **when an adoption has been finalized but the child is returned to foster care or is adopted by another family**
- Wrongful adoption: **when an adoption agency, attorney, or facilitator suppresses information that would have caused the adoptive parents to decline the adoption**

---

above: Juan, Colombia

What causes private infant adoptions to fail?

In private infant adoptions, about one third of expectant mothers change their plans between matching and placement. A smaller—but still significant—number change their minds between placement and the termination of their rights. Many of our families have lived through failed adoptions, and they liken the pain to that of a miscarriage or stillbirth. It is a miserable ordeal for everyone involved, including the birth families.

Social workers say that birth-parent counseling is by far the best insurance against a failed adoption. A counselor will help an expectant mother preview likely emotions before she has to make a decision. When the time comes to relinquish her child, she will already have worked through her grief. When the baby's father is part of the decision, he should also be counseled. If he and the mother are at odds, social workers say the best practice is to have separate counselors, so that each birth parent can come to an independent decision.

Addison, United States

STRAIGHT TALK: Remember Baby Jessica and Baby Richard, two children who were returned to their birth parents years after placement? In both cases, the media focused on the children being torn from the only homes they had known. People were sympathetic to the would-be adoptive parents and faulted the birth mothers, who had lied about the children's paternity. However, in both cases, the birth fathers had challenged the adoption within days of the birth, and much grief would have been avoided if the adoptive parents had recognized the inevitable outcome and returned the children immediately. Neither scenario could be repeated today; as a direct result of these cases, states have instituted "putative father registries," where men who believe they may have fathered a child must register in order to file a claim of paternity later.

Karson, United States

We've Been There: Coping with a Failed Adoption

1. Take time to grieve. You may need to experience the stages of grief—denial, anger, bargaining, depression, and acceptance. Take time off work if you can. If you don't want to answer questions when you return, have a friend or colleague let your co-workers know that. And postpone making any major decisions for a while.

2. Accept help. An adoption that falls through is emotionally shattering; you may need the comfort of others. If friends or family invite you out for dinner, say yes. It will feel good to vent about what you've been through, or to talk about something else entirely.

3. Talk to a mental-health professional who specializes in grief, loss, adoption, and/or infertility.

4. Realize that people grieve in different ways. While your spouse may want to get back to work, you might feel lost, stuck in your grief, unable even to go out for an evening with friends.

5. Don't try to figure it out. No one can know what's going on inside someone else's mind, so there isn't much point in trying to analyze why an adoption fell through. It can happen for many reasons.

6. Deal with the child's room in your own way. While some can't bring themselves to look at a child's room after a failed adoption, others find comfort sitting in the room to remember and grieve.

7. Get out of the house. Going to a funny movie can help. Long walks, a concert, or revisiting a hobby can also be therapeutic.

8. Express your feelings. Consider writing how you feel in a journal, or in a letter that you might—or might not—send to the birth parents.

9. Have a sit-down with your agency or attorney. If you have residual questions about why the adoption failed, ask them. See if there is anything to be learned.

10. Go slow. You will likely be dubious about resuming the adoption process. You may be cynical about birth parents, bitter about your experience, and resentful that you have to begin again. It's scary to face the possibility of another failure. But if you truly want to adopt, give yourself time to heal, then move forward.

Maya, United States

Our first adoption fell through. A baby was, literally, taken out of our arms. There is not a word to describe that period in our life, short of saying we were devastated, at least until the time our son came home. They say everything happens for a reason, and never could I imagine having any other child, biological or through adoption, that could mean more to us than Bryan. We thank our lucky stars every day.

—NANCY

What goes wrong in international adoptions?

Since parental rights are almost always terminated before a child is available for international adoption, there is little risk of a birth parent changing her mind. But there are other ways an international adoption can fall apart before the child comes home.

Adoption 101: Why International Adoptions Fall Apart

- The sending country suspends or restricts adoptions because of political pressure at home or genuine concern about the treatment of adoptees or because a natural disaster or civil war disrupts the bureaucracy.
- The U.S. government suspends adoptions from a specific country or withholds a visa for a particular child because of concerns about the ways in which children are becoming available for adoption.
- The sending country or the United States suspends adoptions processed by a specific agency, attorney, or facilitator because of concerns about corruption.
- Adoptive parents learn, either through testing or through a pre-adoption visit, that the child has problems that weren't disclosed in the initial referral.

How can I make my international adoption more certain?

There is no magic bullet to cut risk in international adoption, but there are a number of steps you can take up front.

REALITY CHECKLIST
Safe International Adoptions

Before you choose a country:

❑ Check to see how many of its children have been adopted into the United States in each of the preceding five years. Are the numbers stable? A sharp rise indicates that the country may have difficulty processing new applications; a sharp decline indicates that adoptions may be more restricted. To see State Department statistics on orphan visas granted for each country, go to adoptivefamilies.com/internationaladoption.

❑ Check the State Department's flyers for the countries you are considering for any mentions of instability. Go to adoptive families.com/internationaladoption.

Noah, United States

❑ Talk to recently returned adoptive families. Ask what they experienced in-country and in their visa process.

Before you sign on with an agency:

❑ Ask how many children the agency brought into the United States in the previous year.

❑ Ask if any adoption applications resulted in a NOID (Notice of Intent to Deny a visa, issued by the U.S. embassy when it is concerned about an adoption).

❑ Ask about in-country staff. How long have they been working for the agency?

❑ Ask exactly how children become available for adoption. Are they from orphanages? If so, how do they get there? Are they with foster

I knew from the start that I wanted to adopt from overseas. Before I chose an agency, I asked a lot of people in online chat groups and ended up with an agency that worked in several former Soviet Union countries. I started out adopting from Ukraine, but they closed adoptions to single mothers. On the advice of my adoption agency, I switched to Kazakhstan.

—MELODY

parents? How are the foster parents recruited and paid?

❏ Ask about birth parents. Are they identified? If so, do they have continued contact with the child? What support do they have if they choose not to place the child for adoption?

There are no right answers to any of these questions. What you are looking for is an agency that understands the process, knows its employees and colleagues, is sympathetic to the birth family, and can patiently explain the details to you. If you sense that they cannot or will not provide information, move on to another agency.

What if the country stops or suspends adoptions?

If your sending country halts adoptions after you started the process, you will be tempted to persist, hoping for a reopening. Our families' experience is that, unless you have already accepted a referral, you are better off switching to another country. As a general rule, when a country restarts its adoption program, there are many new restrictions, and the entire process slows down.

TRIED AND TRUE: If your adoption agency works with more than one country, it will be far easier to switch mid-process.

What if I meet the child and find problems I can't deal with?

For most of our families, the first meeting with their child is a magical moment—of instant, overwhelming love. For others, it is a time of uncertainty. The child doesn't look like the one in the referral photograph or video. The child has problems that weren't disclosed in the referral. Or you just don't feel right.

First, don't panic. You must separate the normal anxiety of new parenthood from genuine worries about the child. Bear in mind that many—if not most—biological parents have moments of terror before and after their child's birth. This is the moment to rely on your adoption-support team, particularly on the families who have adopted in similar circumstances.

If yours is a domestic adoption, either private or from foster care, you should take time before placement to have the child fully evaluated. If the child has a condition you are truly not prepared to support, your attorney or agency will help you withdraw from the adoption. Most agencies keep lists of parents who specifically want to adopt a child with medical problems.

In an international adoption, your situation may be more complicated. You are in a foreign country, you may not have access to medical experts, there may be translation difficulties. Again, if you feel that you cannot support this child, lean on your agency to provide you with another referral while you're in-country.

> **STRAIGHT TALK:** In some countries, adoptions are completed by proxy before the adoptive parents meet the child. If this is your situation, and you think you can't parent the child, you must get legal advice about your responsibility. Before you travel, locate an attorney with experience in international adoption; bring the contact information with you so you can call or e-mail for help while abroad.

A week before I gave birth to my daughter, I wanted to back out of the whole thing. I wasn't ready to be a mother. It wasn't until she was about two days old, when the pediatrician stuck a needle into her heel for a blood sample and she wept, that I fell for her. When I later adopted my other children, it was a blessing to remember those days of uncertainty. They were about parenthood, not about children.

—*AF READER*

Lost Daughter
Deb Luppino

I'VE HESITATED ABOUT TELLING THIS STORY, BUT I THINK IT DOES need telling. Last May, my husband and I received a referral from China of a little girl named Wen Ying. Our adoption trip to China was a very emotional one because, sadly, Wen Ying was not the child we brought home.

When we received Wen Ying's referral picture, we noticed a droopy eyelid. The medical report, however, indicated that she was normal and healthy, was sitting unaided and turning over. From the growth data included, we knew she was small but not alarmingly so. Our doctor reviewed the referral information and said that a droopy eyelid could indicate nothing more serious than ptosis, an easily corrected muscle condition. To follow up, our adoption agency requested further medical information from the orphanage about a possible eye condition, and we were assured again that the child was fine. We happily accepted Wen Ying's referral and began to plan our trip.

Several months later, a family traveling just before us to the same city graciously agreed to carry some small gifts for Wen Ying and to bring back new pictures of her. When the pictures arrived, we were alarmed again. Not only did her eyelid droop, but she appeared to have a wandering eye, or strabismus, a condition that sometimes indicates cerebral palsy. Also, it seemed clear from the pictures that, at thirteen months old, Wen Ying was not standing or walking.

We became even more alarmed when we learned that our agency had received a call from its representative in China after she had met Wen Ying with the earlier travel group. The representative, knowing that we would travel to China with our five-year-old daughter, Julie, was concerned about the impact on Julie should we decide, once we were in China, to turn down the referral. What did she mean?

By the time we were due to travel, we were convinced that Wen Ying had serious medical problems. However, we had accepted her referral, and we had to meet her. We were very, very concerned about protecting Julie. How would she feel if she met a little sister, only to watch us leave her behind? We decided that Joe and I would meet Wen Ying one at a time, without telling Julie that she was in our agency representative's room. Joe would go first, while I stayed with Julie. After Joe's return, I would go. We would, we decided, make our decision right there.

The child we met exhibited all the classic signs of cerebral palsy, including a wandering eye, protruding forehead, and inability to focus. Her fists were clenched, and one side of her body was markedly stronger than the other. She couldn't sit up on her own. The orphanage director and doctor were quite upset by our reaction. They clearly cared very much for Wen Ying and felt that going to a family would be her best opportunity for care. They left immediately to take Wen Ying for evaluation at a local children's hospital, where pediatricians confirmed the diagnosis of serious mental delays.

Although we were not surprised by this news, it was devastating to have our assessment confirmed. With great sadness, we composed a letter to the authorities declining Wen Ying's referral. It was very difficult to watch our travel mates with their children, knowing that the child we had expected to join our family wouldn't be coming home with us. We told Julie only that her sister was "not ready" yet. Julie was anxious and asked repeatedly about "her baby."

We could have decided at this point to return home, but under Chinese adoption procedures at that time, if a doctor declared a child unhealthy, prospective parents could request a second referral. The next day we were referred a little girl named Chun Jiang, who had just turned one year old in a nearby city. We drove off to meet her, and found her healthy and chubby. It was a joyous moment for Julie, and very bittersweet for Joe and me.

We went through the paperwork process with heavy hearts. What if the orphanage officials, who knew Wen Ying best, had been right about her? Did she really have cerebral palsy? It's usually not diagnosed at such an early age. Would Wen Ying improve in foster care? Would she receive the occupational or physical therapy she needed? Would someone else adopt her?

As we got to know Chun Jiang (whom we decided to name Sarah—the name we had chosen for Wen Ying—to avoid confusing Julie), we talked to our agency representative about our wish to care for Wen Ying. We asked whether the orphanage would allow us to sponsor her for medical treatment and foster care. The orphanage accepted our offer, and we were able to arrange this under the auspices of Families with Children from China of Greater New York and the Amity Foundation, a local organization that provides assistance to children in orphanages. As we left China, I felt as if I was leaving a daughter behind.

Even though we have been home for three and a half months, and all is well—we love Sarah Chun Jiang and she is thriving—I often find myself thinking about Wen Ying. Each time Sarah flashes her adorable smile or reaches another milestone, I think of Wen Ying and wonder if she is smiling, too, if she will ever reach the same milestones.

Chandler, United States

What happens if I can't parent the child I bring home?

Good agencies have social workers and psychologists on staff or on call who can support parents after placement. If you feel you cannot cope with your child, lean on the agency. Don't be embarrassed—these professionals have seen *everything*. They can help you find support, navigate the medical and educational systems with you, and even arrange respite care if you need it.

What if we have finalized the adoption and still can't make it work?

When an adoption is dissolved after finalization, the legal issues are more complicated. Your parental rights must now be terminated in court and transferred to your state or to another adoptive parent. You will need expert advice from a social worker and an attorney; you and the child will also need emotional support.

While dissolutions are, mercifully, rare, they are usually the result of finding that the child has reactive attachment disorder so severe that it doesn't respond to therapy, or that he has a previously undisclosed illness. If you are adopting a child who is at risk of RAD, consult a psychologist beforehand and learn what symptoms to look for.

STRAIGHT TALK: Statistics indicate that about 10 percent of potential adoptions disrupt (between placement and finalization) and between 1 and 3 percent are dissolved (after finalization) because the child has problems that the adoptive parents are not equipped to support. These failures are far more likely to occur in older-child adoptions; social workers estimate that fewer than 1 percent of infant adoptions disrupt or dissolve, while 30 percent of adoptions of teenagers do. If you are adopting a teenager or preteen, line up expert psychological support for yourself and the child before home-coming.

We've Been There: Healing After a Disruption or Dissolution

1. Take time to grieve within your immediate family, and if your grief persists, seek professional therapy.

2. Meet the people who will take over the child's care, if possible. You can share what you know about the child's needs, and this will give you some peace of mind.

3. Reinforce relationships with your spouse or children.

4. Decide whom to confide in. Your extended family may have trouble understanding the disruption process. Some find it more helpful, at least at first, to talk to others who have been through a disruption.

Can I sue my adoption agency or attorney?

If you have reason to believe that an agency or professional didn't give you all of the medical and/or social background information available regarding the child and her birth family, you may want to consider suing. The courts have started to address these issues by al-

We had just begun to recover from a very rare infant-adoption disruption case, in which we had to place our eight-month-old baby in a special-needs home after just five months at home. Our caseworker asked us to both get on the phone. A birth mother had chosen us for her healthy newborn baby. We were completely shocked and incredibly excited! How could we be so blessed! We packed our bags that night and left in the early hours of the morning for a three-hour trip to the hospital, where we met our daughter's birth mother and held our daughter for the first time. We play those moments over in our heads with incredible joy and appreciation, none of which would have been possible without the selfless act of love from our daughter's birth mother—to choose an adoption plan for her child.
—MAUREEN AND MATT

lowing lawsuits, commonly referred to as "wrongful adoption" suits.

Although brought under a number of different legal theories, most wrongful-adoption lawsuits contain a count of misrepresentation or fraud, that is, an allegation that the adoption agency or other professional, intentionally or negligently, failed to make a good-faith effort to find out and reveal material information to the adoptive parents. Not all information, however, is considered "material." "Material information" is information that, if it had been divulged, would have caused the adoptive parents not to adopt the child.

Joaquin, United States

PART III

Parenting Your Adopted Child

above: Kevin, United States

Will We Fall in Love?

Bonding and Attachment for You and Your Child

How can I bond with a baby that "isn't mine"?

Some parents feel an instant bond when they meet and hold their infant. For most, however, bonding is a gradual process, taking weeks and sometimes months. More than 50 percent of our adoptive families, when asked to recall those first days and weeks, report that they felt more numb and scared than connected and competent. (Of course, the big dirty secret of parenting is that half of biological parents feel numb and scared, too.)

You may meet your infant in a hospital room, a hotel room, an airport, or at home, in a quiet room or amid a bustling group. Your child may snuggle into your arms or pull away and cry. Some infants become withdrawn and unresponsive, while others light up with a smile. The more you've prepared by talking with other adoptive parents about the wide range of experiences, the less likely you are to feel taken aback by your baby's reaction.

When I adopted my youngest daughter domestically, attachment was difficult because she was hospitalized for three months. When she came home, I bought a soft-sling baby carrier. It allowed me to hold her close to my heart in a comforting fetal position for much of the day. Not only did this improve our attachment, it improved her health immensely.

—HOLLY

above: Jake, Russia

Many books say that you shouldn't pick up your baby every time she cries, lest she become "spoiled." But when our daughter cried, we went to her. We felt it was important to let her know that we would meet her needs consistently. We quickly learned that our daughter doesn't cry for no reason, and once we figured out what her need was (and met it), the tears would stop. Our efforts have paid off: Our girl is happy, amiable, and peaceful.
—AARYN

All infants, even newborns, need time to adjust and connect with a new environment and family. They may avoid eye contact, become fussy, refuse to take a bottle, sleep excessively or not at all. This has nothing to do with your parenting skills or whether or not you gave birth to this child. So try to relax and give your baby time to acclimate.

We've Been There: Bonding with Your Baby

1. Appeal to your baby's senses. Hold off washing the outfit he came home in, and keep it near him in the crib. Newborns can be comforted by a familiar aroma.

2. Avoid excessive eye contact. A newborn will let you know when it's too much—she'll look away, close her eyes, or fuss.

3. Speak quietly and move gently. Most infants will startle at sudden movement. Leave the room as little as possible. If you can, stay in the hotel room, rest, and hold your baby, rock him, or croon to him—these early moments of bonding are priceless. Try to avoid distracting visitors, noise, and commotion.

4. Snuggle up. Hold your infant as much as possible, to facilitate bonding. A baby cannot be spoiled by too much holding. Consider using a baby sling or a front carrier.

5. Respond to your child's cries immediately.

6. Playfully imitate your child; let her know she's the center of the universe. Play peekaboo!

7. Talk to your child as you perform nurturing actions, like cuddling and feeding.

8. Stay with your child and comfort him through crying and screaming.

Elissa, United States

STRAIGHT TALK: Newborns who were exposed to drugs in the womb may suffer withdrawal. They may wake often during the night, require prolonged feeding, and be irritable and easily distracted. It is tough to bond with a baby who won't sleep or eat and can't be soothed. If you are adopting a drug-exposed child, ask a nurse or social worker to teach you comforting techniques. And don't worry: These symptoms may persist through the first year of life, with absolutely no long-term implications.

We were fortunate to have an open relationship with our daughter's birth parents, with whom we spent a great deal of time before our daughter was born. She was first placed in foster care, where we visited her at least twice a week. By the time we brought her home, we felt we had bonded already. We brought familiar items—blankets, toys, and clothes—home from her foster situation. We kept as much as possible the same: bottles, diapers, lotions and soaps, formula, and—most important—routine. We bonded quite easily and had little difficulty with our daughter's transition into our home.

—LISA

Becoming a Mother
Claire Houston

SOMEWHERE ALONG THE WAY, BETWEEN "GOTCHA" AND TODAY, I became her mother. It's hard to say when. The day I first saw her, I was an independent, forty-four-year-old woman and she was a cute ten-month-old baby girl. Now when I look at her, I know that I am her mother and she is my daughter.

After a year and a half, and mountains of paperwork, a child was placed in my arms. We were strangers. She was leaving the known world of her foster home, and my husband and I were taking on this unknown baby from an unfamiliar land, where Caucasians are rare. We retreated to our hotel room and began to play house. It was that strange. We knew there were four things she needed: food, diapers, stimulation, and sleep. We began to go through the motions of all four and, several hours later, collapsed into bed, laughing quietly. She was sound asleep as we remembered the Talking Heads' lyric, "My God, what have I done!" We weren't confident about our parenting skills, but somehow, it all worked.

More days of meticulous paperwork ensued—interviews, signatures, passports—to prove that we were who we said we were. My husband and I tag-teamed very well, but still, we felt we were spectators.

During the adoption process, you spend a lot of time saying, over and over to officials, that you want this baby, that you will treat her like gold, and that you promise never to abandon her. Then you finally get the baby, and all the hoops disappear. The reality of this being's presence begins to come into focus. Yet I continued to feel more like a curious observer than a mom.

A loving homecoming at the airport brought friends and family out to celebrate our return to American soil. We entered our house to find balloons, gifts, meals in the fridge, and plenty of good wishes. The baby girl looked around, then smiled. She liked the house that, she would soon learn, was her new home.

Jet-lagged and sick, I had trouble feeling like myself, let alone like a mother. But slowly, new routines began to emerge at home. My husband and I marveled at her intelligence, at how fast she learned and applied her learning. She laughed. She laughed a lot. We could see that she was a happy girl.

It was delightful to engage her and get the reward of a baby's belly laugh. She liked to see that she could make us laugh. Days slipped by, and our souls were secretly being woven together.

I saw the first glimpse of this elusive bond about a month after her arrival. Acquaintances stopped by to give her a gift, yet they seemed more attentive to each other than to her. She handed them her favorite toys, and they absently took them and put them down. She played peekaboo with them, and they vaguely participated. She looked somber. At first, I didn't think much of it, but after a while, I noticed a dulling of her eyes.

I swept her up and announced that we had to make dinner. Our guests departed, and I turned my full attention to her. We looked at her toys and our cats and played peekaboo in earnest. We laughed together. Her light quickly returned.

Then I understood: I had become Mom to Evie.

A definitive peacefulness has followed that realization. I am clear about my purpose with this little girl. And I recognize the mother lioness in me. The mysterious bonding thread has formed, and, although we are not genetically formed, one from the other, genetic programming has kicked in. I am genetically programmed to take care of this baby human, and she is genetically programmed to bond with me, her mother. All is well with the world, working perfectly.

How can I bond with a toddler or preschooler?

Toddlerhood is a particularly difficult stage for a child to be moved to a new home. He's had time to build attachment to a caregiver, and now his greatest fear—losing that person—has come true. His cognitive and language abilities are not developed enough to understand adoption easily. Children adopted at this age may cling to the new parent for fear of losing that person.

Maizie, United States

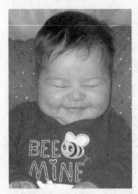

Aubrey, United States

Gena wanted to be in physical contact with me all the time. She would plaster herself to the shower door and whimper for me, or she would climb up on me just about anywhere I would sit. I somehow learned to do everything with one hand.

—SUSAN

We've Been There: Bonding with Your Toddler

1. Stick to a consistent schedule when you first come home, and introduce change gradually.

2. Use humor. Laughter can defuse a standoff and relax a tense toddler.

3. Don't worry about spoiling her with too much attention. Your child needs to trust that you'll be there to get comfortable in a new home.

4. Don't take tantrums or oppositional behaviors personally.

5. Keep your expectations flexible. Remember that a toddler or preschooler adopted from an orphanage may be emotionally much younger than his actual age.

What about older children?

When older children are adopted, they are not just getting new parents and a new home. The "new" list includes new friends, new school, new teachers, new rules, new books, new procedures—and maybe even a new language. And they are experiencing all this new-ness under the shadow, most likely, of some level of grief for what they have lost.

At the first meeting, an older child might be shy and reserved, happy and excited, or nervous and boisterous. For the next weeks or months, it's common for families to have a "honeymoon" phase, during which the child stays on his best behavior. Then, as family members be-come more comfortable with one another, a child may begin to test his new parents' limits, to see how much he can get away with. Sometimes there are bouts of grief, confusion, or even rage over his new circumstances.

Parents may be surprised to see how deeply a child can grieve his losses. An institution, whether it was good or bad, may have been the only home a child has known. He may miss familiar routines and people, especially foster parents and friends. Though rough patches are usually brief, adjustment problems are sometimes severe enough to warrant professional help. Generally, however, grief is a positive sign. It means that a child formed strong attachments in her home country—and is emotionally equipped to form attachments again.

We've Been There: Bonding with Your Older Child

1. Children arriving from other cultures— including other cultures within the United States—need time to adapt to your family's habits and rhythms. Preserving some element of a child's previous life can smooth the transition. Find out what you can about the schedule at the child's orphanage or foster home, and see if you can duplicate some of it.

2. Don't underestimate the significance of dietary changes. Smell and taste are evocative senses, and a child who is stressed takes comfort in familiar foods. Though some children eat new foods willingly, don't expect a child to enthusiastically sit down to a meal of hot dogs and apple pie right off the bat. Cooking a child's favorite foods, or making weekly visits to a restaurant that serves her home cuisine, can ease her transition.

3. Give your child the childhood he never had. Immediately meeting any need will not spoil a child who never knew the joy of a nurtured infancy.

4. Have fun with your new child. Play, swim, and eat together, so you establish some happy family memories as quickly as possible.

5. Don't sweat the small stuff. Choose your battles wisely. If a child is grieving over the loss of

Routine was very important to my kids. To this day, we eat lunch at noon and dinner at 6 P.M. That kept their schedule the same as it was at the children's home, and it worked for us.
—ROBYN

Christopher was so used to being uncomfortable—cold, hot, hungry, even sick or hurt—that I had to help him identify what his body was experiencing. I had to name the cold he felt when the wind blew, then demonstrate how we block it by putting on a jacket.
—CARRIE

My son came home at almost five, so he had an entire life before we met. Treasuring the memories he has of his foster family and helping him remember and talk about them has helped a lot. It was well worth the effort to bring him home and become a family.
—CATHY

Teresa's attachment to us was an exciting and gratifying adventure. We played, cooked, went to movies, fixed up her room, and talked about the future. She told us one Sunday after worship that she believed angels had brought us together.
—MARY

familiar people and surroundings, don't make an issue out of tooth brushing or mismatched clothes.

6. Have family meetings. Discuss what everyone in the family is doing, what strengths the children have, and how they can use them.

7. Have a new family portrait made early on.

WISE WORDS: *Mary Ann Curran, director of World Association for Children and Parents, says, "Do expect a lot of time to pass before your child feels like part of your family and accepts the change that his adoption entails. This does not mean years of disruptive behavior, but it may be a long time before he feels he truly belongs."*

What can prevent bonding?
Disciplining children while you're working to build attachment requires understanding, especially if there is the chance that a child has been abused in the past. Older children are especially sensitive to discipline that seems to be rejection. Using "time-ins"—sitting with and comforting the child as he rages—rather than solitary time-outs, is one way to discipline without reinforcing a child's feeling of rejection.

Keep in mind that behaviors such as hoarding, stealing, and lying may be a child's expression of anxiety over situations he cannot control. If disruptive behaviors persist, if a child is struggling with grief, or if she has extreme difficulty bonding with family members, working with a qualified therapist is critical.

How do I bond with a child who doesn't speak English?
Developmental psychologists say that communicative language, the skill needed for social interaction and practical applications, is readily acquired, while cognitive language, which we use for reasoning and educa-

tion, takes much longer—up to seven years. As a result, non-English-speaking adoptees learn to communicate basic needs—about food, play, and comfort—within days or weeks. But communicating about grief, loneliness, and homesickness may be impossible. Our families stress the importance of comforting your child without language: cuddling, holding, stroking, even for an older child.

TRIED AND TRUE: If you are adopting a child from another country, recruit someone who speaks her language before homecoming, so that you have a translator in an emergency.

WISE WORDS: Ellen Margolese, a psychiatrist and adoptive mother, says: "Imagine being abducted by strange people who speak a different language. When you think of all the scenarios a child might visualize, his behavior may make more sense."

If we're not bonding, where do we go for help?

First, don't rush. Even in biological parenting, bonding isn't always instant or automatic. But if time has passed, your child has settled in, and you still don't feel attached, it's time to get help. Start with your adoption agency or the social worker who did your home study; they can refer you to psychologists specializing in adoption issues. Also, lean on your support group—especially other adoptive parents.

TRIED AND TRUE: Our families say that even if you don't feel parental love for your child at first, you should act as though you do. Showing affection helps to build real affection on both sides.

The best advice I got was not to parent according to some fixed idea but to let my children show me who they were before I imposed expectations on them. We knew our girls had never been apart, so we figured they would want to share a room. But we were imagining the typical American kid, who wants his own space, even in a shared room. Not so ours, who wanted their beds right next to each other. They could not handle any separation. We also learned that we needed to sit with them and leave a light and a radio on as they fell asleep. Most of that defies conventional parenting wisdom, but if we had rigidly followed how we thought things should go, we would have ended up hurting them—and our family.

—SARAH

You Showed Me

Emily Jamberdino

I KNEW I LOVED YOU BEFORE I MET YOU . . .

Savage Garden is on the radio. "Mom! It's your favorite song!" Jon exclaims.

My son Jon—I had prayed for this child, and put in a few special requests. "Let it be a child who really wants a mom. Please send me a child who needs me." I didn't want to be greedy, but I put in one more: "It would be nice if he likes music."

After three trips to see Jon at the orphanage where he was living, I wondered if God had made a mistake. Whereas my daughter, Dominika, had grown more comfortable with us each time we visited her, my relationship with Jon was strained. Happy and loving at first, he seemed suspicious and manipulative when my husband, Jerry, and I made our second visit. When my mother and I came to take him home a few weeks later, he was interested only in what we had brought for him and seemed leery, at best, about going anywhere with us.

I swore to you my love would remain . . .

"Mom!" Jon interrupts my thoughts. "It's Westlife!"

When Jon came home, he stuck to Jerry, my older son, Jeff, or me on any outing. He bumped into us when we stopped, panicked if he lost eye contact, and refused to enter a restroom without me. After the school bus had initially skipped his stop on the first day he rode it home, I met him at the end of the driveway with a hug. He ducked into my shoulder to hide his tears. But a smile peeked out when I told him how scared I had been when his school bus didn't come, how I had called transportation and yelled at them, and how worried I was even after they told me the bus was on its way.

At McDonald's one day, Jon stood outside the car, staring at me, unwilling to close the door so I could lock it before I got out. Eyeing me suspiciously, he was ready to leap back into the car the minute I showed a sign of driving away. I got out and locked my own door. Then I walked to his smile as he hastened to close the door I now had to open and lock. I told him America was different. The police would arrest anyone who tried to leave a child. And I would never leave him. He was my child forever. He watched me, hoping I was telling the truth. He had no trust in me, though. He knew about moms abandoning children.

One summer day we were at the amusement park. Jerry had gone back to the hotel to rest. Jeff, Jon, Dominika, and I had stayed to go on the water slides. Afterward, towels and wet bathing suits in tow, we stopped for a snack. By the time I had bought the requested snack for each child and settled down to enjoy my own, two of my three children were finished eating. Jon asked, "Mom, can Dominika and I go on that ride?"

I explained that, while the ride was next to us, the line for it was on the other side and I wouldn't be able to see them from where we were. The thrill of standing in the middle of this so-new-to-him fairyland had him dancing under his skin, though. He begged. Tired, I acquiesced. "Go ahead, Jon, if you want. Stick together, though. I'll be at the exit gate when you get off."

I watched them go, then turned to my older son, Jeff. "They'll be back in less than two minutes," I assured him. "As soon as Jon realizes he can't see me from there, he'll be back. I just hope Dominika comes with him."

We waited. We ate. We waited. Jeff ate more. I was too nervous. I rushed around to the front of the ride, terrified that they were lost or kidnapped. There they were, standing in line, oblivious to me. When I finally got their attention, they waved back with fearless smiles. I was filled with wonder and delight. Jonny finally trusted me.

"Mom?" He hesitates, and I do not encourage him.

"Hmm."

"Mom, there's this song I'd really like you to listen to. It's called 'Perfect Fan.' "

"Oh, Jon, not now. I'm busy making supper and I can't stop."

"It's okay." The quickness of his response doesn't cover up his disappointment as he turns away from me.

"I'll listen to it later, okay?"

"Okay." He smiles then. It's a candid smile—one that's full of acceptance and trust. It's a boy's smile—full of adventure, mischief, and happiness. It's a smile that diffuses anger, suspicion, and reproach. He smiles his love from the pool, the basketball court, the other side of the church, and the top of the Ferris wheel. Can he see my love for him as I smile back?

"Mom?" He hesitates as he approaches.

"What, Jon?" I ask, looking over the newspaper.

"Do you think you have time to listen to that song now—you know, 'Perfect Fan'?"

"Oh, Jon, not right now. I want to—"

"I understand." He withdraws hastily, and I sigh a little relief.

"Mom?" He's back. I try to think up an excuse, knowing I have none, until I see those eyes. They are a wistful shade of pleading. "Do you think you have time to listen to that song now—you know, the one by the Backstreet Boys, 'Perfect Fan'?"

"Sure."

Jon's eyes flicker at my unexpected answer, but he eagerly hands me the headphones.

"Do you like it, Mom?" he asks anxiously. The music is just starting.

You showed me how to care / You showed me that you would always be there . . .

"Oh, Jonny . . ." I slowly grab him into a hug and duck into it to hide my tears. "I love it!"

Pleased, he leans his head back to see my face. My tears don't surprise him, but they make him suddenly shy. His smile spreads bashfully, but it's as wide as usual when he nods his eagerness. His response is almost a whisper, as we grab each other and hug. "Me, too."

Will my spouse bond with the baby?

If your spouse was initially reluctant to adopt, you may worry that he will be slow to bond. Our families report that, oddly enough, the reluctant spouse is often the one with the first and most passionate attachment. However, as with biological parents, one spouse may bond more slowly than the other.

How do I help siblings bond?

If you have children already, whether adopted or biological, you can help them to bond—beginning long before the adoption itself. Younger children can take part in choosing the baby's name, deciding where he should sleep, buying a special toy. If your child is older, involve her in the adoption process.

We've Been There: Helping Your Children Bond

1. Get your first child involved. Many agencies hold sibling-education sessions. If your agency does not, or if you are adopting through an attorney, involve your child in family discussions.

2. Give your child permission to ask tough questions. With the freedom to feel what he honestly feels, your child can engage emotionally with the new sibling at the right pace.

3. Having granted your child the right to her feelings, don't be disappointed if they're negative, especially after the new child arrives. Even a child who eagerly awaited a new brother or sister may be resentful when the reality of the change sinks in. Help your older child express feelings, and work together on solutions.

4. Enlist your child in readying the house. Imagining where a crib or new bed will go helps anticipate the changes to come.

5. If possible, take your child on the adoption trip. Families that don't need to travel a long distance might set aside some time at home, without visitors, to give each member a chance to spend time with the new baby.

6. Give your child some breathing room. Though siblings are usually encouraged to share, let your child decide which of his things are off-limits. Keep his social life untouched, too; children of all ages need to spend time with their peers without siblings tagging along.

Quite loudly at the supermarket, my daughter exclaimed, "Mommy, I told you I want a baby sister from China, not a baby brother from Russia." It was as though I'd put Froot Loops in the shopping cart instead of Honey Nut Cheerios.

—JOYCE

We had less than two days to prepare to be parents, let alone to think about the specifics of bonding with our son, so we relied heavily on our instincts. The most important thing was to remain as relaxed as possible. We wanted Caleb to be in a soothing environment, so I didn't sweat the small stuff. I would always feed Caleb while holding him close to me, and I rarely let others feed him. My husband would hold him with his shirt off, to make skin-to-skin contact (which we now know is immensely helpful in bonding). I would bathe with Caleb, sing, make eye contact, the things that every healthy mom does with her baby. We did what felt natural, and made our home our sanctuary.
—CHRISTINE

7. Expect sibling rivalry, and remind yourself that it is the norm for biological siblings, too. Even if sibling rivalry isn't an issue, there may be times when the younger child needs or receives more attention and the older one feels left out. Deputizing your older child as a special helper—having her hold or feed the baby—may let her feel involved rather than ignored.

8. Promote togetherness. Look for family activities that all ages can enjoy. Remember that many older siblings love an excuse to revisit early childhood joys, such as cartoons, blowing bubbles, and running through the sprinkler.

How do I continue bonding after I go back to work?

Children who have been in orphanages or in multiple foster-care placements, with a history of several caregivers, learn to attach quickly to each new adult they meet (it's a survival mechanism). When you return to work, you may find that your child attaches too easily to a child-care provider. It's important to reinforce your existing bond, with voice and with touch, throughout the day, despite your absence, and remind the child that your relationship is primary.

We've Been There: Bonding While You Work

1. Call home and speak briefly to your child every couple of hours.

2. Prepare snacks. Ask the babysitter to say, "Your mom (or dad) made this for you" when offering the food.

3. Tape-record yourself as you cuddle with your child and read a story. When the babysitter plays it, it will evoke the warm memory of being held by you.

4. Develop a special hug or bath and bedtime ritual that only you share with your child. Ask the babysitter never to share that same kind of hug or ritual.

5. Leave a transitional object, such as a stuffed animal that you both hug at bedtime, with your child.

Can I breast-feed my adopted baby?

An increasing number of adoptive mothers are putting their babies to the breast. Like biological mothers, they find the practice can be frustrating, discouraging, and immensely rewarding. If you plan to nurse, contact La Leche League (a breast-feeding advocacy group) when your home study is approved and ask for an adoption specialist. You will need to prepare for several months before your child comes home.

> TECH SUPPORT: For instructions on breast-feeding your adopted child, go to adoptivefamilies.com/medical.

What is cocooning?

Many of our most experienced families recommend that new parents delay baby showers and other celebrations and instead stay quietly home alone with their new child for the first few weeks. Some suggest that, to promote attachment, only the parents hold the child. If you plan to follow this advice, make sure you warn visitors (especially grandparents and other family members) ahead of time, so they will not be offended when you ask them to back off.

Can adoptive parents get the "baby blues"?

Adoptive parents, accustomed to thinking of postpartum depression as a matter of hormones, are unprepared for the reality of post-adoption depression (PAD). The fact is that some postpartum depression results

We adopted our son at three days old, and I wanted to share with him the closeness that comes with breast-feeding. With the help of a lactation consultant, I prepared to try to breast-feed by taking various medications in the months leading up to the adoption. When our son came home, we tried breast-feeding with a supplementation system for about a week. Although it didn't work in the end, we had a special week of bonding time. And I know that inducing lactation can work!
—MELISSA

*When I adopted
my son, I had
planned to take a
year off work. But
he was the baby
from hell. He had
terrible colic, which
continued long after
the usual three-
month mark, and
was impossible to
comfort. When he
was five months old,
I found a marvelous
caregiver and went
back to work part-
time. Working saved
my sanity and made
me a much better
mother.*
    —AF READER

from exhaustion—both physical and emotional—and
is as likely to strike a parent who has just adopted as it
is to strike a parent who has just given birth. In rare
cases, it can trigger full-blown clinical depression,
which should be treated by a doctor or therapist.

REALITY CHECKLIST
Exhaustion or Depression?

If you have recurring thoughts about death or
suicide, or if you have several of the following
symptoms, get help.

❑ Loss of interest in being around other people

❑ Feelings of being always on the verge of tears

❑ General fatigue or loss of energy

❑ Difficulty sleeping or an increased need for
  sleep

❑ Significant weight gain or loss

❑ Excessive or inappropriate guilt

❑ Feelings of worthlessness or powerlessness

❑ Loss of enjoyment in life

❑ Irritability

Do I Love Him Yet?

Melissa Fay Greene

WHEN I FOUND MYSELF WEEPING IN THE LAUNDRY ROOM OVER being forced to put my children's sheets on the interloper's bed (because, at age four and a half, he was wetting the bed), I knew I was in trouble.

Refusing to take photos of him during his first weeks in America (because it might mean he was staying, because the photos might be used as evidence that he'd been here) also might have been a clue. Refusing to let anyone else take a picture of the whole family (because his presence in the family portrait, among our four kids by birth, would mar the effect) similarly could have sounded a warning note.

Lying awake at night considering, "If I drive all night and check in to a motel in Indiana, will anyone ever find me?" also might have signaled that I was having some issues with our son, Jesse, whom we had adopted from Bulgaria three weeks earlier.

My husband knew. I couldn't stop myself from shaking him awake at night to sob and complain. I insisted, in the small hours of the morning, that we'd spoiled our lives and the lives of our children, then ages seven, eleven, fourteen, and seventeen. "It just doesn't feel like when we brought the other kids home from the hospital," I said, weeping.

Don answered softly, with some surprise, "To me it does." I turned away from him and let the ridiculous man go back to sleep. All night long I thrashed and pummeled my pillow, in the grip of panic and grief and regret.

"Can you remember why you wanted to adopt?" asked a friend, at a loss as to how to help me. The child looked fine to her, cute, even.

"No!" I sobbed. "I can't. It wasn't me. I can't even remember that person. What was she thinking?"

I knew what she had been thinking: "Our children are so wonderful, our house is so full of love, we're good parents. Let's bring in another little kid from somewhere and prolong the fun."

Ha-ha. What a mistake. Instead of prolonging the fun with our four children, I now grasped, I'd never see them again. Every time I tried to spend a moment alone with one of them, Jesse came barreling into the room and threw himself onto my body. He was thrilled to have been given a mother, even a rumpled, disconsolate one like myself. He pulled me into the bathroom with him. He wanted me to watch him eat. He couldn't fall asleep unless I was sitting on his bed. Whenever I disappeared from his line of vision, he went berserk, falling to the floor in a fit, screaming and thrashing.

The landscape flattened. I drove slowly through my neighborhood, heartsick at how the houses and yards had become two-dimensional, like comic-strip sketches, almost colorless. I recognized everything, but I could no longer insert myself into the scene.

"Post-adoption depression" never crossed my mind. I didn't know that it was quite common among adoptive mothers of older children. The reasons vary. But surely it is, in part, because adults are hardwired to attach to wide-eyed, helpless babies; a fit-throwing, non-English-speaking, snarling Bulgarian four-year-old does not, at first glimpse, invite adoration. The crucial period of mother-infant courtship is missed as sorely by adult women as it is by the kids who suddenly parachute into their lives with their boots on.

In the orphanage in rural Bulgaria, the director had taken the little boy by the shoulders, turned him to face me, and said, "Mama." That was it for Jesse—a light went on in his mind. An archetypal image was personified: "Mama." He felt instantly devoted to me, instantly cared for.

Jesse was not having bonding or attachment issues, but I was. I couldn't figure out how on earth I would survive the coming years. I was reeling with the tremendous and terrible revelation that all the daily subservient tasks I'd done thousands of times for my older children were impossible to perform for a child I didn't love. He was like the sleepover friend who overstays his welcome. "When is that family going to pick this child up?"

It wasn't until the afternoon in the laundry room, awash in a feeling of pity for our old sheets, that I first thought: "You're crying over sheets. You're losing it."

Followed by: "You'd better get help."

"You're completely exhausted," the physician said the next afternoon. "Are you sleeping?"

"No."

"Are you eating?"

"No."

"Have you caught up on your sleep since the jet lag of flying back from Bulgaria?"

Though I'd been back three weeks by then, I still hadn't.

"I'm going to give you something to help you sleep," she said.

I burst into tears. "I need something stronger! I'm crying over sheets."

"Okay, okay," she said. The doctor, who had known me for fifteen years, had never seen me like this. She brought me some sort of pharmaceutical sample. I grabbed it. In my car, I snapped open the package and swallowed the tablet whole, dry, without water. Instantly I began to feel better. I didn't care that the instructions said to allow six weeks for the medication to take effect; the placebo pulled me back from the brink.

There were other things I did right: I told my friends I was in bad shape. I'd never reached out for help from such a scared and vulnerable place before, and my good friends flew to my side. They sat with me. They helped me watch Jesse.

My friends also gave me good advice. "You don't have to love him," one said, consolingly, over coffee. "You can just pretend to love him. He won't know. Jesse's never been mothered in his life. Jesse's in heaven. Just fake it. Your faking it is the greatest, sweetest thing that's ever happened to him."

While faking it, while pretending to love him, I discovered that my body was okay with mothering him—my lips knew how to kiss him, my hands enjoyed stroking his hair, even as my heart was in total rebellion, my brain frozen with regret.

"Do you love him yet?"

Such an awful thing we adoptive parents do to ourselves and our newly adopted children, asking ourselves this question. We don't pursue this line of questioning about the children to whom we give birth. Yet here sat this little guy at the table, painstakingly peeling a hot dog before eating it, looking up, with his shaggy haircut and sparkly eyes, and all I could think was, "Do I love him yet?"

Well, he loved me, and that little, steady, unwavering beacon of love began to lure me.

He was intoxicated with everything I did. One night, as I dressed to go out somewhere, he sat high on my bed, swinging his legs, watching me.

On went the stockings, on went the slip, on went the low heels; before I could finish buttoning the satin blouse, Jesse flew off the bed and into the closet to hug me. "Oh, Mama!" he cried, utterly starstruck.

Under such an onslaught of tenderness, I began to soften. I no longer assumed he was leaving, and he began to trust that I was staying. He began to let me out of his sight for minutes on end. I was able to walk seven-year-old Lily to school in the morning, savoring every step, every breath of the fall air, like heaven had been restored to me. I was able to listen to my older daughter practice her upright bass, and to my older son play his trombone, seated on the beds in their rooms, without a small Bulgarian draped across me.

One afternoon, feeling irascible and weary, I gave in to his pleas of "Bagel, Mama? Bagel?" and hacked so hard at a stale bagel that the knife glanced off the roll and slashed my finger. Jesse followed me upstairs in a panic, his eyes huge and filled with tears. He stood beside me as I sat on the closed toilet trying to stanch the bleeding. He patted and patted my shoulder. "Mama!" he announced. "Mama, nay bagel! Mama, nay bagel!" He was trying to help, after the fact, by un-requesting the bagel.

Later he stood on his tiptoes, reached into the kitchen drawer, extracted the big, guilty knife, and said, "Nay Mama this. Daddy. Nay Mama. Daddy." Meaning you should not use the knife anymore; let Daddy use it.

Still later, he had an updated announcement to make, pointing at the knife: "Nay Mama, nay Franny" (our rat terrier, whom he already adored). I don't know if the policy statement was meant to protect the two individuals he most loved from the bad knife, or if he now put me in the competence department with the dog.

Finally, toward the end of the day, he came to me with a plastic picnic knife he'd found somewhere. He put it in my bandaged hand and said firmly, "Mama."

What was it I felt at that moment, as I laughed and wept and accepted the picnic knife and hugged him? Was it, actually . . . could it be? Well, by then I was trying hard to stop grilling myself a dozen times daily. I had learned about post-adoption depression and realized such interrogation was getting me nowhere.

I had an appointment with a psychologist scheduled for a few days after the bagel mishap. But after Jesse handed me the plastic knife, I canceled it and scheduled a haircut instead.

I took Jesse with me. If he thought I was beautiful before the haircut, he really thought I was beautiful after the haircut. He thought the whole haircut experience was a glamorous and magnificent thing, full of the scents of perfumes and hairsprays and peppermints in a dish. As we drove home, I glanced back at him in the backseat, his cheek big with a peppermint. He gave me a huge, sticky smile. Did I love him? I didn't ask.

WHAT DO I DO NEXT?

Wait. Don't expect to bond immediately. Even biological parents don't always fall in love at first sight.

Cocoon. Stay close to home, and keep parties and distractions to a minimum.

Rest. A new child is an adjustment for everyone; make sure that you make time for yourself. Follow the advice given to all new parents: Sleep when you can, forget housework, take it easy.

The best thing we did after we came home from Russia was to ask that friends, and even family, leave us in peace for two weeks. That gave the four of us time together to adjust in relative calm.

—RENÉE

Madeline, United States

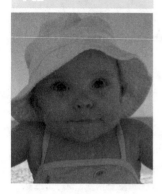

Is There a Greeting Card for This?

Your Child's Birth Mother and Other New Relatives

The best part about being a birth mother in an open adoption is that I am at peace. Colin and I are still a part of each other's lives, yet he is so happy and deeply rooted in his family that sometimes I forget that he's not their flesh and blood. Knowing he has the life I wanted for him allows me to move forward in mine.

—JEN

What is "open" adoption?

In an open adoption, birth parents and adoptive parents know one another's identities. Once a novelty, openness is now routine in U.S. newborn adoptions and is even spreading to foster-care and some international adoptions. Our families say that openness—even without ongoing contact—helps children understand adoption, relieves the fears of adoptive parents, and helps birth mothers resolve their grief.

How much contact is there in an open adoption?

At one extreme are families who know one another's names but don't meet or communicate. At the other are the adoptive and birth families who socialize once a month or more. Most open adoptions lie somewhere in the middle, with families exchanging letters, pictures, and phone calls and meeting once or twice a year, often tailing off as the children—and the birth families—grow older.

above: Amanda, United States

Families (both birth and adoptive) who want access to information while preserving their privacy can opt for "semi-open" adoption, where the two families have some contact (letters through an intermediary, or even meetings in a neutral area) but don't know one another's names or addresses.

What No One Told Me
Leigh Kaufman Leveen

THE JOURNEY THROUGH DOMESTIC INDEPENDENT ADOPTION is filled with professionals, all supporting you in myriad ways. From finding you a birth-parent match to supporting that relationship and then legally binding it all together, there is one person or another by your side. And yet, my husband and I were adrift from the start. All the reading in the world did not prepare us for the things that we did not know and about which no one talked to us. We are intelligent professionals; we are used to running offices, deals, and whole projects. But we had no idea how to handle the murky, gray areas as we tried to become adoptive parents.

The first thing we realized is that independent adoption attorneys all work differently, and these differences are not apparent until you are presented with a placement. We interviewed three top lawyers in our area, each of whom highly recommended the other, and each of whom said we would be in good hands, regardless of which one we chose. So far, so good, we thought. It wasn't until we actually started speaking to birth parents and evaluating matches that we began to see how different each lawyer was.

Most lawyers actively advertise, in one way or another, to reach out to birth parents seeking adoption information and situations. Some want the prospective adopter to be the initial recipient of the birth mother's phone calls. Others want to vet those calls themselves, then put you in touch with the birth mother. We chose to be the initial recipients of the calls. We installed a toll-free line in our home and waited for the phone to ring. Our lawyer preferred this method, which allowed a quick personal connection with any birth situation that arose. To us, it felt like we were taking charge. After years of failed attempts to grow our family, the desire for control was all-consuming.

After our second call, it was clear we were in over our heads. We were emotional puddles trying to sound like coherent adults to scared and confused birth parents. We were neophytes lost in a strange land. Why wasn't our attorney making the important first impression? Well, because that was not what we had chosen. In hindsight, I realize how much work our lawyer abdicated to us. We hadn't been counseled enough to know what we would feel when answering those calls.

It wasn't just the emotional ride, there were also prank calls. After the second one, I dreaded hearing the phone ring. I would look at the caller ID and shiver. Was this call a real birth parent, or would I be asked to send a photo of me in a bathing suit again? I wondered what on earth makes someone see an adoption ad and decide that this would be a good person to call on a sadistic whim.

After months of calls, some real, some not, most dead ends, we finally matched. I dove into a relationship with our birth mother. She lived out of state and was planning to come to us for the delivery. We developed an intimacy very quickly; we were sharing the emotional roller-coaster ride of an impending birth, as well as her daily life issues. And yet, it was a false closeness. There were huge chunks of information that we did not know about one another, and never will. The basics were shared—medical information, background about her and the birth father, family details about us—but I cannot say that I know the core of our birth mother, nor does she know me. We probably never will. No one seems to tell you the truth about the relationship with your child's birth mother: It is honest only to a point. You are not looking for a co-parent, a life partner, or a new best friend. So you strive for truth, hope that it is given to you in return, but you are ultimately taking a leap of faith in binding yourself to this person or family. There is no other relationship like it, and it tested our capacity to trust, more than anything I have ever experienced.

When Jane arrived in town, we spent a lot of time together, and I have a wealth of stories to share with our daughter. But we were not prepared for how it would feel to be with her for such an extended period of time, and it got really sticky. We didn't know what to talk about and what not to talk about, what might upset her or what she may or may not want to know about her child's future with us. I needed to learn to handle this new friendship while guarding myself and my family. Other families we knew who had adopted domestically did not have such relationships with their birth mothers, our friends from home-study class were all in earlier stages of adopting, and our lawyer was not available all the time. Our social worker was kind, but she was not the person to turn to. I wanted to make sure that when relinquishment happened, our birth mother knew how much she meant to us, and what a gift she was giving us. But what if—that horrible, gnawing fear—what if, at the last moment, she didn't relinquish? I needed to protect us from that possibility.

There are therapists who specialize in adoption, and I wish that I had sought help from one of them. But you keep thinking that this will pass, the baby will be born, and life will return to a proximity of normal. What I did not figure on was the aftermath of so much internal drama; as the cliché says, everyone needs someone to lean on.

And then there were the kids. Jane is parenting two other children, and they came with her when she came to town. We had a four-year-old, and the three children together became a source of deep pain. They were all struggling with what adoption meant, from various developmental places and from different sides of the placement equation.

We had talked with our lawyer about bringing our birth mother and her kids out all together. He focused on the logistical aspects and said he had overseen numerous situations like this. It would be manageable, he said. But no one can prepare you for driving on the freeway with no exit in sight while three kids fight in the backseat. One of them is yours, two of them are your birth mother's. She is sitting next to you, ready to deliver any moment and needing to go to the bathroom worse than anything. Who did I attend to first? My child? The one who was crying the hardest? Jane? Disciplining someone else's child is treacherous at best, and in this situation it was near impossible.

I asked my husband later if this was really worth it. Were we permanently damaging our other child, putting him through all of this? No one told us what it would mean to have all the kids interact on such a regular basis. I hadn't understood that it wasn't done very often, and that advice would be in short supply. A little forethought, a shred of counsel from a friendly professional, would have gone a long way.

I thought, if I could arrange everything, and keep everyone happy and taken care of, that it would all turn out fine. This was my need to control at work again. And again, how wrong I was. When Jane went for appointments, to her social worker, to the agency, to her doctor, I had to take her. That meant someone else had to take care of the kids. Between family and babysitting agencies, we were able to manage. But once she went to the hospital to deliver, it all fell in on us. Her kids missed their mother, and they were afraid, in a strange, rented apartment, in a city where the only people they knew were us. We had a new baby at home, and we wanted to spend every moment with her. I called our lawyer to say we were past our limit handling all this. He told us that the week after birth is the hardest, hold tight, it will pass. That was it, "It will pass."

And then there was this wonder, this beautiful child in our arms, our daughter. And it was all happening because we were meant to be her parents, this was our journey toward that goal. It was not the journey I intended to take, nor the one I'd planned for, nor one I would repeat, but it was meant to be. We made it through those final five days, sleep-deprived, anxious, but happy, too. We gathered our strength to support our birth mother, her kids, and our own, one day at a time. But each day I said to myself, "If only someone had warned us, if only I had known what to expect, this would have been easier."

The day before our birth mother and her children were supposed to go home, both families got together one last time. We went to a park. We had a picnic in the high winds and ended up hanging out at the mall. We spent a whole day together, just together. Then it was time to say good-bye.

Doesn't open adoption confuse a child?

Our families say their children in open adoptions are not confused about who their parents are. In play groups, at school, and on television, they see blended families and other nontraditional structures. Children incorporate birth-family members into their extended families quite easily.

Can open adoptions be legally enforced?

Some U.S. states allow adoptive parents and their child's biological families to make enforceable, written agreements about how much ongoing contact the two families will have. Each state has its own requirements; you should work with an attorney to make sure your agreement conforms to your state's laws. If, over time, either the birth family or adoptive family wants to enforce or change the agreement, they can seek mediation or bring an action in family court. The court will decide what is in the best interests of the child (in practice, they almost always abide by the wishes of the adoptive parents). Breach of a contact agreement does not affect the legality of the adoption or the adoptive parents' rights.

In states where statutes don't address post-adoption contact agreements, adoptive and birth families can make an informal agreement, based upon the goodwill and trust between the parties.

Adoption 101: Making an Ongoing-Contact Plan

Whether you are making a legally enforceable contract or just a mutual agreement, topics to cover should include the following:

- The kind of communication you will have, including whether it will be direct or through an intermediary, and whether it will include letters, telephone calls, photographs, audiotapes or videotapes, and visitation.
- The frequency of communication or visitation and the circumstances under which the birth family may visit, such as whether they can take the child without supervision, and if so, at what age.
- The type and frequency of contact between the adoptive family and other members of the birth family.

The premise of open adoption is telling the truth, and that jives with our family values. There are some practical benefits, too. My son has someone other than his parents to go to for firsthand answers to his questions. He can see a family resemblance in her, and that is important beyond words. Open adoption squelches the tendency to fantasize about his birth mother, about the reason she made an adoption plan, and about the life he might have led.

—JANA

My husband and I met our daughter's birth mother during the eighth month of her pregnancy. After that, I would drive her to her weekly doctor's appointments. The drive wasn't far, but it created a wonderful opportunity for the two of us to talk and share the stories that have shaped our lives. That short month of parenthood preparation was a very sweet time, in which we developed a special relationship with our birth mother. During the pregnancy, our baby didn't seem real— everything was still like a dream. We feel fortunate that we took the time to get to know our birth mother and that we maintain our friendship. Our daughter (now very real!) will be the one to benefit as she grows up.

—JESSICA

Ian, United States

- How information about the adoption will be shared with the child.
- How birthdays and other special occasions will be celebrated.
- How the agreement will be modified to meet changes in needs and circumstances, and how conflicts will be resolved, including who will pay for the cost of counseling, mediation, or legal services, if required.

WISE WORDS: *Lois Melina, an adoptive parent who has been writing and lecturing about adoption for thirty years, says: "Instead of thinking of your open adoption as a new, untested kind of adoption, think of it as just another family dynamic. I suggest that families use their relations with in-laws as a model. While some people have close, warm relationships with their in-laws, for many others, in-laws are the people we have to get along with because we are connected through the one person we all love. Likewise, in an open adoption, an adoptive and a birth family form a relationship because they all love the same child."*

A Lasting Relationship

Brenda Romanchik

ON OCTOBER 17, I HAD MY FIRST VISIT WITH MY SON. HE WAS three weeks old. Physically, I was still unaccustomed to my post-pregnancy body and was still healing from a C-section. Emotionally, I was just beginning a heart-wrenching journey into the loss of my son. I was brittle with grief.

Earlier in the day, I had been to court to sign away my parental rights. While the judge was as gentle as he could be, the language of relinquishment hung heavy in the air. I was giving up all "rights and responsibilities" from this day forward. I was to "be as a stranger" to my son. While I understood that I no longer had any legal responsibilities to him, I knew I had a moral responsibility. I was determined that, even though I was no longer parenting, I would not "be as a stranger" to him. Visiting my son that day was an affirmation of the decision I made to have an open adoption, despite the legal language.

Did I really need to see my son being mothered by another? Did I really want to walk into a house I could never afford and see the stability I could never provide? The answer to both questions is a resounding *yes!* At that time, was visiting the most comfortable thing for me to do? Absolutely not. But even then, I knew that comfort is not what this open-adoption stuff should be about.

Open adoption is not designed to make the adults involved comfortable; it is about providing for the needs of a child. Much of the open-adoption experience is awkward, especially in the beginning. Many birth parents in the crisis of planning for an adoption or in the throes of grieving look upon continuing contact as too painful to contemplate. Many adoptive parents just want to be a family, without the added complication of visits with their child's birth family. Open-adoption agreements that are guided by feelings that occur around the time of placement do not allow contact to ebb and flow according to the needs of all involved and, most important, the needs of the child.

Adoption is a lifelong process. As time goes on, birth parents, adoptive parents, and the child often find that they want more contact but feel they are not able to ask for it because of the original agreement. If the child is to be the primary beneficiary of open adoption, we need to see open adoption as a covenant, instead of a contract or agreement. In *Webster's Revised Unabridged Dictionary,* the word *covenant* is defined as one of the strongest and most solemn forms of contract. It is also described as sacred. For open adoption to work best, birth parents and adoptive parents need to see their involvement with one another as a sacred commitment, a covenant they make with one another for the sake of the child.

When birth family members are accepted into the adoptive family, it gives the child a sense of wholeness. Children in these situations do not have to worry about "splitting their loyalties" between two families, because they come to see their adoptive family and their birth family as one. In the early years in particular, birth parents and adoptive parents take up the responsibility of maintaining connection with one another. A toddler or a child cannot carry the burden of connecting his two families. An adopted child whose birth family and adoptive family come together in a positive way will grow up with greater certainty. There is a saying that the greatest gift parents can give their children is to love one another. I think this applies not just to married couples but to all parents.

Treat one another as the family members you are. You don't have to spend every holiday together, but at the very least you should find ways of remembering one another on holidays and birthdays. There is a tendency in open adoption to create artificial boundaries that one would never dream of imposing on other family members, friends, or even acquaintances. When considering the contact you are going to have with one another, instead of asking "Why?" ask "Why not?"

Honor one another. In addition to sending one another Mother's Day and Father's Day cards, birth parents and adoptive parents can honor the unique roles that they have in the child's life. For birth parents this means supporting and respecting the parental decisions that their child's adoptive parents make. For adoptive parents it means acknowledging the similarities that your child shares with his or her birth family, as well as encouraging the birth family to share family history and pre-placement history.

Honor your differences. Everyone has different ways of communicating, showing affection, and celebrating. Learn what these differences are, and respect them.

Let the child be the witness. Ask yourself, twenty years from now, "What will my child think of my actions?" Too often, adoptive parents and birth parents base their actions on fear, insecurity, or uncertainty. If you think about the contact you have with one another as a way to build memories for your child, decisions will be based on the child's needs, not solely on the needs of the adults involved.

Be there when it is important to be there. We all lead busy lives, and sometimes it seems impossible to coordinate schedules and activities. However, as my mother often says, "Ninety percent of friendship is showing up." Birth parents need to make time to be present at a dance recital or a basketball game. Adoptive parents need to extend the invitations to these events, and to "show up" at important events in the lives of birth-family members.

Have fun with one another. Remember that, in open adoption, birth parents and adoptive parents choose one another for a reason. Focusing on your similarities will help you relax and enjoy yourself.

Do birth fathers stay involved with their children?

Of the 25 percent of birth fathers who take an active role in their child's placement, only about 20 percent continue contact with the adoptive family. Many of our families have open adoptions with their child's birth mother but have what are, in effect, closed adoptions with the birth father.

Micayla, United States

Should we keep the birth grandparents involved?

It's not unusual for biological grandparents to be interested in maintaining contact after the adoption of their grandchild. In a case of an older child who had an established relationship with birth grandparents before the adoption, it is often in the child's best interest to maintain that relationship. Some of our adoptive families, believing that children cannot have too many people who love them, incorporate biological

We get together with our two daughters' birth parents and extended birth family whenever possible. We visit each other's homes, we have them over for Christmas, and we have even taken a weekend trip with one daughter's birth mother. We've been to birth-family graduations, funerals, and weddings. My children's birth parents come to watch the kids play softball. Every two years we host a birth-family picnic and invite the extended birth families of both our daughters. We usually have about thirty-five people—it's wonderful!
—DIANE

grandparents and other relatives into their child's life. The degree of contact varies, from occasional letters to frequent meetings.

However, biological grandparents do not have any enforceable rights to visitation with their grandchild after the adoption is finalized, unless there is a written contract between the adoptive parents and the child's biological relatives guaranteeing visitation, and you live in a state that allows such contracts.

Will the birth family always be part of our lives?

Often, the birth parents move on with their lives after the child's first year or two. They resume the roles they had before the birth or take on new ones. This is particularly true for young birth parents; as they become involved with school, peers, careers, and new relationships, their focus is on themselves and not on the child. This is as it should be. One of the reasons they placed the child for adoption was that they needed to concentrate on themselves before taking on responsibility for another person.

Birth parents may want less contact with the adoptive family after they have other children, because they have less time for other relationships, and because it can be hard to see all the children together and wonder what it would have been like to raise them together.

If birth parents pull back from the open-adoption relationship to move on with their lives, the adoptive family might still have regular, ongoing contact with other members of the birth family.

TRIED AND TRUE: In our experience, adoptive families enter into open adoptions worrying that the birth parents will want too much contact. After the first few months, our families find they have *less* contact with the birth family than they would like.

We've Been There: Keeping in Touch

There are many ways to share information with your child's birth mother. Choose those that feel right for your level of contact.

1. Give her a small photo album of your child. Include shots of everyday routines, not just special occasions.

2. Share a list of the words your child can say, or tell her about his favorite foods.

3. If your child no longer plays with a favorite toy or stuffed animal, consider giving it to her birth mother as a keepsake.

4. Share your upcoming vacation plans and adventures.

5. As your child begins to doodle with crayons, give a drawing to his birth mother.

6. Share the results of your child's latest healthy checkup.

7. Mail a postcard "from" your child, telling her birth mother about her day.

8. Share the dates on which your child reaches major developmental milestones over the first two years.

JD, United States

We welcome our three children's birth parents into our lives. There was a time, though, when they weren't physically present, because that would have caused our children some confusion. Even then, we continued writing and calling, and when the time was right, we welcomed them back. The reason our openness works so well is that we all trust one another. All of our decisions have been based on the best interest of our children.

—ANNETTE

How do I deal with a birth parent whose child was taken away?

If you have adopted a child who was removed from the birth family because of abuse or neglect, your instinct may be to protect your child by cutting off contact. Psychologists who deal with abused children recommend that you maintain some kind of relationship. If you reject the birth parents, you are rejecting a part of the child. Social workers can provide a safe and neutral place for supervised meetings; if this isn't

Patrick, United States

For my last birthday, my mom organized a big party. All my grandpas and grandmas, aunts, uncles, and cousins were there. My birth mother came, too. My mom says every family is different. I have a mom, a dad, a brother, a birth mother, and many people in my life who love me. Whether we are together or apart, we are always in each other's hearts.
　—CHRISTINA,
　　as told to her mother,
　　SHARON

possible, try to exchange letters and photographs. Our families say the relationship is like that of divorced parents: You may not like each other much, but you all want the best for your child.

> **WISE WORDS:** *Sarah Gerstenzang, associate director of the Collaboration to AdoptUsKids, a federally funded initiative to promote and facilitate the adoption of children in foster care (and herself an adoptive parent), says: "If you have a relationship with the birth parent, you may have a better relationship with the child, who will feel fully accepted by you."*

Should I maintain contact with the foster parents?

Social workers used to advise cutting off all contact with previous placements when children were finally adopted. Now ongoing contact is encouraged, especially for older children who formed bonds with their foster families. In some cases, the foster family is the only link between the child and the birth family—the first foster family may have met the birth family during the termination process.

Are there open international adoptions?

Until recently, openness in international adoption was very rare; some adoptive parents even chose intercountry adoption to avoid encounters with their child's birth parents. Today, however, parents are meeting their children's birth families across international boundaries. Few countries establish open adoptions from the start, but many provide enough identifying information so parents can attempt contact with birth-family members later.

> **STRAIGHT TALK:** Open international adoptions are different from open domestic adoptions in one critical way: If foreign birth parents express any

desire for ongoing contact, the child may not qualify for an orphan visa and will not be able to enter the United States. There is nothing to stop the adoptive family from making voluntary contact with the birth family—but it can't be, in any way, a condition of the adoption.

If we have a closed adoption, or if the birth parents disappear, can we find them later?

Our families say that parents should resist the temptation to search on their child's behalf. On the other hand, if it's your child who wants to search, you should enlist professional support from a therapist who has experience with adoption-related issues. Adoptees should be prepared for all of the possible search outcomes, including rejection by a birth parent, learning that a parent has died, realizing that there's a disparity between fantasy and reality, or—in the best-case scenario—building a relationship with and integrating the birth parent into their lives. Families will also need help in setting appropriate boundaries with a birth family, as well as in guiding their child through the search-and-reunion process.

STRAIGHT TALK: Many adult adoptees feel that initiating contact with birth parents should be the child's prerogative, not their parents' decision. They note that the decision to search, and the searching itself, can be important to a child's quest for identity.

We have open adoptions for all three of our children. Our two girls have the same birth mother, and they have many photos of her, though we don't see her often because of distance. The only difficulty is that the girls have different birth fathers. We have met our older girl's father, and his family is in frequent contact. But our younger daughter's birth father is known to us by name only. We have never even seen a photo. At times, she seems sad that we know more about her sister's birth father.

—KERRY

Our Leap of Faith
Janice Pearse

MY HUSBAND AND I ALWAYS KNEW WE WOULD TAKE OUR CHIL-
dren back to their countries of origin. Our daughter, Marina, entered an
orphanage when she was seven, after her father died and her mother,
Elena, could no longer take care of her. We adopted her four years later.
Over the years, she's often wondered if Elena was okay. Last summer,
when Marina was eighteen, after much family discussion, we decided it
was time.

We boarded the plane to Russia, with a few addresses for her birth relatives, little information about her birth mother, Elena, and no guarantee
that we would meet anyone.

The staff of Marina's orphanage confirmed the addresses we had. The
next morning, as we approached the town, we had to decide whether to
turn left, toward her cousin's address, or right, toward her aunt's. Something steered us left.

As we walked through rows of marketplace stalls, Marina whispered to
me, "I don't know if I'm ready." I replied that I was about to throw up, and
that made her laugh.

As we neared the end, a woman at a vegetable stand looked up. It was
Elena! Marina walked toward her, holding out her arms for a hug. At first,
they were both too stunned to show much emotion. Soon, though, they
both started to cry. Elena reported that she was living with her boyfriend
of several years. Marina was relieved to hear that Elena was doing well.
My daughter now had peace of mind, for the first time in seven years.

Our day of searching was not over. Marina's paternal aunt, Alla, invited
us all to a family birthday feast, which was under way. I asked Alla if she
had any photos of her brother, Marina's birth father. I remembered vividly
the night, soon after her adoption, when I found Marina crying in bed because she couldn't remember what her dad looked like. Alla brought out
an album and gave Marina a picture of her father holding her when she
was a baby. Tears ran down Marina's cheeks as she gazed at the photo.

The evening was fantastic, with conversation and vodka flowing freely.
Our family has expanded—they are all wonderful people. Marina has

added photos of her birth family to the collection on her wall, and she is no longer anxious about her birth mother's well-being. Now Marina has a more complete sense of self and an increased sense of security in us as a family.

Grace, Russia

WHAT DO I DO NEXT?

Clarify. Make sure that you and your child's birth family share an understanding about on-going contact.

From the beginning, we have encouraged our sons to stay in touch with their foster families. These efforts help our sons build and sustain important relationships. They have already experienced too much loss and grief in their young lives. The boys enjoy saving favorite photographs, school-work, and crafts for their other families. Our family-tree projects include all members of our sons' families— birth, foster, and adoptive.

—LINDA

13

What Do I
Tell My Child?

Creating the Adoption Story

When do I tell my child she was adopted?
Early, and often. Speaking about birth history helps all family members get used to the words and narrative and lets your child know that she can always come forward with questions and emotions about birth parents. Some children will have an easier time talking about birth-family history than others, but all should be given opportunities to hear, absorb, and retell their stories.

Adoption 101: Age-Appropriate

Children need to have the adoption story repeated, because they will focus on different aspects of it at different developmental stages. At one age, a child wonders how old his birth parents were when he was born; at another, he's more interested in the

above: Rhyan, Canada

legal process of adoption. Fortunately, we now have some understanding of what children need to know at certain stages of development.

- Birth to age seven: Tell the child's story as a story, not a dry recital of facts. Limit any negative details.
- Eight to twelve: Children at this age can understand abstract concepts and will begin to ask more questions about the adoption story you've already told. This is often the ideal age for sharing thorny realities.
- Thirteen onward: If the adoption conversation has been open thus far, it's likely to remain so during adolescence. Be prepared for some turbulence as your child struggles to figure out who he is, but don't assume that your child will be troubled (plenty of children sail through the teen years with ease), and don't automatically pin problems on adoption (biological teens have been known to act out, too).

WISE WORDS: *Ronny Diamond, director of the Adoption Counseling Team at Spence-Chapin, a New York agency that has been placing children since 1908, says: "The best experiences are when children say, 'I just always knew I was adopted.' It's like gender: There's no one time to inform your child that she is a girl. Most children can't remember a time they did not know their gender."*

My advice for new adoptive parents is to start talking about the adoption story right away. Incorporate it into your everyday conversation. This does a couple of things. Even if the child is too young to understand, it gets you comfortable with the words and ways of talking about it, so that when he or she is ready to understand, it is easy to do. Also, it gives the child the idea that there is nothing secret or wrong with this way of forming a family, and that this is something they can talk to you about. Be calm and matter-of-fact. Children pick up tone of voice and feelings, as well as words.
—DONNA MARIE

You must tell your child he or she was adopted, or risk a terrible breach of trust. I've seen men in their fifties destroyed when, at a parent's funeral, some relative spilled the beans. Talking about adoption will defuse negative effects. Your child will ask more than once, reflecting different needs at different ages. So get information, meet his or her birth parents. Be honest but not critical. Remember, your child will incorporate your interpretation of his or her birth parents into his or her self-identity.

—ABIGAIL

What do I say about why they were placed for adoption?

Children are self-centered and, despite parental assurances to the contrary, may decide that they were placed for adoption because of something they did. It's usually not enough to assure your child that adoption is a choice made by adults and was not prompted by anything he did. You should tell your child that the birth parents chose adoption or lost their parental rights because they were unable to care for *any* child. As they get older, it helps to explain the social context of the birth parents' actions. Learning about conditions such as extreme poverty, drug or alcohol addiction, or prejudice against unwed mothers can be very important in helping children make sense of their past.

We've Been There: Good Lines
- "Some families are formed by birth, and some are formed by adoption." This helps your child learn that there are different ways to create a family, and they're all equally wonderful.
- "Your birth mother couldn't take care of any child just then." This statement stresses that your child did nothing "wrong" that led to the adoption. If you know your child was relinquished because of his or her gender, say: "Your birth mother couldn't take care of any baby girl/boy just then."
- "We will be your family, even when you're a grown-up." Kids sometimes worry that you could decide to place them for adoption, too. Make sure you let your child know that adoption is for keeps, and that you'll be there for her for the rest of your life.
- "I wish you'd grown inside my tummy, too, but that's not what happened." This last line responds to the common reaction as a child

begins to understand adoption: "I wish I'd grown in your tummy." The desire for closeness is one you can meet with empathy.

If I don't know my child's background, should I make something up?

Our families caution against inventing a story about your child's past, if for no other reason than you're likely to forget exactly what you said. Children are notoriously quick at picking up tiny discrepancies, and it will undercut their trust in you.

However, if you have no information about the circumstances of your child's birth, don't assume that there's nothing to talk about. Talk about general circumstances—youth, lack of education, poverty, government policies that might have led a birth parent to adoption.

My child's birth story is traumatic—how much should I tell?

Parents sometimes hesitate to tell children difficult details of their personal histories (conception from rape or incest, a parent in prison). But most secrets eventually come to light. And when they do, the fact that they remained secrets tells the child that he or she should feel ashamed. Adopted children need to know their entire life stories, not just the good parts.

Most parents' first inclination is to put it off until the child is a teenager. But adolescence, hard enough for most young people, is probably the worst possible developmental stage for children to learn about difficult family history. A better time to first share difficult information is around the age of eight. This allows a few years for the child to work through the "hard stuff" and for you to emphasize that poor choices made by one generation are not genetically predestined for repetition in the next.

You may want to consult a psychologist or social worker for guidance. You might also turn to this pro-

I started when we first went for walks in the stroller, and my daughter pointed to an airplane. I told her that she had been on four airplanes, that was how she got home with Mommy, Daddy, and her sister from her birth country. Repeating this over and over, she finally learned the answers, even if she didn't understand them. Now she asks why was she in that country, and I tell her that is where her birth parents lived, but they couldn't take care of her, so they let us adopt her. She asked me today if they were dead. I told her I didn't know and we may never know, but that there are lots of reasons why parents may not be able to take care of their children by themselves.
—DONNA MARIE

We met my son, Carlos, when he was two years old, in Colombia. His adoption story was always a part of his life, but at age seven or so, he began to want more information than we have available. He and I are both dissatisfied with the scant information we were given, and we're told by the Colombian government that this is all that is available. We have only his biological mother's name and her age. If I could do anything differently, I would have insisted on obtaining more information, and conducting a search, before I left Colombia. I would suggest to internationally adopting parents, get as much information as you can in the country.
—ILANA

fessional for family and individual counseling as your child deals with the information.

> **STRAIGHT TALK:** If you have been told that your child was the product of rape, be extremely cautious about passing this along to the child, at any age. The birth mother may have said she was raped to avoid being punished for having consensual sex outside marriage. Don't let your child think her birth father was a rapist unless you have absolute proof that it's so.

What should I tell my child about the cost of his adoption?

When adopted children become aware of adoption's expense (often through exaggerations, in the media, or through friends' remarks), they may ask, "What did I cost?" Our adoptive families say the best response is first to explain that you paid for the process, not for the child, and then to give the rough final net of all fees (after any reimbursements). You can add, "If we had given birth to you, we would have paid doctors and hospitals about the same amount."

How can I keep the adoption conversation going?

Many of our families say their children have no interest in talking about adoption. Social workers caution that the children may be clamming up because your subtle cues tell them that talking about adoption is difficult for *you.* You may want to prompt your child with books and movies about adoption; some of our families say that making a life book for your child is a particularly useful exercise. Whether it's a simple scrapbook with documents and photographs or an elaborate album, it can be an excellent way to keep your child talking.

Thirty Nagging Questions
Laurie Elliott

THROUGH MY WORK AS A COURT-APPOINTED AGENT FOR ADOPTEES searching for their birth families, I have learned that many older adoptees have nagging questions about their adoptions. As they grew up, they wondered about very basic information and were afraid to ask their parents.

To help other adoptees avoid these adoption-related identity issues, I made a list of the things that the adoptees I worked with most wanted to know about themselves, their birth parents, and their adoption circumstances. I recommend that adoptive parents try to gather as many answers to these questions as they can when their children are young and the information is easier to find. I have been gathering information to share with my own nine children. It has provided them with another piece of who they are.

I encourage parents to share this information with their child before adolescence, to promote a stronger sense of identity and avoid problems later on. Information that would be matter-of-fact to children at a younger age becomes a crisis if they're older and don't have it.

1. What are my birth parents' first and middle names?
2. Where was I born?
3. What time was I born?
4. Were there any complications at the time of my birth?
5. Did my birth mother see me or hold me?
6. Who else was present at my birth?
7. What were the circumstances surrounding my placement?
8. Did my birth mother pick my adoptive family?
9. Did my birth mother know anything about my adoptive family? Did she meet my adoptive parents?
10. What did my birth mother name me?
11. Does anyone else in my birth family know about me? Who knows what?
12. How old were my birth parents when I was born?

13. Were my birth parents married when I was born?
14. Where did my birth parents go to school? College?
15. What kind of students were they?
16. What religious backgrounds do my birth parents have?
17. What is my ethnic/racial background?
18. Did my birth parents marry each other or anyone else after I was born? Do I have any biological siblings? Do they know about me?
19. Did I go to a foster home or orphanage?
20. What was my foster family's name? How long was I there?
21. What do my birth mother and birth father look like? May I have a picture of them?
22. Are my birth parents still alive?
23. Do my birth parents love me?
24. Do my birth parents think about me? Did they ever regret their decision?
25. Do my birth parents have any special talents, hobbies, or interests?
26. What traits did I inherit from my birth parents? Personality? Looks? Talents?
27. Did my birth parents write to me over the years (journal/letters in a file)?
28. Are there any medical concerns I should know about?
29. If I called my birth parents, or wanted to meet them someday, what would they do?
30. What should I call my birth parents?

WHAT DO I DO NEXT?

Rehearse. Get comfortable with the adoption story you want to tell your child.

Record. Make a scrapbook (or a memory box, or a file) with everything you know about your child's beginnings; scraps of information gleaned now can answer big questions later.

14

Who Needs to Know?

Talking to Teachers, Doctors—and Strangers

Who has to know my child was adopted?

The only people who *have* to know your child was adopted are those who will provide medical or dental treatment. When you first visit the pediatrician or dentist, make sure the child's file carries a prominent note about adoption, with as much information about ethnic background and birth-family medical history as you can find. If you change doctors, see that this information is transferred. Your child's pre-adoption background affects what a doctor will look and test for. A pediatrician who sees two white parents with a light-skinned African American child may not think to screen for sickle-cell anemia, for example, while a Norwegian American child with a Jewish parent could undergo unnecessary testing for Tay-Sachs disease.

above: Max, United States

How much privacy should my child have?

Children who have been adopted have the right of privacy. Privacy is not the same as secrecy. A secret is something that is kept from someone to whom the information pertains. Privacy involves sharing personal information only with people who have a relevant need to know. For example, if a child has a birth mother who was an alcoholic, that fact is important information to give the child's pediatrician, who can be aware of signs of fetal alcohol syndrome or fetal alcohol effect, while maintaining professional confidence. It isn't information that needs to be shared with other people, however, including close family members. The adoptee might choose to share that information, but it is his choice—not the choice of his adoptive parents. Once information is given away, it's out—no one can control how it spreads.

Dylan, United States

TRIED AND TRUE: It's important that kids know it's okay not to answer questions. Parents can demonstrate this when a friend or stranger intrudes with a question. A polite "We don't care to discuss it" is fine.

WISE WORDS: *Lois Melina, an adoptive parent who has been writing and lecturing about adoption for thirty years, says: "I'm quite willing to answer people's questions about the adoption process, the practices of different agencies, our reasons for adopting, and how my children reacted to what was a major change in their life. I consider information to be private if it refers to a child's genetic and social history. My rule of thumb: Would you readily share that information about yourself?"*

Do I need to tell the school?

Our families are divided on whether to tell their child's school about the child's adoption. Many parents say, yes, they must inform the school and teacher that their child was adopted. The subject will come up—during the ubiquitous family-tree assignment, or through thoughtless comments made by kids and adults—so they feel that it's best to prepare staff to handle such situations when they arise. Others feel that adoption is private, a family matter, and not relevant where school is concerned. They do not want their child singled out for societal misconceptions ("He has separation anxiety because he was adopted"). They feel that when a child is older, it is her choice to tell or not to tell.

Some of our families have compromised by leaving the fact of the child's adoption out of the formal school record but telling the teacher informally at the beginning of the school year, until the child is old enough to make the decision herself.

STRAIGHT TALK: If you have asked your school to provide English-as-a-second-language tuition for an internationally adopted child, or have asked for special-education screening because of a child's past, the adoption history will be part of the child's official record. After the services have been provided, you can ask for the information to be removed from the file.

When Nora was seven, we moved to a new town, and to a new school and new friends. Before school began, I went to see the second-grade teacher and told her that Nora was adopted. We lucked out. The teacher herself was adopted. She asked two other adoptees in the class to look out for Nora, and all four of them—including the teacher—got together to talk about things like not looking like one's parents. Nora, who's now a teenager, still says it made the move much easier for her.

—CHRIS

Henry, United States

We've Been There: The Unfortunately Predictable Questions

Our families report a common set of questions heard after an adoption. How you answer those questions will help a child learn to explain adoption while guarding his privacy.

- What do you know about his real parents?
  We are his real parents now. Do you mean his birth parents?
- Her birth mother was a teenager, right?
  We're keeping information about her birth parents private for now.
- How could anyone give up such a beautiful child?
  His birth mother decided that she couldn't raise any child right now.
- I thought it was impossible to adopt a newborn these days. How many years did you have to wait?
  Adoption is more common than you realize. Most families adopt in less than two years.
- Adoption costs a fortune, right? How did you afford it?
  Adoption is less expensive than you might think, and well within the reach of many families. I'd be glad to talk to you about it if you're interested.
- Aren't you worried that his birth parents will try to take him back?
  No. We're his family by law now.
- Don't you still wish you could have children of your own?
  He is our own child.
- Will she speak Spanish? (Chinese? Russian?)
  She's a baby. She doesn't speak any language yet.
- Are you planning to tell her that she was adopted?
  Yes.

Emily, United States

The Power of Truth
An Adult Adoptee

WHILE I KNEW I WAS ADOPTED, WE DIDN'T TALK ABOUT IT much while I was growing up. My parents' approach to the outside world was to pretend that I was not adopted. This made me anxious, because I was always afraid that someone would find out and I would have to explain. The fact that my adoptive parents are Jewish, and have dark curly hair, brown eyes, and olive complexions, while I am of Scandinavian descent and have blond hair, blue eyes, and fair skin, complicated my feelings.

Even though we didn't look alike, people often commented on how similar my parents and I were in other ways. My father would react to such comments by winking at me, as though we were sharing a sweet and delicious secret. That felt good; we were in on the secret together. Unfortunately, the secrecy also made me feel as though I was strange, somehow not quite as good as a child born into a family. As an adult, I realized my parents were trying to protect me from the negative adoption attitudes of others. Unfortunately, the strategy backfired and made me feel as though I had a dangerous secret that could hurt me if anyone found out.

I wish my parents had given me more information about my adoption and more power over the information. I wish they had done more to reassure me that, although our family was different, it was a good family. Like most kids, I had a great need to belong and fit in.

It would have helped me to practice responses to these questions together, and to discuss which answers work the best. This would have had the added effect of drawing us closer as a family, to share this important family responsibility. Together, we could have rehearsed responses such as, "We may not look alike, but we have the same sense of humor."

WHAT DO I DO NEXT?

Alert. Check that your child's medical and dental files include a notation about adoption.

Repeat. Rehearse with other family members (and with your adopted child, if old enough) what story you'll tell strangers.

Aidan Jane, United States

15

Is This Normal?

Speech Delays, Learning Disabilities, and Other Complications

Is my child likely to have problems?
In studies done in the late 1960s, researchers found that adoptees were more likely than non-adoptees to have psychological, behavioral, and academic problems. Later analysis of these studies pointed out a large flaw: The studies grouped together children adopted in infancy with children adopted as teenagers. Children adopted in their teens have generally suffered neglect and/or trauma—that's why they're available for adoption. Subsequent, better-designed studies show a more nuanced picture.

The Sibling Interaction and Behavior Study (SIBS) at the University of Minnesota, which has followed children in six hundred families since 1999, concludes that by mid-adolescence, adoptees are no more likely than their peers to engage in negative behaviors such as delinquency, substance abuse, or aggression. Their relationships with their brothers and sisters (whether adopted or the biological children of the

above: Brielle, United States

There is an assumption by the general public that all children who have been adopted will have some sort of issue, developmental, physical, or in some other category. I'm living proof that this is just not the case. Adoption is just like anything else—you cannot stereotype based on one anecdote that you hear in the news or from your neighbor. Because someone was adopted does not mean that they will automatically have problems.

—MEREDITH

adoptive parents) were as close and loving as those between bio-siblings, and they reported feeling just as attached to their parents as did biological children.

However, the study also finds that adoptees are "moderately" more likely than their non-adopted peers to suffer emotional or behavioral problems such as anxiety, depression, oppositional defiant disorder (ODD), and attention deficit/hyperactivity disorder (ADHD). Children adopted domestically are at slightly more risk than those adopted internationally; researchers do not know why. Overall, though, the SIBS researchers emphasize that "most adopted adolescents are psychologically healthy."

Curiously, SIBS notes that while the risk of disorder is moderate, adoptees are more than twice as likely as non-adoptees to be referred to a mental-health professional. The researchers theorize that adoptive parents are better educated or have greater economic resources than non-adoptive parents, have had previous interaction with social services, and "may have a lower threshold than the parent of a non-adopted child for reporting behavior as problematic."

In other words, some adopted children are seeing psychologists because their parents are extra sensitive to any signs of trouble. But, even after accounting for this bias, the fact remains that adoptees are slightly more likely to have real behavioral and learning disorders than non-adopted children.

WISE WORDS: *Dr. Margaret Keyes of the Department of Psychology at the University of Minnesota says, "It is important to place this increased risk in some sort of context. The disruptive disorder risks associated with having an adopted child are comparable to or even less than those associated with having a male child. Despite the slight increase in risk among males, no one is overly concerned about giving birth to sons."*

For the latest results from the SIBS study go
to adoptivefamilies.com/sibs.

Someone to Watch Over Me
Janis Cooke Newman

MY BEST FRIEND, MEG, IS AFRAID SHE'S LETTING HER SIX-month-old son spend too much time in the Johnny Jump Up. "I feel so guilty," she tells me. "We should be playing with the Gymini, developing his gross motor skills."

I know what she means. The other day I watched several Babar cartoons with my two-year-old son, Alex, trying to see if I could justify them as a tool for language acquisition.

Like most parents, I've become an expert on child development. I know that playing peekaboo establishes object permanence, that the Legos all over my kitchen floor will help Alex develop his fine motor skills, and that the squeaking rubber ducky that's starting to grow mold shouldn't be thrown out, because it teaches cause and effect. I have read that the first three years are the most important time in a child's life for learning, so I try to give Alex as much educational stimulation as I can, before he turns three and it's too late.

The downside to having all this expertise is that I'm terrified I'm not doing enough. I think that if I let Alex watch the cartoon elephant in the green suit instead of the real elephants in the National Geographic special, I'm sentencing him to a lifetime of summer school.

This is when I make myself go back and remember how Alex spent the first half of his all-important three years.

For the first fifteen months of his life, Alex lived in an orphanage in Moscow, an old building with mint-green walls and a smell of boiled cabbage. He and eleven other children spent their days in a large playpen, surrounded by a painted pink-and-white railing. Four women took turns caring for the children, never more than two at a time for all twelve. Most often, it was Nadia, a woman who dressed in a white lab coat, a babushka, and men's tube socks with sandals.

There was no *Sesame Street,* no *Mister Rogers' Neighborhood,* no *Barney*—only a small plastic radio that was left on all day, tuned to a station that alternated between disco music and loud Russian talking. The toys Alex played with had not been chosen for their educational value. Some had been bought by the orphanage, some were left by Americans who had come to pick up the children they were adopting. The nicer toys were kept out of reach, on a shelf. During the two weeks my husband, Ken, and I spent visiting the orphanage, waiting for Alex's papers to be signed, I never saw them taken down.

Although all the children in Alex's group were well over a year old, none of them had learned to walk. During that first week, I began to take Alex out of the big playpen and put on a pair of canvas shoes from a communal pile over his footed terrycloth jumpsuit. Back and forth, along the long wall where twelve cribs were lined in a row, I'd walk Alex while Ken videotaped. The day he walked the short distance between the cribs and the railing of the playpen by himself was the first day we saw him smile.

Once or twice a week, Nadia would climb into the big playpen with a large stuffed dog. She'd hold the dog up and point to its ears, its nose, its eyes, saying the word for each, while the children gathered around, mostly just to touch her arm, her leg. Then she'd sing a Russian song, with a lot of clapping, and the lesson was over.

At fifteen months, Alex didn't talk. None of the children did. They didn't try out sounds or babble. Even when they played together in the big playpen, they were silent. Watching them was like watching television with the sound off. The only time I heard any noise was when Nadia took one of them out to be fed. Then the rest would crowd around the pink-and-white railing and cry to be next.

At the orphanage, Ken and I talked to Alex constantly. Sometimes we'd sing to him, old songs from musicals by George Gershwin and Irving Berlin. One day Nadia let us take him outside, to the weeds and patches of dirt and the old swing set, where the older children played. We sat by a small carved wooden playhouse that looked as if it belonged in a Russian fairy tale, and Ken sang "Someone to Watch Over Me," our wedding song. When he stopped, he heard a soft, high voice in his ear. Alex was singing along.

After we brought Alex home, I opened my books on early-childhood development. I read about infants playing with rattles that developed coordination, newborns being given teddy bears that stimulated their sense of touch, and parents who spoke French to their babies while they were still in the womb. I was afraid that Alex's time in the orphanage would mean he'd have to go through life with one hand tied behind his back.

Today Alex is almost three. His fine motor skills are so well developed that he can open a childproof lock faster than I can. Not only does he run and jump and climb with no problem, he can also do a pretty impressive flip over the headboard of our bed. And his language skills are so strong that he can ask a theoretical question in the future tense, such as, "When you get bigger, Mommy, will you have a penis?"

I find this question comforting. It makes me remember that children are incredibly resilient, and that Alex will not have lifelong learning problems if I sometimes let him play with a Power Ranger instead of his phonics desk.

So I remind Meg that Alex did not hear one word of English until he was fifteen months old, and that he can now carry on a five-minute conversation about dog poo.

Then I go into the living room and hold Alex, and while I'm at it, I pick up the wooden puzzle of farm animals, so we can work on his spatial relationships.

Which children will need extra support?
Children who have spent significant time in an overseas orphanage may not have had sufficient stimulation and may arrive with poor language skills in their own language, which can lead to later learning problems. A child over the age of two should be evaluated in her native language, so that any delay can be addressed as soon as possible.

Children who are of school age when they are adopted should be screened for potential learning disorders. Public schools are legally required to provide a free assessment if there is any suspicion of a risk for later learning problems—even if the child in question attends a private school. You can also request testing for your preschooler if he shows language delays, poor coordination, or other hints of a problem.

What happens if my child is diagnosed with a learning disorder?

If your child is found eligible for special-education services, you'll meet with school officials to design an individualized education program (IEP). The plan might include special attention from remedial-reading teachers, speech or occupational therapists, or other specialists. It will list accommodations to help your child compensate for her weaknesses—extra time on written tests, for instance, or a copy of the class lesson. It should also arrange for assistive technology devices, if needed, such as audiobooks or computer software to help children organize their thoughts.

What do I do if my child has emotional or behavioral problems?

Sometimes even the best parenting can't overcome everything a child and his family faces. Most children's difficulties can be chalked up to normal childhood development rather than to problems stemming from adoption. But if you've tried different parenting and discipline methods and your family's difficulties persist, a professional can give you the tools you need to parent successfully.

Joshua, United States

We've Been There: Before Going the Therapy Route

There are no hard-and-fast rules for when to seek professional help. Before you do, consider these options:

- Your child's behavior may well be normal for his developmental stage. Read up on child development.
- Consider the family situation. Is there a change in the household (conflict, new sib-

lings, divorce, a move) that may be prompting the behavior?

- Seek out parenting classes or advice from a parenting expert.
- Make sure your child knows that it's easy to talk about adoption. Watch an adoption-themed movie or read adoption books together. Show your interest in talking about adoption and your availability to address any concerns.
- Make sure your child has a chance to interact with other adopted kids by joining a support group, attending a workshop, or taking part in summer camps.
- Join a support group yourself.

How do I know if a problem is adoption related?

The therapists who support our families say that, in their experience, adoptive parents are too ready to assume that a child's emotional or behavioral problem is about adoption rather than a normal developmental stage of childhood—and too quick to sign a young child up for one-on-one therapy.

Is there such a thing as "adoption trauma"?

If you troll adoption-related websites, you are likely to trip over discussions of "adoption trauma" or "the primal wound." This is the theory that all adoptees, even those adopted as newborns, are permanently scarred by being separated from their birth mothers. (The theory has been expanded to cover children born to surrogate mothers as well.) While there is no doubt that people who say they suffer from adoption trauma are genuinely suffering, there is absolutely no objective evidence that the primal wound is a real psychological phenomenon. The Sibling Interaction and Behavior Study doesn't directly address the primal wound theory, but its findings contradict the idea that adoptees

We have a daughter from Thailand who was two and a half when she came home. She had nightmares that were long, loud, and a bit scary for us. We called an adoption pediatrician who said this is very common for children who are adopted at an older age. "This is not abuse, or mental illness, this is just a way for children to handle the amount of change in their lives." The behavior lasted about six months, and the loss of sleep was difficult, to say the least, but one year later we are all sleeping well, in our own beds!

—JULIE

Hannah, United States

are automatically troubled: The adoptees in the study scored as well on measures of self-esteem as their non-adopted peers.

WISE WORDS: Anu Sharma, a psychology professor and a lead researcher on the University of Minnesota's Sibling Interaction and Behavior Study, says: "Adoption is often a subtlety in children's problems—a part of who they are—but not usually the main issue."

When should we try therapy?

If your child has emotional or behavioral problems, whether adoption related or not, and isn't making any progress, you may want to consider therapy.

REALITY CHECKLIST
Finding a Therapist

You're looking for someone who neither overemphasizes the effects of adoption nor ignores its influence. The ideal therapist should have knowledge of and experience with adoption and should encourage you to take an integral role in your child's treatment. Use local adoption resources. Start with referrals from your adoption agency, lawyer, or parent support group. Some states have post-adoption offices that offer referrals. Contact your local mental-heath association for referral to therapists who have indicated an interest in adoption. Don't limit yourself to psychiatrists and psychologists. Clinical social workers, family therapists, and licensed counselors may also be able to effectively treat an adoptee. Once you've compiled a list of therapists, arrange interviews and ask the following questions:

Myrisa, United States

❑ What is your experience with adoption?

❑ What issues do you believe may affect adoptees and can be helped by therapy?

❑ Are you comfortable talking about adoption?

❑ Do you believe adoption always has a negative impact on a child? (Steer clear of any therapist who answers yes.)

❑ What do you need to know about our family? (Parents are critical to a child's treatment and should be included in the plan.)

❑ What experience do you have in dealing with situations like ours?

❑ For children in open adoptions: Have you ever worked with a family involved in a birth-parent search? Have you ever included a child's birth family as part of treatment?

❑ If yours is a multiracial family: What experience do you have of working with people of my child's culture?

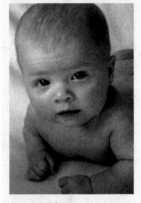

Elliot, United States

❑ How does your practice work? Who covers the practice when you are not available?

❑ What are your fees, and have you worked with our insurance company?

Are support groups for adoptees helpful?

Social workers encourage adopted children to take part in adoptee support groups. Our families often say that their children resisted the idea of such groups but, once they have taken part, find them extremely rewarding.

WHAT DO I DO NEXT?

Step back. Don't jump to conclusions. All children have bumps in their development.

Compare. Talk to your adoption support group: Are other families facing similar issues with their children? And talk to friends with biological children of the same age and gender; if your child is having problems, the likelihood is it's not adoption related.

Evaluate. Ask your school system and your pediatrician for help in finding an expert who can examine and diagnose your child.

Get help. If there really is a problem, lean on your adoption agency or adoption support group to recommend professionals who have worked with adoptees.

Autumn, United States

Ana, Guatemala

16

Will We Live Happily Ever After?

Adoptees on Adoption

Meredith

My experience is that families are families, period. It doesn't matter if the people in the family share DNA. It doesn't matter if kids have come from their mother's bodies or not. Kids are kids, and parents are parents. That is the bottom line, as far as I am concerned. In fact, in all of my years of interacting with various friends, co-workers, and acquaintances, I've had a hard time finding many people who had a relationship with their moms even half as close as the one I've had with mine. We finish each other's sentences, know exactly what the other one is thinking, and spend life as close to best friends as we could possibly be.

Don't get me wrong—we've had our ups and downs, just like any other parent-child relationship. We've had our share of yelling matches, and I'm pretty sure she wanted to bean me throughout my whole thirteenth year of life. But it's so funny . . . we share so many traits that most of the time I feel as though I am, basically, a younger version of her. Because of that, I am a very strong proponent of nurture over nature when it comes to familial relationships. That's not to say that both aren't involved, because I am well aware that they are. However, in addition to having experienced life the way I did growing up, I also have the unique perspective of being a stepparent, so I get a front-row seat at the biological parent-child relationship show every day of my life, without actually being in it. I can tell you that based on my observations, nature does not always outweigh nurture.

Jennifer

My relationship with my family is very special. My mom, Janet, was my best friend in the whole world, and the most wonderful mom I could have ever hoped for. When she passed away, from cancer, I was twenty-one, and I have missed her every single day since. I feel very lucky to have such a wonderful mom, dad, brother, and stepmom. They are the only family I know. I also feel very lucky to have had the wonderful birth family that found my adoptive family for me.

Adoption is very special. It's not about us. It's about what we bring to the world, how we help one another.

An Adult Adoptee

The discrepancy between my appearance and the ethnicity of my surname has inspired comments my whole life. Occasionally a stranger or acquaintance would comment on my being the only member of our family with blue eyes. I think my parents set an excellent example of flexible responses. To total strangers who exclaimed, "Where did you get those eyes?" my mother might laugh and say, "Recessive gene." She would later wink at me and point out that it was the truth. But people who knew my parents for any length of time also knew we were adopted, and their questions were answered differently, with something such as "We know her background is Irish, so the eyes probably come from that." I learned only as an adult that they worried about stigmatizing me by being so open about our adoptions. At the time, what I noticed was that they never acted as though adoption was something to keep a secret.

As time went on, I took a more active role in answering those questions, depending on my mood. My mother still laughs about the time after church when someone commented on my last name not matching my looks, and I replied simply, "Well, I'm not related to my father."

Nosy questions are a fact of life, and most of the adoptees I know become adept at deciding, on the spot, how much or little information to share. I don't think it's necessary to bring up adoption to just anyone who asks, but by modeling responses that are appropriate in different situations, you can set the stage for the day when your child can answer the questions himself.

Jane

As a black child living in a mainly white town, I felt alienated from African American culture. My mother bought me black dolls, showed me movies about the Underground Railroad, and taught me about civil rights heroes. Instead of embracing these symbols of my culture, I shunned them. Yet, even though black culture seemed somewhere far away, I harbored a tiny connection to it. A second-grade project required that we do a paper on an important person in history. Immediately, I felt an obligation to do mine on an African American. I chose Harriet Tubman.

My mother was the one who encouraged me to connect with other African Americans. Even though Mom is white, she has been the one to teach me racial pride. The most important thing she did was to drag my siblings and me to another town to attend a black church. The church was located in a small apartment complex, next to a McDonald's. I was afraid of it, and I thought it smelled strange.

My desire to be white, like everyone else, began to fade as I entered my later teenage years. In junior high, I still wanted to be in the majority, not the minority. I felt that I had nothing in common with anyone black, because I did not know many black people. I finally began to come to terms with myself as I moved through the preteen and teen-idol years. Something inside me changed. I saw black faces on television and began to feel a connection with them. With the rise of hip-hop and black artists in the music industry, I felt pride in my heritage for the first time.

The part of me that felt isolated from my race has not disappeared. I often feel caught between two worlds as I ask myself: "Where do I belong?" I look in the mirror and see a black girl with nappy hair and light brown skin. On the inside, I am a girl who has always been at home in this mainly white town. I look forward to walking out into a diverse, multicultural world.

Hollee

It took four years of exploring my American, Korean, and adoption identities before I embarked on a journey back to my birth country to meet my birth father and his family. The night before I left for Korea, I sat with my parents on our back patio. I feared the only parents I knew might feel I did not love them if I met my birth family. But my dad dispelled my worries. He said, "We always knew we had family in Korea."

During the trip, two days before I was going to meet my birth father, the director of my orphanage surprised me with a phone call. "Hwa Yong-ah," he said, using my Korean name. "I decided to look for your *umma*—your mom—and I found her. You want to meet her, too?" I'd had four years to prepare myself to meet my birth father, but I never thought I would be able to meet my birth mother.

Two brief days rushed by as I met not only my birth father but my birth mother, half-siblings, grandparents, and cousins. I thought I was prepared for the reunions, but the experience was filled with surprises.

Years later, I was able to meet the priest who started my orphanage, a man who really understood the human heart. He said he had always expected that the children he helped to place overseas would come back to Korea. Old practices of secrecy have set the expectation—for some, a reassurance—that internationally adopted people will never encounter those connected to them by blood. But human nature does not always obey laws or follow the perceived "best practices."

Eight years later, it seems the journey has only begun, and I'm not sure how the story will continue to unfold. I continue to travel to Korea, exchange e-mail with my half-siblings, and attempt to learn the Korean language. But meeting my biological family has in many ways strengthened my relationship with my adoptive family. I have a future now with my birth family, but nothing can take away the years of nurture my parents gave me. Meeting my birth family answered some questions I had while growing up, but it also raised new questions that I may never be able to answer.

Sharon

When my husband and I adopted twins, I wasn't worried about forming a bond, because I was adopted as a child, too. My children know that they are adopted and that it is a special relationship, not to be ashamed of but to be celebrated. The key to a good relationship is making sure your children know that they are secure and loved. Spend quality time with them, and tell them that you love them often. I know that is all I ever wanted from my parents.

Brenda

My daughters and I have something important in common: We share the experience of joining a family through adoption. When I was adopted, in 1956, the topic was not openly discussed. People were just beginning to recognize the importance of birth parents and genetic connections, and while my parents referred frequently to my adoption, I sensed their discomfort with the subject. As I became a teenager, my curiosity about my birth parents increased. Physical similarities that my friends shared with their parents, which most took for granted, fascinated me.

Over time, my curiosity became a powerful yearning to know about my genetic heritage. Growing up with so many unanswered questions, I never expected to become an adoptive parent myself. In fact, when I had difficulty getting pregnant, in my mid-thirties, I was adamantly opposed to adoption. I wanted to have the kind of genetic ties that I had envied in my friends' families while I was growing up. And I didn't want my child to feel the ache that had taken me more than twenty years to resolve.

Over time, my mind started to open to the idea. I knew that family ties forged by adoption were as true and deep as those made by biology. Love was not the issue. In the end, I had to relinquish my hoped-for biological connection to my children. I learned that that hope was a minor part of my desire to be a parent. When my first daughter, then five months old, was placed in my arms for the first time, I loved her instantly and completely. Over the years that followed, I've come to see how fortunate it is that my daughters and I share the adoption experience.

Most important, just the fact that we have this common experience makes my children feel good. I recently asked my daughters how they felt about my being adopted, too. "Happy," my eight-year-old said immediately. My ten-year-old thought for a moment and then said, "Connected."

Melanie

For many of us who are adopted, the hope of having a child biologically helps fill the gap of some unanswered questions of the past. For me, the inability to have a child biologically was another loss I had to grieve before I could get on that plane to bring home my son.

I couldn't believe how beautiful he was. I was in complete awe of him. When we took him home forever, my husband and I could not contain our emotions any further. We held our son—our son!—and each other, and cried. But this time, these were not tears from grieving—these were tears of utter joy. It didn't matter how we became a family, only the fact that we were a family. I thought of my own mom and dad and what it was like for them the first time they held me. With my son asleep in my arms, while I walked the streets that I proudly call my motherland, I realized I had come full circle—from a Korean adoptee to an adoptive parent.

I know that my son will grieve his past in his own way, but knowing we share that bond of adoption will, I hope, make grieving those losses a bit easier. There were times in my past when I wondered why I was adopted, and why God had chosen this path for me. Watching my son while he slept close to my heart, I knew—this was the plan God had in store for me when I boarded that first airplane all those years ago.

Abigail

Children need homes, and parents need children to create a family. Mothers teach how to fold towels, make Grandma's recipes, and play fair, and they introduce us to literary classics. Dads teach us how to drive, how to handle conflict, favorite ball teams, and the best political party. I'll sleep in your arms, play peekaboo, bring "I love you" drawings to put on the refrigerator, alarm you with my adolescent fashion sense, and ask for the car keys. Families never stop growing and learning from one another. Understanding teaches courage; courage teaches stability; stability teaches trust; trust teaches acceptance; acceptance teaches love; and love makes the human heart elastic enough to make adoption less of a commodity transaction and more of an extension of family. That is an adoptee's advice about good adoptive parenting.

Kahleah (age nine)

I was born in Guatemala and now live in Quebec, Canada. I would like to share my thoughts about family *and* adoption. There are two ways of building a family, by giving birth to a child or by adopting a child. Some people do both! Some people cannot give birth, so adoption helps them to have a child, a child of their very own. Adoption also gives a child a forever family. It is not just children who are adopted. My parents are adopted, too.

Being a member of an adoptive family means having two families. One birth family and one forever family. Both families are important in different ways. Some people ask me if Mommy and Daddy are my *real* parents, and if Tristan is my *real* brother. I answer, "You can't get more *real* than my family!"

I think adoption is a great way to build a family and to make people happy. To me, a family is people who love each other, take care of each other, help and teach each other, and will always be together.

Justin

I am thirty-five years old and was adopted at age two and a half from Korea. Quite simply, I have never been aware of any longing to find my birth mother. Nor am I aware of any indelible feeling of loss and sadness associated with not knowing her or her life story. I have heard the stories about others who have been driven to find and meet their birth mothers, and while these stories are often poignant and touching, they don't stir any similar drive in my soul.

Susan

I was adopted as an infant almost thirty-five years ago, and I don't remember having sad feelings about it. I was always proud of being so wanted by my parents. I believed what the adoption paperwork said—that my birth parents were young and not married and wanted me to be raised by parents who could give me everything that they could not. It all made sense to me. I didn't feel any sort of loss because I didn't grow in my mom's tummy.

As a teenager, I thought a little more about it. I had no less pride in my adoption than before, but I was also very interested in the birthdays of my friends, because I felt like I didn't really have one. I knew I had been born, of course, but no one could tell me about that day. Sometimes it seemed strange to me that people celebrated my birthday, when nobody celebrating with me had actually known me on that day. However, I loved my birthday, and knew in my heart that my birth mom was thinking of me as I celebrated with my family and friends.

As I approached adulthood, I would write about adoption. I began to wonder about my birth mom more and more, especially as I reached the age she had been when I was born. My writings had a melancholy tone, but not for me. I was sad for her, because I was starting to understand how difficult her decision must have been.

I remember when I gave birth to my daughter. After twelve hours of labor, I held her in my arms. I looked at her and my husband and remarked that I couldn't believe someone had done that for me and then loved me enough to let me go. In my eyes, my birth mom was a hero for thinking of me first and herself second. It must have been so hard, because there was no way that anyone was taking my baby out of my arms. What a strong young woman she was, to do that for me.

Today, as I write this, I wait for my son to wake, which he does often during the night. His birth mom is half a world away, in South Korea, and she is another hero in my eyes. Without her, this incredible baby boy, who brings so much joy into my life, would not be sleeping across the hall, would not wake to snuggle in my arms, and would not grow up calling me Mommy.

Just as I felt sadness for my own birth mother, I feel sadness for his, because she is not knowing this incredible boy to whom she gave birth. My hope for her is that she can find peace in her decision, and can know in her heart that our son is being loved and is being taught that her actions were heroic.

Phil

I grew up in a family of seven children. While I'm not the youngest, I was the last to arrive in what was an adoptive family with two children from Korea; one Caucasian (my brother, who had been left on the stoop of a local church); myself, a biracial African American; and three children born to my Norwegian parents.

The one thing I would say to parents adopting children of another race is: "Be not afraid!" Go outside your comfort zone to embrace your child's culture of origin. Attend services at faith institutions in communities where your child's culture of origin is dominant. Patronize the local businesses in those neighborhoods, and make acquaintances. Those allies can be useful later, as they might be willing to act as mentors to your child, should that be necessary. Recognize that there will be things—culturally speaking—that you cannot give to your child. It's good to have others in your life whom you can rely on for that. I would also suggest that you move to such neighborhoods, if possible, or consider placing your child of color in a diverse school environment, if nothing else.

Do this not only for your child's sake but for yours as well. It can be a life-enriching experience beyond your imagination, but it requires a commitment that will sometimes be uncomfortable. Ultimately, though, it will make you the truly multiracial family that you have become, and give your child a fighting chance at having a positive self-image in a world that doesn't necessarily promote it.

Kaitlyn

My brother, Jason, and I were both adopted. Jason was born in Michigan, and I was born in Korea. Together with my parents, we made a family. We lived in a large city, and through my parents' adoption agency, they were able to locate other parents who had adopted from Korea. When I was young, my mom made a real effort to get together with two of these families for dinners and picnics. It was probably good for me that we did this, but I still chose a Caucasian as a best girlfriend, not because she was white but because she could ride no-handed on her bicycle and because we were experts at getting into trouble together in Ms. Lytel's third-grade class. It wasn't until I was in my teens that I really started to realize that I came from another country and another culture, that, given different circumstances, my life would be completely and totally different.

My teen years were definitely the hardest, for me and for my family. I felt different for the first time. I felt unsure about who I was and had a hard time resolving that. At first, I denied my heritage. I wanted to be like everyone else. Fortunately for me, I have the most wonderful parents in the world! They stood by me, and when I finally was ready to explore my feelings and needs, they were there to guide and share with me.

From one extreme, I went to the other, and immersed myself in learning about my Korean heritage and the history of my birth country. Slowly I moved toward the middle ground and am now at peace with who I am. I want to say, however, that having a supportive and loving family was key in reaching the place where I now am. I don't think that this crisis of self was totally based on being adopted or being Korean. I believe that all people have things that they must deal with and times in their lives when they must resolve them. Those of us who are very, very fortunate have the love of family.

If I am asked one question more than any other, it is, "Do you ever want to go and find your real mother?" I understand why people ask this, but it is a pretty insulting question. I have a real mother. And in regard to finding my birth mother, I just don't have that burning desire. If I could be granted one wish, however, it would be for my birth mother to know that she made the right choice.

My parents told me that they didn't like it when people used to say, "Oh, she is so lucky to be adopted by you." Just between you and me, I want you to know that they are right. I feel pretty lucky. I am loved.

Adoption Terms

Adoption jargon is imprecise; a term can have one meaning when used by a particular social worker, attorney, or agency, another meaning altogether when used by someone else. In international adoption, foreign languages add to the confusion. As you work on your adoption, never hesitate to ask, "What exactly do you mean by that?"

adoptee. A person who was adopted. Some people prefer the terms "adopted child" or "adopted person."

adoption. The complete transfer of parental rights and obligations from one parent or set of parents to another. A legal adoption requires a court action.

adoption agency. An organization, usually licensed by the state, that provides services to birth parents, adoptive parents, and children who need families. Agencies may be public or private, secular or religious, for-profit or nonprofit.

adoption assistance. Monthly federal or state subsidy payments to help adoptive parents raise children with special needs.

adoption attorney. A lawyer who files, processes, and finalizes adoptions in court. In some states, attorneys may also arrange adoptive placements.

adoption consultant. An individual who helps would-be adoptive parents decide on an adoption path and assists in choosing an appropriate agency or attorney.

adoption facilitator. An individual whose business involves connecting birth parents and prospective adoptive parents for a fee (allowed in only a few states). In international adoption, a facilitator may help adoptive parents complete an adoption in the child's country of origin.

adoption plan. Birth parents' decision to allow their child to be placed for adoption.

adoption tax credit. Nonrefundable credit that reduces taxes owed by adoptive parents who claim adoption-expense reimbursement on federal taxes (and, in some states with similar legislation, on state taxes). The credit calculation can include adoption expenses, court fees, attorney fees, and travel expenses.

adoption triad. The three major parties in an adoption: birth parents, adoptive parents, and adopted child. Also called "adoption triangle" or "adoption circle."

agency adoption. Adoptive placements made by licensed organizations that screen prospective adoptive parents and supervise the placement of children in adoptive homes until the adoption is finalized.

birth parent. A child's biological parent.

closed adoption. An adoption that involves total confidentiality and sealed records.

confidentiality. The legally required process of keeping identifying or other significant information secret. Also, the principle of ethical practice that requires social workers and other professionals not to disclose information about a client without the client's consent.

consent to adopt or consent to adoption. A birth parent's legal permission for an adoption to proceed.

decree of adoption. A legal order that finalizes an adoption.

dossier. A set of legal documents used in international adoption to process a child's adoption or assignment of guardianship in a foreign court.

employer benefits. Compensation to workers through employer-sponsored programs, for example, financial assistance, reimbursement of adoption expenses, and/or provision of parental or family leave.

finalization. The final legal step in the adoption process; involves a court hearing, during which a judge orders that the adoptive parents become the child's legal parents.

foster parents. State- or county-licensed adults who provide a temporary home for children whose birth parents are unable to care for them.

Hague Adoption Convention. The Convention on Protection of Children and Co-operation in Respect of Intercountry Adoption, an international treaty to improve accountability, safeguards, and cooperation in intercountry adoption. Its terms govern adoption among almost eighty countries, including the United States.

hard-to-place. A classification given to children whom agencies consider difficult to place because of emotional or physical disorders, age, race, membership in a sibling group, history of abuse, or other factors.

home study. A process through which prospective adoptive parents are educated about adoption and evaluated to determine their suitability to adopt.

ICPC. The Interstate Compact on the Placement of Children, a statutory law that establishes uniform legal and administrative procedures governing the adoption of children between states within the United States.

identifying information. Information on birth parents or adoptive parents that discloses their identities.

independent adoption. A child-placement adoption process that takes place primarily under the auspices of an adoption attorney, rather than under the auspices of a licensed adoption agency.

legal guardian. One who has legal responsibility for the care and management of a person (such as a minor child) who is incapable of administering his or her own affairs.

legal-risk placement. Placement of a child in a prospective adoptive family when the child is not yet legally free for adoption.

open adoption. An adoption that involves initial and/or ongoing contact between birth and adoptive families, ranging from sending letters through the agency to exchanging names and/or scheduling visits.

photo listings. Photos and descriptions of children who are available for adoption.

placement. The point at which a child begins to live with prospective adoptive parents; the period before the adoption is finalized.

post-placement supervision. The range of counseling and agency services provided to the adoptive family after the child's placement and before the adoption is finalized in court.

private adoption. An adoption process that takes place outside the auspices of the state, via either an adoption attorney or a licensed adoption agency. In a private adoption, the birth parents' parental rights are transferred directly to the adopting parents (as allowed by state law) or, usually briefly, to an adoption agency and then to the adopting parents.

private agencies. Nongovernmental adoption agencies licensed by the state.

public agencies. Social service agencies run by state or county governments that deal mainly with children in foster care.

readoption. For a child adopted in another country, a second adoption in a U.S. court.

referral: The document that identifies a child available for international adoption.

relative adoption. Adoption by a biological relative of the child.

relinquishment. Voluntary termination of parental rights. Some prefer the phrase "adoption plan."

reunion. A meeting between an adopted person and birth parents or other birth relatives.

search. An attempt to locate and/or make a connection with a birth parent or a biological child.

semi-open adoption. An adoption in which a child's birth parents and adoptive parents may meet once or twice but exchange only non-identifying information.

special-needs children. Children whom agencies consider difficult to place because of emotional or physical disorders, age, race, membership in a sibling group, history of abuse, or other factors.

transracial adoption. An adoption in which the child and the adoptive parent(s) are not of the same race.

waiting children. Children in the public child-welfare system or in foreign orphanages who cannot return to their birth homes and need permanent families.

What Kind of Adoption Is Right for You?
The Decision Matrix

Work your way through this decision matrix for a preliminary indication
of the adoption that may be right for you.

Prospective-Parent Characteristics	International Adoption	U.S. Infant Adoption	Foster-Care Adoption
1. My age is: ❏ **Under 25** ❏ **25–45** ❏ **Over 45**	Age requirements vary by country. Most countries require parents to be between the ages of 25 and 45 for any infant referral. Older parents may adopt toddlers and older children.	No specific age requirements. Birth parents, however, may more readily select parents perceived as neither "too young" nor "too old."	No specific age requirements.
2. I have the following financial resources to dedicate to adopting a child: ❏ **Less than $10,000** ❏ **$10,000–$25,000** ❏ **More than $25,000**	Most international adoptions cost between $15,000 and $30,000. Many families are eligible for a federal tax credit.	The cost of U.S. infant adoptions varies widely, from $5,000 to $30,000. Average cost is $20,000 to $25,000. Many families are eligible for the federal tax credit.	Expenses are none or minimal. Additionally, many families are eligible for the federal tax credit.
3. I am: ❏ **Part of a married couple** ❏ **Single** ❏ **Gay/lesbian**	For married couples, guidelines on length of marriage and number of previous divorces may apply. For singles, countries may prohibit or limit the number of children placed.	Typically, there are no fixed rules regarding marital status, but some birth parents prefer married couples. However, adoptions of U.S. babies by singles (both straight and gay) are not unusual.	There are typically no specific requirements regarding marital status. Research requirements for single and gay/lesbian adoption in your state.
Characteristics of the child			
4. I am interested in adopting: ❏ **A newborn** ❏ **A child under 1** ❏ **A toddler or older child**	40% of children adopted internationally are under 1 year old; 43% are 1–4 years, 17% are older than 4.	Almost all U.S. private adoptions are of very young babies. Many newborns go home from the hospital with their adoptive parents.	Children adopted from foster care range in age from infants to 17-year-olds. Many foster children have siblings with whom they are placed.
5. It is important to me to know the complete medical and social history of my child.	The quality of medical and other background information varies widely by country and by adoption situation. Parents will want to research the availability of information in countries under consideration.	Medical and other background information is usually, but not always, available in domestic adoptions.	Although background information for a child in foster care may be incomplete, current medical information will be available.

Characteristics of the Child	International Adoption	U.S. Infant Adoption	Foster-Care Adoption
6. I can consider parenting a child with some level of disability.	Quality of early care varies widely by country. Where foster care is available, children usually fare well. Where children are adopted from orphanages, there are often developmental lags and sometimes other medical consequences.	Keep in mind that there are no guarantees of perfect health for any child.	Children in foster care may experience consequences from neglect prior to entering care.
7. I am prepared for the visibility and responsibilities of raising a child who is racially dissimilar to me.	The majority of children adopted internationally are Asian, African, or Hispanic. About one third are Caucasian (primarily from Eastern Europe).	Infants adopted domestically can be of any race.	Of children in foster care currently waiting for adoption, 40% are white, 30% are African American, 20% are Hispanic, and the rest are "other."

The Adoption Process

	International Adoption	U.S. Infant Adoption	Foster-Care Adoption
8. I hope to adopt a child within: ❑ 1 year ❑ 1–2 years ❑ Longer is okay	The average international adoption process is 2 years from start to finish, but wait times vary widely by country.	The time line is unpredictable. The average adoption is complete within 2 years.	Both the wait for placement and for adoption are unpredictable, but placement can be rapid.
9. I would like to know the total cost of the adoption in advance.	Total adoption expenses usually fall within a predictable range.	The cost of a domestic adoption can vary widely depending on advertising costs to identify a birth mother as well as birth-mother medical expenses.	Total adoption expenses are negligible.
10. I am emotionally prepared for uncertainty in the adoption process.	In most cases, international adoptions follow a predictable path. Families can normally count on becoming parents by the end of the process.	Families who want to adopt a newborn domestically can almost always count on doing so. However, along the way, as many as 50% of birth parents who initially consider adoption decide not to place the baby. Post-placement revocations, however, are rare.	Children may be placed with foster families who hope to adopt them before they are legally free for adoption. There can be uncertainty as to when or whether a child will become free for adoption.
11. I prefer the following level of contact with my child's birth parents: ❑ None ❑ Some ❑ Significant	In most international adoptions, there is little to no contact with birth parents. This is changing; an increasing number of parents are opening international adoptions.	Most birth and adoptive parents meet at least once. It is unusual to have no significant ongoing contact with birth parents.	If you foster your child before adoption, you may have some contact with the birth parents. If not, you are unlikely to have any contact with them.
12. I'd like to control the way the adoption proceeds and the professionals I work with as much as possible.	In international adoption, parents typically choose the adoption country and agency. Beyond that, the process is dictated by the requirements of the U.S. government and those of the child's country of origin.	Adopting parents will choose their social worker, their attorney, and sometimes the process by which they identify a birth mother. The timing of a birth-parent match will not be predictable.	Adopting from foster care involves state adoption offices and courts. It is difficult to have control over the process.

Credits

Fostering Love: Rosemary Shulman is the mother of Matthew. Copyright 2009 Adoptive Families.

A Boy Like Him: Deirdre Levinson is the mother of Malachi and Miranda. Copyright 1982 Deirdre Levinson.

Did I Steal My Daughter? Elizabeth Larsen is a freelance writer and the mother of two sons and a daughter. This piece was excerpted from a longer article that ran in *Mother Jones* magazine; you can read the full text at MotherJones.com. Reprinted with permission from *Mother Jones* magazine, 2007, Foundation for National Progress. Copyright 2007 Mother Jones magazine.

Chapter 3: Can I Choose a Child?

Special Delivery: Kate McKee Robertson is a freelance writer and the mother of Derek, Arielle, and Courtney. Copyright 2009 Adoptive Families.

Small Wonders: Rochelle Green is a freelance writer and editor and the mother of Julian and Lauren. Copyright 2009 Adoptive Families.

An Unmatched Set: Jana Wolff is the author of *Secret Thoughts of an Adoptive Mother* and the mother of Ari. Copyright 2002 Jana Wolff.

All's Fair (originally "All's Fair in Love and Waahh"): Corey Halls is the mother of Siena. Copyright 2009 Adoptive Families.

Chapter 4: Where Do I Start?

From the Bottom of My Heart: Deborah C. Joy, M.A., L.P.C.C., is an adoption therapist, the author of two adoption books, *Benjamin Bear Gets a New Family* and *Henry the Hermit Crab,* and the mother of four. Copyright 2009 Adoptive Families.

Chapter 6: Can I Adopt a Healthy Child?

Facing the Unknown: Theresa Reid, Ph.D., is the author of *Two Little Girls: A Memoir of Adoption* and the mother of Natalie and Lana. Copyright 2009 Adoptive Families.

Burden of Choice: "Linda Claire" is a pseudonym to protect the privacy of the author's family. After accepting a second referral, she is the mother of an adopted child. Copyright 2009 Adoptive Families.

Great Non-Expectations: "I. D. Steinberg" is a pseudonym to protect the privacy of the author, an entertainment publicist and the mother of Jack. Copyright 2009 Adoptive Families.

Chapter 7: Why Is There So Much Paperwork?

It's Home-Study Day and I'm Not Perfect Yet: Jeanne Marie Laskas is the author of *Growing Girls: The Mother of All Adventures* and the mother of Anna and Sasha. Copyright 1999 Jeanne Marie Laskas.

Motherhood in the Balance: Emalee Gruss Gillis is a freelance writer and the mother of two sons. Copyright 2009 Adoptive Families.

The Final Step: Eliza Newlin Carney is a freelance writer, contributing editor to *National Journal,* and the mother of Beth. Copyright 2009 Adoptive Families.

Chapter 8: Why Does This Have to Take So Long?

My So-Called Friends (originally "What's Wrong with Foreign Adoption?"): Barb Reinhold is legal counsel to the Bureau of Milwaukee Child Welfare. This article first appeared in Salon.com, and an online version remains in the Salon archives. Reprinted with permission. Copyright 2001 Salon.com.

Having Faith (originally "What the Books Didn't Tell Us"): Matt Forck is a writer, motivational speaker, and father of Natalie. Copyright 2009 Adoptive Families.

Picturing Love (originally "Picture of Love"): Barbara Sinsheimer is an athletic trainer, substitute teacher, freelance writer, and the mother of Tyler and Mary. Copyright 2008 Adoptive Families.

Chapter 9: Is This My Child?

Hold On Tight: Michelle Farrell is an emergency room nurse and the mother of Joseph. Copyright 2009 Adoptive Families.

Vital Signs: Victoria Moreland teaches English composition at Queens University in Charlotte, North Carolina. She is the mother of Olivia. Copyright 2009 Adoptive Families.

Chapter 10: What If It Doesn't Work Out?

Lost Daughter: Deb Luppino is the mother of Julie and Sarah. Copyright 2009 Adoptive Families.

Chapter 11: Will We Fall in Love?

Becoming a Mother: Claire Houston is a psychotherapist, director of the Women Supporting Women Center in Exeter, New Hampshire, and the mother of Evie. Copyright 2009 Adoptive Families.

You Showed Me (originally "Jon's Smile"): Emily Jamberdino is the mother of Jeffrey, Dominika, and Jon. Copyright 2009 Adoptive Families.

Do I Love Him Yet? Melissa Fay Greene is the author of *There Is No Me Without You: One Woman's Odyssey to Rescue Africa's Children* and the mother of Molly, Seth, Lee, Lily, Sol (Fisseha), Jesse, Daniel, Helen, and Yosef. This piece is reprinted from *A Love Like No Other,* edited by Pamela Kruger and Jill Smolowe, by arrangement with Riverhead Books, a member of Penguin Group (USA), Inc. Copyright 2005 Melissa Fay Greene.

Chapter 12: Is There a Greeting Card for This?

What No One Told Me: Leigh Kaufman Leveen is a freelance writer and the mother of two. "Jane" is a pseudonym. Copyright 2009 Adoptive Families.

A Lasting Relationship: Brenda Romanchik is the author of *A Birthparent's Book of Memories* and executive director at Insight: Open Adoption Resources and Support. Copyright 2009 Adoptive Families.

Our Leap of Faith: Janice Pearse is the international director of Adoptions Together in Maryland and the mother of three. Copyright 2009 Adoptive Families.

Chapter 13: What Do I Tell My Child?

Thirty Nagging Questions: Laurie Elliott is the mother of nine children. Copyright 2009 Adoptive Families.

Chapter 15: Is This Normal?

Someone to Watch Over Me: Janis Cooke Newman is the author of *Mary* and *The Russian Word for Snow* and the mother of Alex. Copyright 2001 Janis Cooke Newman.

Chapter 16: Will We Live Happily Ever After?

Meredith: Meredith C. Keith-Chirch. Copyright 2007 Meredith C. Keith-Chirch.

Jennifer: Jennifer Jue-Steuck. Copyright 2009 Adoptive Families.

Jane: "Jane" is a pseudonym to protect the author's privacy. Copyright 2009 Adoptive Families.

Hollee: Hollee McGinnis. Copyright 2009 Adoptive Families.

Sharon: Sharon Thurner. Copyright 2009 Adoptive Families.

Brenda: Brenda M. Cotter. Copyright 2009 Adoptive Families.

Melanie: Melanie Edwards. This quote was excerpted from an article that appeared in *Adoptees Today,* Holt International's newsletter. Reprinted with permission. Copyright 2005 Melanie Edwards.

Abigail: Abigail Lovett. Copyright 2009 Adoptive Families.

Kahleah: Kahleah Maria de Lourdes Guibault. Copyright 2009 Adoptive Families.

Phil: Phil Bertelsen. Copyright 2009 Adoptive Families.

Kaitlyn: Kaitlyn Kerry. Copyright 2009 Adoptive Families.

One Last Thing

Now it's time to hear from you. Did you decide to adopt? How did you make your decision? If you adopted, where did you find your child? Who helped to bring your child home? Were there bumps along the way? What advice would you give to someone starting this journey? Go to www.adoptivefamilies.com/youcanadoptstories and tell us *your* story.

above: Natalya, Russia

Acknowledgments

For their guidance, our agent, Chris Tomasino of the Tomasino Agency; Nancy Miller, who encouraged us to tackle this book; Caroline Sutton, who brought us to the Ballantine Publishing Group; and our wonderful editors, Jane von Mehren, Evan Camfield, and Christina Duffy.

For their wisdom: Susan Freivalds, founder of *Adoptive Families*; Peg Studaker and Kristine Huson, Children's Home Society and Family Services, Saint Paul, Minnesota; Sarah Gerstenzang, AdoptUsKids; Kris Faasse and John Van Valkenburg, Bethany Christian Services, Grand Rapids, Michigan; Mark McDermott, Esq., Washington, D.C.; Ronny Diamond, Susan Watson, Amy Silverman, and Rhonie Lester, Spence-Chapin Services, New York City; Merrily Ripley, Adoption Advocates International, Port Angeles, Washington; Dr. Jeri Ann Jenista, Ann Arbor, Michigan; Dr. Jane Aronson, International Pediatric Health Services, New York City; Dr. Deborah A. Borchers, Cincinnati, Ohio; Lillian Thogersen and Mary Ann Curran, World Association for Children and Parents, Seattle, Washington.

For sharing their extraordinary expertise so generously in the pages of *Adoptive Families* magazine over the last ten years: Robert Barnett, Laura Broadwell, Jane Brown, Eliza Newlin Carney, Mary Ann Curran, Fran Eisenman, Sue Gainor, Lois Gilman, Melissa Fay Greene, Holly van Gulden, Carrie Howard, Deborah Johnson, Annie Kassof, Gregory Keck, Ph.D., Steve Kirsh, Esq., Carrie Krueger, Marybeth Lambe, M.D., Joni Mantell, Kay Marner, Lee McClain, Lois Melina, Julie Michaels, Lisa Milbrand, Vicki Peterson, Debbie Riley, Brenda Romanchik, Jayne Schooler, Diana Schwab, Kathleen Silber, Jill Smolowe, JoAnne Solchany, Ph.D., Sarah Springer, M.D., Lee Varon, Peter Wiernicki, Esq., Jana Wolff, and many others too numerous to name who wrote honestly and openly about their adoption experiences for the readers of *Adoptive Families*. Neither the magazine nor this book would be possible without you.

For their hard work, devotion to accuracy, and impeccable taste: the staff of *Adoptive Families* magazine, especially Eve Gilman, Orin Brecht, and Marie Kiernan.

For their passionate advocacy on behalf of all our children: the readers of *Adoptive Families* magazine.

Index

About the Authors

SUSAN CAUGHMAN has edited and published *Adoptive Families* magazine and website since 2000. A longtime adoption advocate and journalist, she was a founder of Families with Children from China, the national parent support group, and a member of the board of directors of Adoptive Families of America. She is a former executive at Time Inc., where she was responsible for the consumer marketing activities of a number of the company's magazines.

ISOLDE MOTLEY is the former corporate editor of Time Inc., where she was responsible for the editorial content of its women's magazines, including *In Style, Real Simple, Essence,* and *Parenting.* She is a former chief editor of *Life* magazine and the founding editor of both *This Old House* and *Martha Stewart Living* magazines.

Between them, Susan and Isolde have five children, three of them adopted, from China, Ethiopia, and New Jersey.